MY ANCESTOR WOMAN AT WAR

by Emma Jolly

SO

Published by
Society of Genealogists Enterprises Limited
14 Charterhouse Buildings, Goswell Road
London EC1M 7BA.

© Emma Jolly and the Society of Genealogists 2013.

ISBN: 978-1-907199-18-9

British Library Cataloguing in Publication Data.
A CIP Catalogue record for this book is available from the British Library.

The Society of Genealogists Enterprises Limited is a wholly owned
subsidiary of the Society of Genealogists, a registered charity, no 233701.

About the Author

Emma Jolly is a genealogist and writer. She is a member of the Society of Genealogists,
the Association of Genealogists and Researchers in Archives (AGRA) and the Families In
British India Society (FIBIS). The author of *Family History for Kids* (PQ Publishing, 2007),
Tracing Your British Indian Ancestors (Pen & Sword, 2012), and *Tracing Your Ancestors
Using the Census* (Pen & Sword, 2013), Emma runs the Genealogic research service
www.genealogic.co.uk. She lives in London with her husband and two children.

Cover Images - *F* ... rator, Radar Chain Home
system station.) R) ... ctor Operator for the ATS
(in boiler suit, in c(... h anti-aircraft guns, Hyde
Park, London, 193 ... hleen Divall 1945-6. First
World War muniti ... s of the Territorial Force
Nursing Service w

CONTENTS

List of Photographs

Acknowledgements

At the Society of Genealogists, I am grateful to Anthony Mortimer, the members of the Publications Committee, Else Churchill, and June Perrin for commissioning the book and for their support and help with planning and editing. Special thanks to Roy Stockdill for editing and to Graham Collett, who has done a wonderful job with the design and layout.

My research has benefited enormously from the vast collections and dedication of staff of a number of archives, especially those of The National Archives, the Imperial War Museum, the SoG Library, the RAF Museum, The Women's Library @ LSE, the Liddle Collection and the British Library.

Tudor Allen and the staff at Camden Local Studies and Archives Centre have been very generous in allowing me to use several items from their wartime collection. David Vickers of www.forthefallen.co.uk kindly allowed me to reproduce his transcriptions of the Women's Screens in York Minster.

Ken Divall, author of *My Ancestor was a Royal Marine* (SoG, 2008), has been a huge support, sourcing images and giving the benefit of his wide military expertise.

I was very privileged to speak with Bletchley Park veteran, Gwendoline Page, about her wartime experiences in the WRNS, and to Eileen Piggott about her war work in Enfield. Thank you to Mark Piggott, also.

Thanks to my grandfather, former RAF Flight Sergeant Owen Jolly, for sharing his memories of the WAAFs and ATA; to my parents, Barry and Alethea Jolly; my sister, Charlotte Jolly, for reading through the chapters and contributing comments; and mother-in-law Carol Causer for help with reading material.

I am immensely grateful to Nick Newington-Irving for his excellent indexing.

I should also like to acknowledge my friends and fellow genealogists for their support, reading and allowing me to use sources, memories and images from their and their families' collections. Thank you to Kirsty F. Wilkinson of www.myainfolk.com, Rosemary Morgan of www.londonrootsresearch.blogspot.co.uk, Paul Reed of greatwarphotos.com, Jamie Baker of jamiebaker.posterous.com, Suzie Grogan of www.suziegrogan.co.uk, the Gainsborough District & Heritage Association, www.gainsboroughheritage.com, Chris Paton of britishgenes.blogspot.co.uk, Kathryn Hughes of www.bradfordww1.co.uk, Lynne Cleaver of tetburyfamilies.co.uk, Society of Genealogists Chairman William Bortrick, and Sue Light of www.scarletfinders.co.uk. Further thanks go to Matthew Ward of www.historyneedsyou.com/index.html for Civil War details, and Gillian Mawson, author of *Guernsey Evacuees* (The History Press, 2012), for kindly sharing some of her extensive research.

As ever thank you to Simon, Jacob and Oscar for their good humour and patience.

ATS wireless operators learning Morse code at the Special Operators Training Battalion at Trowbridge in Wiltshire, 24 November 1941, by Spender (Lt), War Office official photographer. Public domain image.

INTRODUCTION

Researching female ancestors at war requires a different approach from that of standard military history research. This book is intended to explore women's military roles in the past, and to discuss the wide range of occupations that women could undertake during a war.

Researchers who are tracing more than one female ancestor should find this a useful aid, enabling research into ancestors' war careers, as well as encouraging further research into the war roles performed by women.

Although some veterans have spoken to family members about their wartime activities, details of many women's war work has only been discovered after their deaths. This is particularly true of those who worked in the intelligence services, such as Joan Nicholson, who died in May 2010, aged 87, who worked in Bletchley Park but did not tell even her own mother. (In her war records, Joan is described as a Foreign Office linguist. Some of her papers will be archived at the Armitt Museum, Ambleside, Cumbria.)

Another example is that of Florence Green, who died in February 2012 at 110 years old - the last known surviving veteran of the First World War. She served in the Women's Royal Air Force. This organisation and its members have often been overlooked in the study of women's war. Florence's existence as a surviving veteran was not even mentioned publicly until shortly before she died. This followed the death in 2008 of Gladys Powers at the age of 109 in British Columbia, Canada. In the First World War, Powers served in the Women's Army Auxiliary Corps - joining at just 15 years old - and later the WRAF. Some women did war work even when they had children, particularly in the Second World War. However, they may not have felt comfortable about revealing this in the post-war era, with its focus on domesticity.

Debate continues about whether women served in war or whether they worked, particularly after 1939. After the Second World War, women's roles in the military and civilian nursing services, in auxiliary services and the operational branches of fighting forces were acknowledged, not least by Prime Minister Clement Attlee in October 1945. The line between war service and war work is blurred. This is reflected in the resources available, where they are located and how they are referenced.

Women did serve as auxiliaries to the armed forces: around 80,000 women served in the forces as non-combatants in the First World War. Women also risked their lives not only on the battlefields but in service behind the lines and in factories on the home front. Not all women who died while undertaking these roles are recorded on memorials. The Commonwealth War Graves Commission Roll of Honour lists names that have been provided by the Ministry of Defence, but those of many women are missing.

A number of problems exist in researching this subject. For example, most service records of women who served in the First World War were destroyed in 1940; thus it can be difficult to discover details of what an ancestor did. Besides general lack of record survival, other problems include difficulties in tracing records of those in the secret services, and a general lack of knowledge within the family. Although some official records do not survive, there are other ways of exploring your female relatives' wartime activities.

Standard genealogical resources may not always be helpful: General Register Office (GRO) birth records, for example, do not always give the occupation of the mother, even if she was working at the time. This is not to say that these records should be neglected. These and other general records, such as published memoirs, can be very helpful in locating an ancestor during wartime or providing useful clues that can aid further research. Where no service record survives, careers must be pieced together from unconnected documents. Researching siblings' or aunts' work during the war may also help to discover more about your direct family line.

On the other hand, there are many publications that deal with certain aspects of women's war work in detail: for example, land girls or women's lives 1939-1949 drawing on Mass Observation Archive records.

Women often did more in wars than is popularly assumed. Even if your ancestor did not serve officially, there were other areas in which she may have worked. During war, women worked in the roles left by men who had entered the armed forces; these roles include working in mines, on farms, in factories, in transport, in civil defence and at home. These women made an invaluable contribution to the war effort.

This book seeks to highlight the connections across women's war work, through time and between different areas of service. Some women may have served in different organisations in one war, for example, or may have served in both world wars. Researching women at war requires flexibility and dedication. Hopefully, this guide will help.

Boudica statue near Westminster Pier, London, 2007, by Aldaron.Public domain image.

CHAPTER ONE

History of British women in conflict up to the mid-nineteenth century

> *'Her Husband was a Souldier, and to the wars did go,*
> *And she would be his Comrade, the truth of all is so.*
> *She put on Man's Apparel, and bore him company,*
> *As many in the Army for truth can testify.'*

Ballad of 'The Gallant She-Souldier' (1655).

General Background

Histories of medieval and modern conflict have tended to focus almost exclusively on male involvement. Where women are mentioned it is often as casualties of war, such as victims of the raping and pillaging of foreign invaders. Recent scholars have looked more closely at the roles of female camp followers, but the martial participation of women ancestors can be difficult to find. For example, there are few lists of names for women in this period.

Warrior queens were in evidence before the modern period. Perhaps most famous among these were Boudica, who drank hemlock after failing to prevent the march of the Romans, and Matilda, daughter of Henry I, who fought to retain the inheritance of her father's throne during The Anarchy of 1135-1153. Lesser known queens include 'the Lady of the Mercians', King

Alfred the Great's daughter, Aethelflaed (869/870-918). She ruled Mercia from 911-18 and led campaigns against the Welsh and the Vikings. Aetheldflaed's earliest success was at Tettenhall in 910.

The Middle Ages

Among the peoples of medieval Europe, female camp followers and even some female soldiers have been recorded from as late as the 14th century[1]. Most of these women were from the lower social classes, and several will have descendants alive today. Women in the lower classes who had no family or little financial support were tempted to follow their husbands or sweethearts along with the camp to ensure that they and their children received food.

Camp followers fulfilled a variety of essential roles to support the soldiers. Among these were laundry, foraging, needlework, carrying arms, working as 'horse-boys' preparing meals and tending to illness or injury. Also in the camp were pedlars of various goods and services, including sutlers (who sold provisions to armies) and prostitutes.

Other women were not connected to the armed forces and did not choose to be involved in war. These women were drawn into their military roles through circumstance, or through the actions of their husbands and fathers.

Among the many noblewomen who inadvertently became caught up in her husband's political and military affairs was the beautiful, red-haired Lady Isobel Lindsay (died 1577). Lady Isobel was married to John, fifth Lord Borthwick, who supported the Earl of Arran for the regency, rather than the Queen Mother, Mary of Guise, in the civil war. For this political error, on 4 September 1544, Sir George Douglas had him taken and imprisoned in Dalkeith Castle. During her husband's stay in prison, Lady Borthwick was visited by another supporter of Mary, the then Earl of Bothwell. According to accounts from Lord Eure[2] and Lord Wharton[3], she led him on for a short time, then had him swiftly overpowered and shut up in the castle, vowing not to release him until her husband was freed. 'Bicause the Lady Borthwyke was faire' wrote Lord Eure to Francis, Earl of Shrewsbury at the time, 'he came to her for love, but she made hyme to be handled and kepte'.[4]

The English Civil Wars 1642-1651

The Civil Wars, now referred to by historians as the Wars of the Three Kingdoms because they were fought throughout the British Isles, plunged British civilians into war. Women were forced into conflict when their homes were besieged or their husbands attacked. Others were keen to take an active role in either the Royalist or

Parliamentarian causes. There are recorded instances of women beating drums, pushing pikes, firing muskets, wielding swords, and throwing halberds. Some women raised female armies, such as the 'Maiden Troop' of London and Norwich.

There were others, including wives, fiancés and mistresses, who would wear soldiers' breeches and became known as 'She-Souldiers', which helped to avoid accusations of prostitution. However, women dressing as soldiers was not encouraged. Plowden writes that 'when the king got to hear about it, he was deeply shocked at such defiance of 'Nature and Religion', and issued orders that any woman who presumed to counterfeit her sex by wearing man's apparel should be subject to the 'severest punishment which law and our displeasure shall inflict'.'[5]

The tradition of camp followers continued through these wars. Women, including several Irish women who are known to have been attached to the Royalist armies, followed their husbands or boyfriends when they served away from home. The camp followers took on duties such as nursing and other basic tasks. Depending on where they were living between 1642 and 1651, your female ancestors may have been among them.

Battles took place before the official start of the war. Opposition to Charles I grew due to his claims to rule by divine right. In 1637, Charles attempted to impose the new English prayer book on Scotland. When the Scottish people resisted, the king's forces invaded resulting in a conflict known as the Bishops' Wars. On the 5 June 1639, the Calvinist Lady Ann Cunningham rode at Berwick against Charles' men with pistols and daggers: 'All her attendant women had been obliged to become expert marksmen.'[6] Lady Ann and her fellow Scots succeeded in forcing the king to retreat. He signed the Treaty of Berwick in 1639 declaring his peace.

In October 1641, Irish Catholic upper classes and clergy rebelled against the English Protestant administration causing violence to erupt across Ireland. Charles I had aligned himself with the Irish Catholic gentry when he had needed their army to repress the Scottish revolt following the Treaty of Berwick. Many in Scotland and northern England took this as a sign of Charles I's support for Catholicism. Irish women became embroiled in the conflict. In December 1641, Lady Elizabeth Dowdall raised and commanded a force of 80 men, for the defence of the castle.[7] This rebellion spread, merging into the conflict of the English Civil War, with the newly-formed Irish Catholic Confederation fighting on the side of the Royalists.

On 22 August 1642, Charles raised the royal standard in the precincts of Nottingham Castle. With him were the Trained Bands of England. War had begun. Although a battle took place at Powick Bridge, near Worcester on 23 September 1642, the first major battle was at Edge Hill, near Banbury, on 23 October 1642.

On 19 July 1643, Alice Thornton (1626-1706), daughter of the Lord Deputy of Ireland, was under siege in Chester. She recalled, 'Standing on a turret in my mother's house, having been at prayer in the first morning, we were beset in the town; and not hearing of it before, as I looked out at a window towards St Mary's Church, a cannon bullet flew so nigh the place where I stood that the window suddenly shut with such a force the whole turret shook.'[8]

By the summer of 1643, many women had taken against the war and were keen to protest against it. On 9 August 1643, The Women's Petition was presented to the House of Commons by 'two or three Thousand Women', who were described variously as 'oyster wives'[9], or 'generally of the meanest sort'. This was the petition desiring the preservation of the 'True Reformed Protestant Religion' of 'many Civilly-Disposed Women, Inhabiting in the Cities of London, Westminster, the Surburbs and Parts adjacent. Women demonstrated in Palace Yard.' Three or four MPs were sent out to speak to them, but clearly their words were not well received. By noon, their number had increased to 5,000, including 'some Men of the Rabble in Womens Cloaths'.

Volume 5 of Historical Collections of Private Passages of State 1642-45[10] tells us that:

'... having Brickbatts in the Yard, threw them apace at the Train-Band, who then Shot Bullets, and kill'd a Ballad-Singer with one Arm, that was heartning on the Women, and another poor Man that came accidentally. Yet the Women not daunted, cry'd out the louder at the Door of the house of Commons, Give us these Traiters that are against Peace, that we may Tear them to pieces; Give us that Dog Pym, &c. At last Ten of Waller's Troopers, (some of the Cornets) having his Colours in their Hats, came to pass by the Women ... and call'd them Waller's Dogs, &c. Whereupon they drew their Swords, and laid on some of Flatways, but seeing this would not keep them off, at last cut them over the Hands and Faces, and one Woman lost her Nose; whereof 'twas Reported, she afterwards Died. As soon as the rest of the Women saw Blood drawn, they ran away from the Parliament House, and scatter'd themselves in the Church-yard, the Palace-yard, and Places adjacent ... Serjeant Francis, and one Mr. Pulford were committed for encouraging this Female Riot.'

In Hull women built the town's defences. In Gloucester, also, women helped to build and to mend breaches in the barriers. It was not unusual for women of the labouring class, well accustomed to hard manual work and every bit as tough as the men, to join in the digging and building of fortifications, but when London had been threatened the previous year women and girls of every class had turned out to help. According to the poet, Samuel Butler, these women had:

> Rais'd rapiers with their own soft hands
> To put the enemy on the stands;
> From Ladies down to oyster-wenches
> Labour'd like pioneers in trenches,
> Fell to their pick-axes and tools,
> And help'd the men to dig like moles.[11]

The List of Prisoners taken on 29 January 1644 in Nantwich (Namptwych) included '120 Women, that followed the Camp; of whom many had long Knives with which they were said to have done Mischief.'[12] Women in Nantwich were exchanged by Fairfax for Roundhead prisoners.

During the siege of Lyme in Dorset in 1644, some upper class women were evacuated but the vast majority of Puritan women remained and fought alongside the men. Details can be found in records of Bulstrode Whitelocke and A R Byley, *The Great Civil War in Dorset* (Taunton, 1910). In *Joanereidos, or Feminine Valor discovered in Western Women at the Siege of Lyme:*

> The Roman Capitoll by Geese was kept
> They wake't, poore foules, when the dull Souldiers slept.
> Alas! who now keepes Lime? poore femall Cattell
> Who wake all night, labour all day in Battell,
> Geese, as a man may call them, who doe hisse
> Against the oppossers of our Countries blisse.
> And by their seasonable noyse discover
> Our Foes, when they the Workes are climing over.

In 1645, following the Battle of Naseby, over 100 female camp-followers were slaughtered by Parliamentarians in the mistaken belief that they were Irish. The Royalists attacked the baggage train of Sir Thomas Fairfax's parliamentary army, and 'killed above one hundred women, whereof some were officers' wives of quality.'[13]

Plowden writes:

'The Scots were reported to have made use of females to swell their numbers when they marched on Newcastle in 1644 ... When Shelford near Nottingham was taken for the Parliament in 1645, one of the royalist prisoners is said to have been a woman corporal, and a popular ballad of 1655 told the story of a woman who had served for some years in her husband's regiment under the name of Mr Clarke [see *Sydney Papers, Letter and Memorials of State ... from the Originals at Penshurst,* ed. Arthur Collins (London, 1746)].'

Women were not just active on the ground in the Civil War, they also influenced the political and religious process behind the scenes. Martha Simmond (1624-1665) was one of the earliest Quakers, having converted in the 1650s. Martha was passionate in her faith, challenging the Quaker leadership and becoming close to the charismatic Quaker preacher, James Nayler (1618-1660). She gained employment with Oliver Cromwell's sister, Jane Disbrowe, as a nurse. Jane and her husband, Major-General Disbrowe, were so appreciative of her services, that they granted an order for Nayler's release, which Martha took to Exeter where he had been imprisoned. Unfortunately for Nayler, he was arrested again shortly afterwards under the Blasphemy Act of 1650, accused of impersonating Christ. Although he escaped execution, Nayler was pilloried, whipped, branded and imprisoned for two years' hard labour.

Peace came to Britain with the Restoration of King Charles II in 1660. Charles' brother, the staunchly Catholic James II, proved less popular after he became King in 1685. This led to Whig politicians plotting to overthrow him and all remnants of popery. In the consequent Glorious Revolution of 1688-1689, James' Protestant daughter and son in law, Mary and William of Orange, seized power through what was claimed to be a bloodless coup. While little blood was shed in England, hundreds died during the struggles in Scotland and Ireland.

In 1690, for example, William's forces besieged the city of Limerick in Ireland. Thomas Macaulay wrote that 'The very women of Limerick mingled in the combat, stood firmly under the hottest fire, and flung stones and broken bottles at the enemy.'[14]

Georgian Camp Followers

Restrictions on women accompanying men to campaigns had been in place since the end of the Civil War. After the seventeenth century, fewer women followed the camp. Only ten women per company were attached to regiments in the West Indies in 1758[15]. The British regulations for the Corps of Riflemen 1801 stated 'the number of women allowed by Government to embark on service are six for every 100 men inclusive of all Non-Commissioned Officers' wives, which should never be exceeded on any pretext whatsoever, because the doing so is humanity of the falsest kind.'[16]

Despite the rules, many women were present. The numbers of women allowed at camp officially tended not to include hired nurses, for example. Also, many soldiers married without permission, particularly once their sweethearts had become pregnant.

Below the rank of sergeant, only six out of every 100 soldiers were given permission to bring their wives to camp after 1792. These women did not have fighting roles. The main dangers were from being injured, the insanitary nature of camp life, exhaustion from marching, rape, and drowning sea as they travelled with the regiment abroad.

Napoleonic Wars

The early nineteenth century in Europe was overshadowed by the French Revolutionary and Napoleonic wars. Napoleon's dominance of European conflict came to an end at Waterloo in Belgium on 18 June 1815.

Many British women had travelled to Belgium with their husbands and sweethearts. Most of them provided company for the journey rather than military support.

Englishwoman, Charlotte Ann Waldie, recorded her experiences of the scene when the troops departed from Brussels:

> 'Numbers were taking leave of their wives and children, perhaps for the last time, and many a veteran's rough cheek was wet with the tears of sorrow. One poor fellow, immediately under our windows, turned back again and again, to bid his wife farewell, and take his baby once more in his arms; and I saw him hastily brush away a tear with the sleeve of his coat, as he gave her back the child for the last time, wrung her hand, and ran off to join his company, which was drawn up on the other side of the Place Royale. Many of the soldiers' wives rushed out with their husbands to the field, and I saw one young English lady mounted on horseback, slowly riding out of town along with an officer, who, no doubt, was her husband.'[17]

Even though they were not fighting, several women were killed or injured by the conflict: 'A shell inflicted two wounds on the wife of an injured sergeant of the 28th Foot as she carried him from the field. Other British women were found dead after the battle; a cannonball killed one female, who lay with her child at her side.'[18]

The best source for identifying women who were present at Waterloo is in the form of eye-witness accounts, such as that of, 'The wife of Quartermaster Alexander Ross of the 14th Foot remained at his side for some time after the firing began. Her friends feared that she might be hit and urged her to quit the field, but she was reluctant to go, in case she could help the casualties. They then told her that a battlefield was not a suitable place for an officer's wife, so she retired to the belfry of a church, where she enjoyed a fine view of the action ... Another woman at Waterloo was 26-year-old Jenny Jones. Her tombstone at Tau y Ilyn in Wales records that she was there with her husband of the 23rd Royal Welsh Fusiliers and remained on the field for three days.'[19]

Some women did become actively involved in the war. Philip Haythornthwaite identifies a Mrs Maguire:

> '... who saved the Colours of the King's Own from capture. A genuine 'daughter of the regiment', born within the sound of gunfire at Bunker's Hill, she was the wife of the 14th Foot's surgeon, and was aboard the transport *The Three Sisters* when it was captured by a French privateer off Land's End, en route from North America in 1797. To prevent the Colours from falling into French hands, Mrs Maguire wrapped them around her flat-irons and dropped them into the sea. Until an exchange of prisoners she was the only woman in the prison-camp at Brest, with her young son Francis, where she gave birth to a daughter. Surgeon Maguire transferred to the 69th before the Peninsular War, but the family connection with the 4th was maintained because in due course the child Francis was commissioned into it, and was killed in circumstances of great gallantry at the storming of San Sebastian[20]. Mrs Maguire lived until 1857, the recipient of three pensions, one for her husband who died of yellow fever on service, one for Francis, and one for her son Peter who was lost at sea.'[21]

With the rise of Napoleon, women across Europe were becoming increasingly aware of their need to be able to defend themselves. In 1803, some British women proposed 'a Corps of Ladies, in the present exigency of the country; and the Duchess of Gordon, it is said, has offered to command it'[22].

During this period there were several examples of women disguising themselves as men in order to be allowed to fight. Examples include Christian Davies, alias 'Mother Ross', of the Scots Greys, and Hannah Snell of the Royal Marines.

Haythornthwaite mentions only one woman who is known to have fought with no disguise in this period - Madame de Bennes, a Frenchwoman 'who followed her husband into French royalist service in 1792, and after he was killed in 1793 had an additional motive for continuing the fight.'[23]

Notes on researching British women in conflict up to the mid nineteenth century

The genealogist in this field is, therefore, required to be even more of a detective than usual. It is necessary to focus on the tiniest of clues and to read extensively around the subject. However, with perseverance, it will be possible for many family historians to identify their female ancestors' military involvement in pre-Victorian battles.

There are references in both contemporary and historical accounts of women defending themselves from attacks from the invading armies of the Romans, Saxons, Angles, Vikings and Normans. Contemporary accounts of attacks on women survive in published and archived material. These accounts may not always give many names, but they will identify places. We know, for example, that Exeter, was besieged by the Normans in 1068 and that women participated in the fighting. However, women are unlikely to be numerous in these sources - there are only three women depicted on the Bayeux Tapestry, for example - but they can be found.

Useful records for tracing women at war in this period are sparse. Of those that do exist, it can be difficult to confirm their accuracy. Also, after the Commonwealth, there was no standing army until the nineteenth century. Thus researchers of ancestors in this earlier period need to search extensively for clues in the records that are available. One way of tracing female camp followers is through military records. If a soldier is found, and his wife's name is known, this gives a foundation for more detailed research. Unfortunately, no permanent professional standing army existed in England until after the Civil Wars during the reign of Charles I.

No official records or statistics are given specifically for women in the Civil Wars, so a useful approach in assessing whether female ancestors were involved in either the fighting, protection or nursing in the Civil War, is to identify where they were living at the time. Knowledge of militia, battles and armies can help you to fit the Civil War activity to the whereabouts of your ancestor. Militia records for this period are held at The National Archives (TNA) in reference SP 17. One problem for family historians of this era is that the Civil War disrupted everyday life, including the efficient keeping of parish registers. The dearth of records continued into the Interregnum of 1653-1660. This period is sometimes described as the 'Commonwealth gap' due to the lack of records available. Where records do exist, births may have been recorded rather than baptisms. However, all parishes were different and many continued to record as previously.

If your ancestor was living in a town or area where a battle took place, research can be done into the battle using contemporary resources at local history centres. Civil war tracts and contemporary newspapers can be found in the Thomason Collection at the British Library. The Protestation Returns may help you to locate your male ancestors in 1642, when all adult men were asked to swear an oath of allegiance to the Protestant religion. Your ancestors may also have been eligible for paying 'ship money', a tax levied at times of war for those who lived by the coast. Charles I brought in the unpopular tax for those inland and on a permanent basis in 1634, but it was made illegal in 1642.

Land records can also be useful, particularly where your ancestors owned property in this period, and it was threatened or taken from them during this war. Women on both sides such as Anne Savile, Brilliana Harley, Mary Bankes, Charlotte Stanley, Mary

Winter, and Ann Fanshawe were prominent in defending their property from the enemy. Your ancestor may be named in details of post-war resettlement held in the State Papers Domestic at TNA.

Women sometimes performed different roles throughout the wars. 'Parliament Joan' Elizabeth Atkin served first as a nurse, but became a spy later during the Portsmouth, London and Harwich sieges. This may be useful to note when searching for your ancestor in records.

CHAPTER TWO

The Victorian Era - army schoolmistresses and the emergence of military nursing

'I need hardly repeat to you how warm my admiration is for your services, which are fully equal to those of my dear and brave soldiers...'

Letter from Queen Victoria to Florence Nightingale, 1856.

After the Napoleonic wars, women were less welcome as unofficial camp followers. Those female camp followers who remained served in a far limited capacity. No more than six wives of men below the rank of sergeant were granted permission to remain with their husband's regiment on campaign. These followers took on unofficial roles like laundry work. Their names, and those of officers' wives, can be found on regimental rolls. They may also be identified through the birthplaces of their children.

In the early nineteenth century, as the armed forces became more bureaucratic, newer and more formal roles emerged for women. Instead of performing the role of a nurse as a camp follower, for example, women became military nurses. The official rank of army schoolmistress was created to teach soldiers' children.

The Victorian era created a mass of administrative records. Many of these are used by family historians and can be used to identify or locate women

who travelled with serving husbands, or who worked with the forces as a nurse or schoolmistress. The most notable of these are the census, passenger lists, probate records, ships' records, pay lists/musters, and service records. Several private documents, such as letters, diaries or memoirs, survive from this period and may mention your ancestor by name. Fanny Duberly (1829-1903), for example, the wife of Captain Henry Duberly of the 8th Royal Irish Hussars, wrote an account of her experiences during the Crimean War (1854-1856).

Army Schoolmistresses

With the growth of the British Army and the increased deployment of troops overseas, thought turned to the children and orphans of serving soldiers. Schools began to be established across the Empire to care for these children, either for the duration of their father's service or until they reached the age of employment. Many boys would follow their fathers into service, and the schools were often used to prepare them for an army career. From 1796, the army officially enlisted boy soldiers.

No provision was made for families left at home when soldiers were stationed abroad and many eighteenth century army families became homeless. Military authorities were slow to respond to this problem, but eventually they turned to boarding schools as one solution.

One of the most significant of these early schools was the Royal Hibernian Military School (1769-1924) in Dublin. Established as the Hibernian Asylum by the Hibernian Society in the wake of the Seven Years' War, the school initially cared for children orphaned in that war. Later, the school welcomed children of Irish soldiers who were posted overseas. In 1806, the army took over the running of the school, and renamed it the Royal Hibernian Military School. Girls at this school were taught by publicly funded schoolmistresses.[24] This is one of the earliest examples of women being employed officially in army schools.

In 1812, the order was given to all battalions and corps to establish regimental schools. In these schools, soldiers' daughters along with enlisted boys and soldiers' sons were taught by male sergeant schoolmasters. Some wives and daughters of the regiments were employed to teach knitting and sewing. Over time, their role was extended to educating girls in other aspects of domestic life.

By the time Victoria acceded to the throne in 1837, concerns were being raised about the moral upbringing of the thousands of young girls in the camps or depots of the British Army. On 29 October 1840, a Royal Warrant led to the creation of the official post of army schoolmistress. According to the warrant, these schoolmistresses were 'to instruct the Female Children of Our Soldiers as well as reading, writing and the rudiments of arithmetic, as in needlework and other parts of housewifery, and to train them in habits of diligence, honesty and piety'. Most of these women were either wives or daughters of non-commissioned officers (NCOs). They were fully trained and were examined at military barracks, such as Portobello Barracks. From 1863, some of the daughters began their role early as pupil-teachers - a common position in civilian Victorian schools.

From 1850, army schoolmistresses had sole charge of newly established regimental infant schools. Industrial schools were also set up, in which schoolmistresses taught knitting, needlework and domestic occupations.

However, life could be difficult for the Victorian army schoolmistress. Surrounded by children and male schoolmasters and soldiers, the women's position could be lonely. In 1874, *The Standard* declared that army schoolmistresses:

> '... are despised as intellectual inferiors by the schoolmasters, who are their - superiors, and the military education department looks on them as mere auxiliaries ... 'Justice' [a letter writer to the newspaper] tells a very simple tale of hardship ... that the pay and pension of the army schoolmistress are both insufficient. There are three classes of army schoolmistresses, reaping respectively 30l., 36l., and 44l. per annum ... poor remuneration for the arduous labour and numerous qualifications demanded from an army schoolmistress ... If she is the wife of a schoolmaster, or a soldier belonging to the regiment the case is not so hard ...'[25]

From 1858, schoolmistresses were trained to teacher status. Marian Petrie's *Strength, composition, and organization of the army of Great Britain* states that 'Certificate schoolmistresses are not required to undergo an examination or any further training before they can be appointed; but assistant schoolmistresses and pupil-teachers must pass an examination, and must undergo a course of training in an Army School, or at a Training Institution, before they can be appointed army schoolmistresses.'[26] Those who were unqualified were sent to teacher training institutions, such as those at Royal Army School, Aldershot; training at The Model School, Chelsea. Other wives were appointed 3rd class schoolmistresses. Women who applied to become schoolmistresses were aged 18-33, and required a certificate of moral character. Training was thorough and being an army schoolmistress indicated a well-rounded academic, domestic and musical education. Wages were low, however, at around £20 per year.

By 1864-1865, there were 22 first class schoolmistresses, 40 second class schoolmistresses, 35 third class schoolmistresses, 106 assistant schoolmistresses, pupil-teachers and monitresses.[27]

From 1920, Army Schoolmistresses was administered by the Army Educational Corps (AEC), later the Royal Army Educational Corps (RAEC). In 1926, they became the Queen's Army Schoolmistresses (QAS). They served with regiments posted across the Empire, and in the 80 army schools in Britain.

Notes on Researching Army Schoolmistresses

Army schoolmistresses of long service did receive pensions, but these were not generous. A Royal Warrant of 1871 stated:

> 'A schoolmistress shall not have unqualified claim to a pension until she shall have actually served for period of 21 years ... or if disabled before that period for further service through ill-health ... Intermediate periods of non-employment shall not count towards pension. On the promotion of a trained schoolmaster to the rank of sub-inspector, his wife, if an army schoolmistress, shall be entitled to the same pension as if she had been invalided.'

If she became ill before twelve years' service, she would have nothing. Unmarried schoolmistresses, in particular, found it hard to manage financially and domestically. Where pension records survive, they are held at TNA in reference PMG 34.

Regimental (and Garrison) Schools records can be found in the WO 16 muster rolls & pay lists 1878-1898 (TNA).

A Medal roll index for those who served overseas during WWI is held at TNA but has been digitised on Ancestry.

Training records may be held in the archive of the relevant college.

The First World War service records of army schoolmistresses are held in TNA, reference WO 399. Records for those who served more recently are retained by the Ministry of Defence. The names of these army schoolmistresses can be found on surviving muster rolls, held at TNA in reference WO 16. Pension records, in PMG 34 hold BMD, ships' details and military intelligence announcements of military movements in newspapers.

The Army Children Archive (TACA) produces literature and runs a website: **www.archhistory.co.uk**. Although the focus is on children, the site includes details of military postings, healthcare, and schooling. Its schooling section includes passages from Howard R Clarke's *A New History of the Hibernian Military School* containing a history of army schoolmistresses and reference to the memories of former QAS, Dorothy Bottle's *Reminiscences of a Queen's Army Schoolmistress*, which can be read online at: **www.john_bottle.talktalk.net/My_Pages/Transcrs/TranD018.htm**.

Florence Nightingale and the Origins of the Army Nursing Service

Nurses in the early nineteenth century were untrained and often lacking in skill. Margaret Breay's historical account of nursing describes 'the nurse of the day' as being 'not only ignorant but dangerous to the sick upon whom she was supposed to attend'[28]. For Breay, it was the Quaker social reformer, Elizabeth Fry (1780-1845), who was 'the founder of nursing' and 'the real pioneer of Nursing in this country.' In 1840 Fry set up the Institution of Nursing Sisters, a training school in London for private nurses. However, she is probably best remembered for her work with prison reform.

Unquestionably, the formalisation of nursing emerged out of the Crimea War of 1854-56, thanks to the work of Florence Nightingale (1820-1910) and her nursing corps.

The story of the upper class Nightingale's determination to be a nurse against her parents' wishes and her work in the Crimean war as 'the lady with the lamp' is well known. It was the reports of William Howard Russell in *The Times* that focused Florence Nightingale's mind on the horrors of the war between the nations of Russia, Turkey, Great Britain, France and Piedmont-Sardinia, which took place in the Crimea, Asia Minor, the Baltic, the White Sea and on Russia's Pacific Coast. After persuading her friend, Sidney Herbert, the Secretary-at-War, to allow women to nurse at Scutari in Asiatic Turkey, Nightingale was appointed Superintendent of the Female Nurses in the Hospitals in the East. She arrived at the Barrack Hospital in Scutari (then the largest in the world) on 4 November 1854, the eve of the Battle of Inkerman. Her team of nurses tended to thousands of sick and wounded men in insanitary, vermin-ridden surroundings.

In the 1850s, women had not been allowed to nurse male soldiers. They could clean the wards and assist, but male orderlies were responsible for care. Each regiment had a qualified medical officer and a team of untrained male orderlies. When Nightingale and her team of 38 nurses found themselves advising doctors on medical matters, it quickly became clear that the rules needed to change.

Nightingale introduced uniforms, kitchens, discipline and a cleaning regime. In 1855, she wrote to Lady Canning of the differences between her disciplined corps of nurses and female camp followers:

'The rule about wearing the regular dress applies particularly to when they are out of Hospital ... The necessity of distinguishing them at once from camp followers is particularly obvious when they are not engaged in Hospital work'[29].

The 38 nurses[30] who travelled with Florence Nightingale were:

Georgiana Barrie	Eliza Isabella Forbes Keith
S. Barnes	Sarah Kelly
C. [Elizabeth] Blake	Mrs Emma Langston
M. A. Bowmett	Mrs Rebecca Lawfield
Justine G. Chabrillae	Marie Therese MacClean
Mrs Clarke	Georgiana Moore
M. A. Coyle	Elinor O'Dwyer
J. Davy	Mrs Parker
Mrs Elizabeth Drake	Ethelreda Pillars
Miss Harriet Erskine	Frances J Purnell
Emma Fagg	Mrs Roberts
A Faulkner	Miss Clara Sharpe
Sister Margaret Goodman	Elizabeth Smith
E. Grundy	Sarah A Terrot
E. Hawkins	Elizabeth B Turnbull
Mrs Ann Higgins	Elizabeth Wheeler
Maria Huddon	Margaret Williams
Margaret Jones	M Williams
S. Jones	Mrs Wilson

Of these, Mrs Clarke was Nightingale's housekeeper, five were nuns from a convent in Bermondsey, three were nuns from a convent in Norwood, seven were from a Miss Sellon's religious order, and the remainder were civilian hospital nurses.

Other parties of nurses travelled to Scutari separately. Many of these nurses came from the middle classes and some had been trained at Fry's Institution.

One of those who had worked as a private nurse included Elizabeth Davis, who travelled to Scutari with the 'Sisters of Mercy', organised by a Miss Stanley. Elizabeth was:

"a Balaclava nurse', had had a mixed career before nursing in the Crimea. As well as nursing privately and at Guy's Hospital, she had also been a laundry maid, plain cook, and housemaid, and concluded, 'I did not like nursing so well as being in service'. She was highly critical of Florence Nightingale as well as some of the nurses, especially 'the ill-behaviour of two or three of the party, who disgraced themselves by drunkenness'. This recurring complaint was in part the result of the hospitals providing nurses with a generous ration of beer.'[31]

Jamaican boarding-house keeper and daughter of a Scottish soldier, Mary Seacole (1805-1881), was in London at the outbreak of war in September 1854. There she also read Russell's reports in *The Times*. Keen to help her former officer clientele who had been sent to Turkey from Jamaica, she tried to volunteer for nursing. Although she was too late to join Florence Nightingale, and was turned away by others for the colour of her skin, Seacole was determined to help, and arranged her own travel to the Crimea. Contrary to popular belief, Seacole was not a hospital nurse[32], but instead cared for officers in her British Hotel: 'I would willingly have given them my services as a nurse; but as they declined them, should I not open an hotel for invalids in the Crimea in my own way?' Here she cooked meals, organised provisions, employed staff and eradicated vermin. She also volunteered to take refreshments to soldiers waiting to be transported to hospital.

While she was not formally a nurse, Seacole took great care of her hotel guests, giving them nourishing food and drink, and even Creole herbal remedies. Many ordinary soldiers preferred to seek medical treatment at Seacole's hotel than in hospital. Seacole explained the appeal: '... don't you think that you would welcome the familiar figure of the stout lady whose bony horse has just pulled up at the door of your hut, and whose panniers contain some cooling drink, a little broth, some homely cake, or a dish of jelly or blanc-mange...' According to her memoir, she received many letters from grateful patients at the end of the war, such as this:

'This is to certify that Wm. Adams, caulker, of H.M.S. 'Wasp,' and belonging to the Royal Naval Brigade, had a severe attack of cholera, and was cured in a few hours by Mrs. Seacole.'

Despite the best efforts of all the women in Turkey, 22.7% of British Army troops there died. Of these, four times as many died of illness or malnutrition than of death caused by enemy action.

On her return, Nightingale used the 'Nightingale Fund' that had been raised in her honour to establish a training school for nurses at St Thomas' Hospital, London. In 1860, she founded a similar school for military nurses at the Royal Victoria Hospital at Netley. The military hospital at Netley was built in 1856 at the command of Queen Victoria[33]. Built near the port of Southampton, the Royal Victoria Hospital functioned as the main hospital for healing soldiers of the British Empire so that they could return to duty as soon as possible. Military doctors were trained here and the site was home to the Army Medical School.

Some of those who had nursed with Nightingale in the Crimea corps took senior roles at Netley. These included upper-class Jane Catherine Shaw Stewart, who was appointed Lady Superintendent of the Netley Hospital in 1869.

Meanwhile, increasing numbers of British forces were being posted across the Empire. The largest concentration of British forces outside the UK was in India. Troops were often involved in skirmishes and battles across the continent, but women generally remained at the cantonments (army bases). In May 1857, British women were thrust into a war zone when rebels from the 3rd Bengal Light Cavalry, angered by the imprisonment of their colleagues, mutinied. The rebellion spread across the European cantonment in Meerut, near Delhi, and onto further mutinies in Dinapore, Lucknow, Agra and Umballa. Many British women and children were killed or besieged in the struggle. Some of the women present kept diaries or later wrote memoirs of the events. These documents are held in the European Manuscripts section of the Asia and African studies Reading Room at the British Library.

On 19 June 1879, six sisters of Her Majesty's Army Nursing Service (known as the 'Netleys') sailed from Southampton to tend sick and wounded soldiers of the Zulu war at the Military Hospital in Durban[34]. At the time, the Lady Superintendent of the Army Nursing Service[35] was Mrs Jane Cecilia Deeble, who had been trained at St Thomas'. There were several nurse casualties in this period, and Queen Victoria was keen to reward the bravery of the Nursing Sisters with Royal Red Cross (RRC) award - the first military order given exclusively to women. In 1883, the Royal Red Cross award was established. Mrs Deeble was the tenth recipient of the award. Another 14 were given to nurses for the Zulu war.

During this period, a sense of snobbery existed within army nursing. Florence Nightingale and Jane Stewart were from upper class backgrounds and there was a prejudice towards those who were of higher class. In 1887, Mrs Deeble 'was busy observing that many nurses were not ladies but rather offspring from 'the shop girl class.'[36]

By 1881, with the demands of the Empire increasingly straining British forces, the Army Nursing Service (ANS) became officially part of the British Army. There was evidence of the term 'Army Nursing Service' being used to describe the nurses who served in the First Boer War (then known as the Zulu War). Nurses from Netley and others sponsored by the National Society also served in the Egyptian Campaign of 1882, and the Sudan war of 1883-1885. Members of St John's Ambulance also served in Africa.

From 1883, Nursing Sisters were employed in Military Hospitals in Aldershot, Gosport, Portsmouth, Devonport, Dover, Shorncliffe, Canterbury, the Curragh, Malta and Gibraltar. The Naval Nursing Service (NNS) was founded in 1884. It existed under this title and as the Royal Naval Nursing Service up to 1902.

Although there are records of nurses in army hospitals in India from the 1860s, the Indian Nursing Service (INS) for the British Army in India was founded in 1888.

Greater numbers of Nursing Sisters were sent to southern Africa during the Anglo-Boer War of 1899-1902. They also served aboard hospital ships and on troop ambulance trains.

The ANS changed its name to the Queen Alexandra's Imperial Military Nursing Service (QAIMNS) in 1902. This reflected both Britain's imperial mission and its feelings towards the new Queen and ANS President. The Service remained small, comprising only around 300 members by the outbreak of war in 1914. To support the QAIMNS, the QAIMNS Reserve (QAIMNSR) was formed in 1908. This corps was formed from members of the recently disbanded Princess Christian's[37] Army Nursing Reserve, which had been formed in 1897. Some of the PCANR had served in the Second Boer War. The new QAIMNSR consisted of civilian nurses, ready to serve in an emergency, reflected the temporary nature of the newly-formed Territorial Force of the British Army.

In 1896, the civilian Colonial Nursing Association (CNA) was formed, recruiting nurses for the Colonial Office. This organisation would go on to have a more military function in later periods.

Margaret Augusta Fellowes

Mrs Fellowes was a nurse under Florence Nightingale. She trained at St Thomas' Hospital and Netley. She served in the Zulu War, travelling out in 1881, and then in Egypt in 1882. However, Florence Nightingale was concerned that her skills were not being used properly[38] and wrote about this in private correspondence.

A transcription of Margaret Augusta Fellowes' nursing record by Sue Light (taken from TNA ref. WO 25/3955) can be found on Findmypast. This reveals that she was also known by the surnames Kirkland and Makins. She was, in fact, Lady Makins at the time of her death. Kirkland was her maiden name. The transcription reveals that she was born in 1845, she served with the Army Nursing Service, and her father was General John Vesey Kirkland. Fellowes was trained at St Thomas' and appointed as ANS on 9 September 1882. She was a National Aid Society candidate and 'one of Miss Nightingale's nominees'. She resigned on 17 February 1883.

The A2A search engine reveals a number of documents relating to Fellowes in the HO1 reference of LMA, in the papers concerning Nightingale nurses. Letters written to her from Florence Nightingale are held in HO1/ST/NC1. The index tells us 'After the death of her first husband, General Fellowes, in 1879, she trained as a nurse at the

Nightingale School in 1880. In 1881 she accompanied Sir Frederick Roberts' force to the Transvaal. On her return to England in June 1881, she was appointed Sister Leopold (Sister of Leopold ward at St Thomas'). In 1882-1883 she served as a nurse in the Egyptian War. In December 1884 she married Sir George Makins, surgeon to St Thomas' Hospital. The collection includes letters, a passenger list including Mrs Fellowes from the *RMS Durban*, a funeral service sheet and an obituary.

An obituary was published in *The Times*[39]. This reveals details of her personality:

'... exceeding grace of manner and sweetness of temperament', as well as of her early military travels with her father. She accompanied him when he was engaged in military service in Canada and South Africa. The obituary highlights Florence Nightingale's high regard for Fellowes: she 'speedily recognized Mrs. Fellowes's outstanding nursing qualities and powers of leadership'.

Fellowes was one of the first recipients of the Royal Red Cross; this was awarded to her in 1884. Sue Light's transcription of M A Fellowes' award is on Findmypast. This reveals Fellowes received a First Class award for service as a Nursing Sister on Hospital Ship 'Carthage'. Extra notes on the transcription reveal that the award was for service in Egypt, that Fellowes' changed her name by marriage and reported this 2 May 1885, she died 29 September 1931, which was reported in *The Times* 1 October 1931. This record was from Volume 145/1, page 1.

During the First World War, Fellowes came out of retirement to run the Hospital for Facial Injuries in Park Lane.

Notes on Researching the Victorian Era: army schoolmistresses and the emergence of military nursing

Staff records of early nurses are held in the Nightingale Collection at LMA. *Registers of Nurses sent to Military Hospitals in the East, 1854-55* is held at the Florence Nightingale Museum. Letters of applications for nursing in the Crimea and lists of nurses are held at The National Archives.

Details on the Crimean War and the life of Florence Nightingale can be found in the many letters and books she wrote. These include: *Notes on Matters Affecting the Health, Efficiency and Hospital Administration of the British Army* (1858) and her 'Answers to Written Questions', reported in *Florence Nightingale and the Crimean War*, volume 14 in the *Collected Works of Florence Nightingale*.

Mary Seacole's memoir of her experiences in the Crimea, *Wonderful Adventures of Mrs Seacole in Many Lands* (1857) can be read online at **http://digital.library. upenn.edu/women/seacole/adventures/adventures.html**

A list of nurses who served in the Crimean War taken from the index and partial abstract of the Register of Nurses can be read online at **www.dorsetbay.plus.com/ hist/crimea/nurselist.htm**

Fanny Duberly's *Journal Kept During The Russian War: From The Departure Of The Army From England In April 1854, To The Fall Of Sebastopol,* can be read online at: **http://digital.library.upenn.edu/women/duberly/journal/journal.html**

More on the Crimean nurse, Elizabeth Davis, can be read in her memoir, *The autobiography of Elizabeth Davis, a Balaclava nurse, daughter of Dafydd Cadwaladyr*, ed. Jane Williams (2 vols, London, Hurst and Blackett, 1857), published online by Google Books: **http://books.google.co.uk/books/about/The_ Autobiography_of_Elizabeth_Davis_a_B.html?id=bfc5AAAAcAAJ&redir_esc=y**

Elizabeth Davis' letter of application to the Sidney Herbert MP is held at TNA reference WO 25/264.

Newspaper reports of wars or from regimental stations may reveal details of nursing life there. Names are sometimes mentioned. Details of awards and casualties may be found in the *London Gazette*. Records of the Royal Red Cross are available online at TNA Discovery website.

Records of 238 women who served in the ANS are held at TNA in WO25/3955, and transcriptions of these records have been digitised on Findmypast. The online records also contain supplementary information from additional sources, including army lists and the *London Gazette*.

The records contain details such as father's occupation, training hospital, date of appointment to the Army Nursing Service (between 1869 and 1891), and notes on retirement or resignation from the service.

Records of women who nursed at the Royal Hospital Chelsea between 1856 and 1910 can be searched at Findmypast. The original records are held at TNA in WO 23/181.

Ledgers containing details of the Royal Red Cross (RRC) awards are held at TNA in WO 145. Transcriptions of the information contained in these registers can be found on Findmypast.

The Findmypast nursing collections have been published in association with Sue Light. More useful information on army nurses can be found at Sue Light's website: **www.scarletfinders.co.uk**

Records of nurses in India and of the St John's Ambulance Association are held at the British Library. A good overview of researching military nurses in India can be found at the website of the Families in British India Society (FIBIS) **www.new.fibis.org**. When researching nurses in India the Military Collection 262A at the British Library includes letters in the candidate's own handwriting and demonstrating their personality and perhaps manner of speech. Some include letters of instruction on travel, even naming the troop ship on which the nurse would sail. For Dora Maxwell Moore (31 on the 16 July 1890), who was born in Benares to a Chaplain father of the HMIS, and alumnus of Cheltenham Ladies College it was the Serapis, sailing from Portsmouth on the 12 November 1890.

Separate from the Indian Nursing Service was the organisation of Lady Roberts Homes in India. Records for this can be found at the British Library.

The records of the Indian Nursing Service lie within the Military Collections at the British Library (ref. IOR:L/MIL/7) in Collection 262 (ref. IOR/L/MIL/7/11316-11616) and cover the years 1886-1940. Within this are Papers of Sisters appointed to Service (files 81-99 [5]): this is a leather volume comprised of files, including letters. File 99 is that of a Miss M. COOPER and begins with an official form marked Military Collection number 262a, file 99. There is a letter addressed to Miss May Cooper, Victoria Hospital, Tite Street, Chelsea. This follows an interview May had in June 1904 (according to her letter). In May 1905 she was told to forward her certificate and a letter confirms she did so. On 6 May 1904, the Senior Surgeon to the Victoria Hospital for Children, Chelsea certified that Miss Cooper is fit to undertake the duties of a nursing sister in India.

Aside from the correspondence is the Declaration, which gives date and place of birth (30 August 1875, Kilburn), her father's occupation (surveyor), her marital status (single), her place and standard of education (Miss Metcalf's Highfield Hendon and Madchen Austalt, Am Rhine), her medical certificate (very strong), where trained (St Bartholomew's Hospital 5 years February 1899 - February 1904 with matron's and two senior medical officers' names), appointments and referees.

Then are personal and work Statements from referees (a senior surgeon at the hospital; this includes her Tone 'Superior - a highly cultivated lady' although another resounds with 'high moral tone' but elsewhere he notes she is not a good disciplinarian).

This has an index at the beginning but alphabetised by first letter only. There was no May Cooper. Names are indexed in chronological order of appointment - including those that were rejected or those whose applications were withdrawn. Details given are name, address, number & date of application, declaration date, date of birth, supporting document name; health certificate date; institutions trained; their certificates and testimonials; general remarks; and note of parents' social standing,

Medal Rolls for service in Egypt and South Africa are held at TNA in reference WO 100.

Military nursing is discussed further in chapters 5 and 9.

A British government poster used during the First World War to promote the war effort, 1915. Public domain image.

CHAPTER THREE
Women in the First World War

'Without women victory will tarry, and the victory which tarries means a victory whose footprints are footprints of blood.'

Lloyd George, Speech 17 July 1915.

During the First World War, the Great War, there were increasing opportunities for women to serve in formal and informal roles. Throughout the war, the numbers of women in official employment increased dramatically. Many women took up work in positions left by men who had departed for the front. These roles included work in offices, government departments and on public transport. Thousands also worked in war-specific work such as munitions, while others were employed on the land.

Volunteer Corps

After the declaration of war by the United Kingdom on 4 August 1914, the established women's organisations responded quickly. Among these were the army nursing services, the Queen Alexandra's Imperial Military Nursing Service and QAIMNSR, and the Voluntary Aid Detachments (VADs), which are discussed further in Chapter 5.

Away from the battlefields, social, religious and political groups marshalled their members into voluntary activity. One of the first priorities was to

welcome, and provide for, the 200,000 Belgian refugees who arrived in Britain by autumn 1914, exiled from their homeland after the enemy invasion. Up to the summer of 1915, it was mainly aristocratic or upper middle-class women such as Lady Londonderry who established and ran these voluntary groups.

The volunteers busied themselves raising funds for the Red Cross and running canteens at Young Men's Christian Association (YMCA) 'huts'. Other religious societies employing women during the war were the Church Army, Soldiers' Christian Association, and the Salvation Army. In 1914, Decima Moore and the Honourable Evelina Haverfield founded one of the first quasi-military organisations, the Women's Emergency Corps (WEC). The WEC existed chiefly to feed soldiers and refugees. Along with the National Guild of Housework, the WEC also trained girls in domestic work. As none of its members were paid, most were upper class and of independent means.

The Women's Emergency Canteens were run under the London Committee of the French Red Cross. One member, Mrs Mary Stuart Gartside-Tipping was killed in an accident while serving. She was awarded the *Croix de Guerre*. According to *The Times*, she was shot by a soldier whose mind was disturbed. She is buried at Vauxbuin French National Cemetery. Plot III.B.5, after being originally buried in a vault in Compiegne South Communal Cemetery[40].

Other quasi-military organisations were the Home Service Corps (HSC), the British Service Corps (BSC), and the Women's Defence Relief Corps, which was raised by Mrs Dawson Scott in an attempt to free men for work at the front. Volunteers of the Women's Auxiliary Force (WAF) ran canteens, social clubs, worked on the land and in hospitals. The WAF should not be confused with the WAAC or other non-voluntary auxiliary forces that were brought in by the government in 1916.

The Women's Volunteer Reserve (WVR), sponsored by Edith, Marchioness of Londonderry (nee Edith Helen Chaplin; 1878-1959), was formed as a branch of the WEC in 1914 following the aerial bombing of the East coast. The WVR became the largest and best-known of the voluntary organisations. However, not only were WVR members unpaid, they had to buy their own khaki uniforms.

As the war developed and women's organisations became more professional, some of these early volunteer groups became redundant. Nevertheless, their style and uniforms were to influence the auxiliary corps that came after them. Also, key founders, such as the Marchioness of Londonderry, would go on to more significant roles in women's services later in the war. Lady Londonderry was appointed Dame Commander of the Order of the British Empire in the Military Division in 1917. She continued to assist in the running of an officers' hospital at her home in London's exclusive Park Lane.

The early years of the twentieth century had seen a dramatic growth in women's political involvement, following the formation of Millicent Fawcett's National Union of Women's Suffrage Societies (NUWSS) in 1897. From 1903, more militant demands for women's right to vote came from members of Emmeline Pankhurst's Women's Social and Politician Union (WSPU).

By 1913, animosity between the suffragettes and the government had reached its height, following Prime Minister Asquith's last minute retreat from enfranchising women over 30 years of age. On the 5 June, the suffragette movement claimed its first martyr when 40 year old Emily Wilding Davison was struck by the king's horse while trying to throw a suffragette banner over him. By the end of the year, hundreds of suffragettes had been imprisoned and several were force-fed after going on hunger strike, causing the government to pass the controversial 'Cat and Mouse Act'. This act, officially the Prisoners (Temporary Discharge for Ill Health) Act 1913, allowed women, who had been freed for going on hunger strike, to be imprisoned again after they had recovered their strength.

In the summer of 1914, the women's suffrage campaign continued to dominate the news and the political agenda. Yet, on the outbreak of war, leaders of the WSPU along with the NUWSS put aside their campaigning to focus on the war effort. Politically active suffragettes who had previously been mobilised to protest their cause were now readied for their new role as patriots. Emmeline and Christabel Pankhurst changed the name of their journal to *The Suffragette into Britannia*, and helped to recruit volunteers for the forces and to fill industrial roles left by serving men. Meanwhile, the NUWSS funded women-only hospital units.

Emmeline's daughter, Sylvia Pankhurst, disagreed with her mother and sister's patriotic stance and continued the struggle of votes for women. As a socialist, Sylvia was against what she regarded as a capitalist war. Instead of working for war, she used her campaigning skills to demand improved work and childcare facilities for the wives and children of enlisted working-class men. In 1916, Sylvia renamed her organisation the Workers' Suffrage Federation. The following year, the newspaper she helped found, *The Woman's Dreadnought* was renamed *The Workers' Dreadnought* indicating its socialist position.

The suffragette movement in the UK was dominated by middle and upper-class women. Life for the vast majority of British women continued much as before until the middle of 1915, when the severity of war became more apparent. Among the working classes, women were already occupied in roles unrelated to the war effort. One of the largest areas of employment for women was in domestic service. Other women with children worked at home, dressmaking, doing piece work, or taking in laundry or lodgers. Those who worked in factories were busy making textiles, matches or pottery. In areas such as the West Midlands, thousands of women worked in metal trades that were largely unrelated to military use.

In response to news from the Western Front, the government introduced a voluntary registration scheme for women in March 1915, requesting they sign up for military related work or service. But, for most women, the war only brought real change to their lives following May 1915 and the election of the new Coalition government.

Munitions Work

One of the key ministers in the new government was David Lloyd George, who had begun the war as Chancellor of the Exchequer. It was he who, in March 1915, convinced male employers and trade union members that women should be employed in munitions factories, but only for the duration of war.

Munitions workers are examined in more detail in Chapter 4.

Later Voluntary Organisations

After their successful placement in munitions factories, officials felt that women could take over traditional male roles in other areas. The Army Council thus authorised women to work as cooks and waitresses (for example, through Lady Londonderry's Women's League - formerly the WVR). Later the Council encouraged women into other work too, taking over the operations of many of the early voluntary organisations.

A year after war began, the nation had become fully aware that the war that was to be 'all over by Christmas' was having a major impact on all their lives. Women across the nation were being affected as they had with no previous war. On 15 August 1915, the government demanded that all persons (male and female) sign up to a compulsory National Register so that availability for service or war work could be fully assessed.

Conscription and Empty Jobs

The compilation of the National Register led on to compulsory conscription. The Military Service Bill of 5 January 1916 brought in the conscription of unmarried men. Only four months later in May 1916, the government brought in Universal Military Conscription of men, including those that were married. Thousands of these men were to leave wives, mothers and children with little or no income. They would also leave job positions empty and ready to be filled by women.

By late May 1916, the government began a national drive to find women to take these empty roles. Whereas some women were keen to take up work, or move into higher paid jobs, others were unhappy at having to leave home and friends, or an established position. At the time, most women were working in mills or factories, dressmaking, millinery, matchbox-making, as shop assistants, or in domestic service. As a result of this new demand, many women left domestic service positions empty. Domestic service was to suffer a major and permanent decline during this period.

Some women had higher paid roles in skilled work, such as clerks, teachers or professional nurses. Wherever they worked before the war or during, women were paid less than men. The Trade Union movement, particularly, was influential in protecting men's payments at the cost of their female counterparts.

Women's Auxiliary Military Services

In December 1916, the Coalition Government made a cohesive effort to organise work on the Home Front. As part of this effort, the government established Women's Auxiliary Military Services. These were auxiliary to the existing male services of the Army, Royal Navy, Royal Flying Corps and Royal Naval Service. The Women's Army Auxiliary Corps, Women's Royal Naval Service (WRNS) and Women's Royal Air Force (WRAF, formed 1918) are discussed in Chapter 6.

From early 1917, a National Service Scheme was established 'to cover all aspects of civilian and non-combatant employment' for men and women.

Besides the volunteer corps and the auxiliary services, there were other forces employing women for war service and work, including those labouring on the land.

Spies

The vast majority of British women did not serve beyond the Home Front. Nevertheless, this was not without its dangers.

Even women who were involved in secret service work worked mainly in the UK. Women were involved in organised secret service work from as early as 1909 and some continued through the war. Dorothy Westmacott was recruited to MI5 in 1911, although she is shown on the census[41] as 'Living At House'. Her father, who recruited her was described as 'Confidential Clerk To A Private Gentleman', which shows how difficult it can be to identify a secret service employee in public records.

During the war women were employed as spies and in other intelligence roles. Thousands of agents were recruited during the war for various intelligence services. In MI5 alone, there were around 800 women working in mainly administrative roles. Although most were drawn from public schools or women's Oxbridge colleges, surprisingly, MI5 employed Girl Guides as young as 14 as messengers and patrollers.

Women were also involved in signals intelligence, organised from within the Army and Navy. Members of the Women's Army Auxiliary Corps, known as Hush-WAACs, helped the Intelligence Corps to decode German signals. It was out of these agencies that the Government Code and Cipher School (GCCS) would be formed in 1919.

Girl Guides

The Girl Guide movement was founded in 1910 by Agnes Baden-Powell, following on from the emergence of Girl Scouts in 1909. During the Great War, Girl Guides volunteered quickly for many roles, and those unable to work in Voluntary Aid Detachments (VADs) cared for children, collected waste paper, or helped on farms. Guides also acted as patients for VAD training, and some of those from aged 14 upwards worked in munitions factories.

Originally, MI5 employed Boy Scouts as Messengers, but the boys quickly proved 'troublesome' and ended up 'getting into mischief'[42]. So, 'On 15 September 1915, MI5 replaced the scouts with Girl Guides, aged between 14 and 16, who were entrusted to carry secret counter-espionage memoranda and reports.'[43] Not that the girls were perfect: it was just 'their methods of getting into mischief were on the whole less distressing to those who had to deal with them than were those of the boys'.[44] Those employed worked long days, from 9am-7pm, and were paid 10 shillings per week. MI5 were so impressed with the Guides that in January 1917 they employed a small group, the MI5 Guide Company, within the building at Waterloo Road to maintain the typewriters, dust, and clean. Propaganda films were made during the war, showing enemy spies being foiled by Girl Guides.

Work On The Land

German submarine and mine attacks on merchant shipping led to a reduction in imported food. The consequent food shortage created increases in food prices and queues for popular foodstuffs. The problems were reduced by the introduction of rationing in 1918, but from 1916 there was a concern that Britain should reduce its reliance on imports by producing food at home. Britain needed to feed itself.

For this reason, and to replace male agricultural workers away in the armed forces, women were sought to work on the land. In the early years of the war, the Board of Agriculture gave male farm labourers exemptions from military service. Thus women were not needed in large numbers until the situation at sea became more urgent in 1916. That year, Dame Meriel Talbot DBE was appointed to work with the Ministry of Agriculture to find a solution. The Board of Agriculture's Women National Land Service Corps was established in February 1916. That same year, the Board of Trade had appointed Women's War Agricultural Committees in each county; other women were employed as Travelling Inspectors and Group Leaders in villages. The Women's Branch also developed the Women's Institute. These committees helped to create a voluntary register of workers specifically for the land.

In 1917, Rowland Prothero, the Minister of Agriculture (and Fisheries), founded the Women's Land Army (WLA). There was no conscription but women did have to sign documents on enrolling, committing themselves to six months or a year's service. These contracts existed for 'Government schemes such as the National Factories, Women's Forage Corps, and later, the Land Army'. Although this was not an armed service, the WLA did much for the war effort, not least in enabling merchant sailors to restrict their imported cargoes to the bare essentials. At its height the WLA had 17,596 members[45].

1. Member of Women's Land Army Great War - by 1917, a quarter of a million women were working on farms across Britain: 'this unknown WLA worker wears a typical uniform of the period: a wide brimmed hat with the Women's Land Army badge of the period, a rubberised waterproof jacket very similar to an army despatch riders coat, jodhpurs, good shoes and leather gaiters.'

According to Dame Talbot, 45,000 women applied but around half were rejected by Selection Panels, leaving 23,000 who went on to work in diverse roles such as milking, driving tractors, driving carts, ploughing, thatching, looking after sheep and working in the fields. With restrictions on fuel, the work of the WLA returned to Victorian farming methods: women ploughed fields by hand and relied on whatever horses had not been taken to the Front. By July 1918, there were 16,000 members of the WLA; this increased the number of women working on the land to 113,000, compared with 80,000 in July 1914.

Most WLA members came from the middle and upper classes but a large number were drawn from the working classes. Some local women worked part-time, but others from farther afield lived in Gang Hostels. All worked for a minimum wage, although they did receive bonuses for extra days.

The Land Army was divided into three sections:

1. agricultural - Women could enrol for a minimum of 6 or 12 months.
2. timber cutting - Women could enrol for a minimum of 6 or 12 months. The Women's Forestry Corps was run by the Board of Trade (Timber Supply Department) and supplied wood for home and war use.
3. Women's Forage Department - provided food/forage for army horses; minimum of 12 months.

The Women's Auxiliary Agricultural Corps, and Women's Forage Corps were formed by similar government initiatives. These groups helped to perform the roles previously undertaken by the men in the (Royal) Army Service Corps (RASC).

When considering your ancestor's war service it is useful to note that many women changed roles during the war. Norah S. Bristow, for example, began the war serving in the War Office issuing pensions, but later worked as a motor tractor driver with the Women's Land Army in Essex and Norfolk[46]. She was demobilised on 27 Oct 1919 at Canterbury.

The Land Army was disbanded officially in 1919. Women received certificates of appreciation for their services.

Private organisations also existed for agricultural work, including:

- Women's Defence Relief Corps
- Women's Legion Agricultural Branch
- Women's Farm and Garden Union
- Women's National Land Service Corps (later Women's Land Corps)
- Land Service Corps.

During the war, administration of the Women's Institute was moved to the Board of Agriculture.

Industrial Work

Many women who had worked in factories before the war continued to do so. Others replaced men at a variety of factories across Britain. Besides munitions workers, female wartime industrial workers were employed in gas works and as riveters in shipyards.

Transport

One of the largest areas of women's employment in the First World War was transport. This saw the biggest proportionate increase of women's employment from 18,000 in 1914 to 117,000 in 1918.[47]

When the war began, few Britons and even fewer women were able to drive. The few women who could came from the upper classes. In 1915, a group of these women formed the Volunteer Motor Mobilization Corps. This was not an exclusively female organisation, however. Some Corps staff were men.

In the realm of public transport, companies and union members were initially reluctant for women to be employed. In May 1915, tramway workers passed a resolution that the employment of women on the tramways was a dangerous and unwise innovation. When, in August 1915, Salford Corporation engaged women to work on the tramways, a number of men refused to work with them. However, by winter 1915, half the Manchester tram conductors were women and there were several drivers in other parts of Lancashire.[48]

2. Annie Jolly (nee Jones) in the late 1930s (middle).

London saw a marked increase in female transport workers. In February 1916, the London General Omnibus Company was converted to the use of women conductresses (in March there were only 100 bus conductresses in London, but training was taking place for another 500 per month). By February 1917: around 2,500 bus conductresses were being employed. At least half of these new transport workers were former domestic servants. Annie Jones (later Jolly; 1882-1969) had worked in domestic service in Stoke Newington, but during the war she became a conductress for Metropolitan Electric Tramways (MET) on the number 79 tram, which ran from Waltham Cross to Smithfield.

Women were employed not only as conductresses, but also as drivers. For working class women, this was often the first time they had driven. In early 1916, women drivers were employed by the Metropolitan Asylums Board Motor Ambulance Section, and in July 1916, women were running the London County Council Ambulance Corps.

Women's Police Volunteers

Margaret Damer Dawson was appointed the Chief of the Women Police Volunteers in 1914. The Women's Police Movement in Great Britain was part of the Women's Auxiliary Service, and was originally responsible for managing the transport of the Belgian refugees in August 1914. They wore a distinctive uniform of 'breeches and highly-polished riding-boots; naval peaked cap and great coat; and a variety of flashes and rank-badges.'[49]

Later, Women's Police Volunteers were employed in checking for prostitutes near army bases. Similar 'welfare' patrols were also organised by the National Council of Women (previously the National Union of Women Workers). Other women police were employed at munitions factories (including HM Factories, National Filling Factories and Government Controlled Establishments).

Conscientious Objectors

Female conscientious objectors of the First World War usually found avoiding conscription easier than their male counterparts. Where they were active was in disrupting the war effort: 'Nellie Best, an activist associated with Sylvia Pankhurst, was sentenced to six months imprisonment in March 1916 for interfering with recruiting (Liddington, 1989). Alice Wheeldon and her daughter Hettie, involved in aiding fugitive conscientious objectors, were charged with plotting to assassinate Lloyd George in early 1917 (Liddington, 1989).'[50]

Many conscientious objectors and pacifists were Quakers. However, others were women from a variety of religious and social backgrounds. Female poets and other writers expressed their feelings in works that survive today. The Roman Catholic Lady Margaret Sackville, a poet and children's author, worked alongside her sister-in-law Muriel De La Warr in the peace movement during the war. Lady Margaret's notable anti-war collection, *The Pageant of War* was published in 1916.

A Memory (1916)
There was no sound at all, no crying in the village,
Nothing you would count as sound, that is, after the shells;
Only behind a wall the low sobbing of women,
The creaking of a door, a lost dog-nothing else.
Silence which might be felt, no pity in the silence,
Horrible, soft like blood, down all the blood-stained ways;
In the middle of the street two corpses lie unburied,
And a bayoneted woman stares in the market-place.

Humble and ruined folk-for these no pride of conquest,
Their only prayer: 'O Lord, give us our daily bread!'
Not by the battle fires, the shrapnel are we haunted;
Who shall deliver us from the memory of these dead?

British Women Overseas

Outside of the military medical personnel, few women travelled to the Western Front. Some women served in India, but few in the war in the Middle East. One woman who was recruited by British Intelligence for her knowledge of the Arab region was the explorer, Gertrude Bell (1868-1926). At the time, the British feared Arab loyalty to Turkey - one of Britain's enemies in the war. In an attempt to retain Arab loyalty in October 1915, the High Commissioner in Egypt, Sir Henry McMahon, promised Arab independence. This complicated imperial plans, particularly those of the India Office, which had hoped to annex Iraq for itself. In the ensuing difficulties, Britain famously sent T. E. Lawrence to persuade the Arabs to the British cause. Meanwhile, Gertrude Bell was sent to Arab Bureau in Cairo to gather useful information. She also used her diplomatic skill to liaise with the Arab leader, Hussein, and his sons, encouraging them to mobilise against Turkey.

Appreciation of Women's War Service

During the war and in its immediate aftermath, the nation was hugely grateful to women for their service and work. Public declarations of thanks appeared in newspapers and in physical memorials across the nation. The Government showed its appreciation through the medals bestowed from 1918.

In the last months of the war, the Royal Family showed its appreciation with a public statement. The King's Thanks to the Women Workers of the Empire was given on 29 June 1918:

'When the history of our Country's share in the War is written, no chapter will be more remarkable than that relating to the range and extent of women's participation. The service has been rendered only at the cost of self-sacrifice and endurance. Women have readily worked for long hours and under trying conditions in our factories and elsewhere to produce the supplies of munitions which were urgently needed at the Front and to maintain the essential service of the Country. As nurses and V.A.D. Workers, they have laboured in hospital for the care of the sick and wounded with even more than the accustomed devotion which has characterized our Red Cross Service since the days of the Crimean War. They have often faced cheerfully and courageously great risks, but both at home and overseas, in carrying on their work, and the Women's Army has its own Roll of Honour of those who have lost their lives in the service of the county. Some have even fallen under the fire of the enemy. Of all these we think to-day with reverent pride.'

Notes on Researching Women in the First World War

As most service records of women who served in the First World War were destroyed in the bombing of the War Office in September 1940, family historians need to explore the documents that do survive and other ways to find out more.

With few official records surviving for non-auxiliary services, further information can be found by searching local and national newspapers, private papers and local archive catalogues.

Sadly, none of the 1915 National Register records survive. The nearest national register of the population in this period was the census of 1911, which can be searched online at various websites. Many suffragettes refused to appear on the census, but some were enumerated by family members or persistent officials. This census also gives some indication as to what work or otherwise your female ancestor was doing before war began.

The Europeana website holds millions of images, text files, digitised books, oral and film footage relating to the First World War from cultural and scientific institutions across Europe: **www.europeana.com/portal/**. This resource includes over 6,500 items held in the Great War Archive: **www.oucs.ox.ac.uk/ww1lit/gwa** at the University of Oxford. This includes memoirs, such as that of WAAC Violet Nye, photographs of serving women, and documents, such as Ellen 'Nellie' Ogden's Pass giving her 'permission to be absent from headquarters' while serving with the Women's Legion (ref. GWA_3287_nel1.jpg).

One of the main resources for researching women in this period is the Women's Work Collection, which can be searched in Imperial War Museum's Explore History Centre: **http://london.iwm.org.uk/server/show/nav.24479**

Campaigns and letters regarding the Belgian refugees are mentioned in local newspapers; also see local government board/ War Refugees Committee records & the Women collection at IWM.

NUWSS records are held in The Women's Library collection @ LSE and Political Science (LSE).

Copies of the Women's Volunteer Reserve magazine can be found at the British Library and the Imperial War Museum.

The Welsh Experience of World War One

The National Library of Wales, in partnership with JISC, is undertaking a mass digitisation of primary sources relating to World War One. Sources included are printed and manuscript sources as well as moving image, audio and photographic material. Collections to be digitised are from the National Library of Wales, Aberystwyth University Special Collections, Bangor University Special Collections, Trinity St David's Special Collections, Swansea University, Cardiff University Library, the Archives of BBC Cymru Wales and archives and local records offices that are members of ARCW (Archives and Records Council, Wales). The records will also include content from an ongoing project: People's Collection Wales. The unified, mass digital collection that will be created will represent the experience of the entire Welsh nation during World War One; **http://cymruww1.llgc.org.uk/**

The Gertrude Bell Archive is held at Newcastle University: **www.gerty.ncl.ac.uk/**

Memorials

Plaques and other memorials may be found to the work of women volunteers in the towns, cities and villages where they worked. For example, there is a brass plate in the waiting room of Preston Railway Station that reads:

'DURING THE GREAT WAR OF 1914-1919
THIS ROOM WAS, BY THE PERMISSION OF
THE L. & N. W. AND L. & Y. RAILWAY
COMPANIES, OCCUPIED FROM AUG. 19. 1915
TO NOV. 11. 1919. BY THE PRESTON STATION
SAILORS AND SOLDIERS FREE BUFFET
ASSOCIATION VOLUNTARY WORKERS,
WHO SUPPLIED THREE AND A QUARTER
MILLIONS OF THE SAILORS AND SOLDIERS
WHO PASSED THROUGH THIS STATION, WITH
REFRESHMENTS AND COMFORTS. THE ROOM
FROM AUG. 19. 1915 TO MAY 31. 1919 WAS
OPEN CONTINUOUSLY DAY AND NIGHT AND
FROM JUNE 1 1919 TO NOV. 11. 1919 FOR
FOURTEEN HOURS EACH DAY.'

Medals and Awards

Details of awards can be found in the 'Decorations' section of the Women, War & Society link in the IWM Explore History Centre. The database can be searched by name and reveals genealogical details as well as information on medals received (see Lily example of ref. DEC 7/4 Roll of Women of the British Empire to whom the Military Medal was awarded). There are also some photographs for some listings in ref. DEC 1-8.

Medal index cards for women, as well as the Military Medal collection and Indian Army cards, are held at the Imperial War Museum. As such, they do not form part of the Ancestry WWI Medal Card database [provided in partnership with TNA].

Police

A number of police records can be found at TNA (see Records Section), but other useful sources of information can be found at The Police Federation of England and Wales, Surbiton: National Council of Women Collection; the records of the Metropolitan Police Office (series MEPO at TNA], Bristol Training School for Women's Police and Patrols; the Scottish school; and PRONI, which holds the papers of Edith, Lady Londonderry.

A list of original members of the Women's Police Movement can be found in Appendix 4 of *The Pioneer Policewoman.*

WAS records, diaries of policewomen, articles in the English Review, Blackwood's, the Police Chronicle, the Police Review, the Manchester Guardian (online database).

Transport

Corporation Tramway Committee minutes are held at local record offices, London Metropolitan Archives or TNA. Records of tram and bus companies that employed women during the war can be found in local record offices.

The National Railway Museum (NRM) has an online database of over 20,000 male and female railway workers in World War One, including Bertha (Betty) Gavin Stevenson of the North Eastern Railway and YMCA who died 30 May 1918 in France. Stevenson was awarded the Croix de Guerre avec Palme. **www.nrm.org.uk/RailwayStories/worldwarone.aspx**

Some female transport workers belonged to the Amalgamated Association of Tramway and Vehicle Workers, and their names may be found among their records.

Girl Guides

There are references to Girl Guides in The Nameless Magazine, published by 'The Nameless Club', a group of former female MI5 office staff who were unable to join the club of the male staff. A copy of this magazine is held at the Imperial War Museum.

Most secret service files were ordered to be destroyed. Further details may be found in obituaries of former spies in either local or national newspapers, such as *The Times* **http://archive.timesonline.co.uk/tol/archive/**.

Some of the propaganda films that featured Girl Guides, such as *The German Spy Peril,* can be watched online via the British Film Institute Archive: **www. screenonline.org.uk/film/id/1114339/index.html**

Guides signed contracts to work for MI5. They were employed via the BP Girl Guides Employment Bureau at 76 Victoria Street, London. Some records of companies are held at local record offices. For example, membership and administrative records of Lancashire Girl Guides Association 1916-1970 are held at the Lancashire Record Office in Preston, and the Log book of the 1st Rodborough Girl Guide Company 1914-1934 is held at Gloucestershire Archives.

Other aspects to bear in mind when researching women in the Great War are their personal and social lives. Society's mores were altered by the war. The nature of war service and work also led to increased migration, for both women and men.

One of the results of these changes was an increase in illegitimacy: 'In England and Wales, the total of illegitimate births rose to 8.3 per cent of all births in 1917, at its height, nearly doubling the 1914 rate of 4.2 per cent, but it was back down to 6.3 per cent the following year and soon hovered around the prewar standards of between 4 and 5 per cent of all births. What is striking is that while the number of births went down by nearly 200,000 between 1914 and 1917, the actual number of illegitimate births was higher in 1917 by about 20,000 (Mitchell, 1962: 30-3).'[51] Overall, illegitimacy increased by around a third by 1919. When considering your ancestor's war service, you may find it useful to check death dates of husbands, marriage dates and birth dates carefully alongside birth certificate details of all relatives born during the wars. Several illegitimacies were hidden from the statistics by careful wording at registration.

Besides providing clues to your family's history, records of civil registration can present clues to your ancestor's service. A woman's war work may or may not be mentioned but an address can be useful in identifying likely factories or bases where she worked.

Divorce records can also be useful for learning more about women in this period. Divorces increased three-fold from 596 decrees absolute in 1910 to 1,629 in 1920[52]. The papers can be very revealing about your ancestor, her marriage, occupations and residences in the period concerned. Those divorce records that survive can be found indexed online at Findmypast, ScotlandsPeople, or using the J77 reference on Discovery. Otherwise a search of decrees absolute can be made at First Avenue House in Holborn. Reports of divorces and other court cases may be found on *The Times* Digital Archive or at the Gazettes Online website.

Recruitment for the WLA was advertised through leaflets, newspapers and rallies. Local and national newspapers thus hold details on when and where different branches were established. A specific publication was launched, *The Landswoman. Land Girl 1941* has a chapter on the Women's Land Army in the Great War.

Conscientious Objectors can be found in the archives of the Peace Pledge Union and in Quaker resources. One of the largest collections of Quaker records is that held at the Society of Friends' Archive in Euston Road.

Women killed during the First World War are named in the Women's National Memorial in York Minster. Some women appear on the Commonwealth War Grave Commission's Register of Honour.

Screen 12 in York Minster names those killed from the Women's Forage Corps, Women's Legion, Motor Transport Services, Serbian Relief Fund, Friends' War Victims Relief Committee, Women's Emergency Canteens, Young Men's Christian Association, Women's Land Army, and General Service.

CHAPTER FOUR

Women Munitions Workers of the First World War

'Where are the girls of the Arsenal? Working night and day;
Wearing the roses off their cheeks, For precious little pay.
Some people style them 'canaries', But we're working for the
    lads across the sea.
If it were not for the munition lasses, Where would the Empire be?'[53]

Song of the munitions workers of Woolwich Arsenal.

O f all the women who served their country in the First World War, the majority worked in munitions factories. 891,000 of the 1,590,000 non-professional positions for women that were created in this war were in 'industrial occupations'[54], which included a wide range of roles besides the manufacture of munitions. The debate continues over whether producing munitions qualifies as war service. What is not in question is the essential contribution these women made to the war effort, nor that the work was dangerous. Hundreds of women died in the cause of patriotism while working in these factories. Female munitions worker casualties were remembered and most are recorded on Panel 11 in York Minster (see Appendices). The *National Roll of the Great War* gives details of some of the dead, as well as those who served and survived. However, many of those who died as a result of toxic poisoning remain unrecorded outside of their death certificates.

National and Private Factories

In 1914 women were already working in munitions factories throughout Britain. Up to this date all munitions were produced in privately owned factories. In July 1914 there were 212,000 women working in these factories, but this number more than quadrupled to 947,000 by November 1918. Over the course of the war, these 'munitionettes' produced 80% of the British Army's ammunition.

By early 1915, Britain was failing to provide its forces at the Western Front with sufficient ammunition. This was highlighted after Douglas Haig's disastrous defeat at Aubers Ridge on 9 May. Colonel Charles Repington, war correspondent for *The Times*, wrote an attack on the government blaming a lack of shells for the heavy losses: 'The want of an unlimited supply of high explosive was a fatal bar to our success.' He ended the article with a call for munitions: 'It is certain that we can smash the German crust if we have the means. So the means we must have, and as quickly as possible.'[55] *The Times* drew further attention to this problem, creating the 'Great Shell Scandal', which led to the government responding in June 1915 with the creation of a new Ministry of Munitions, overseen by Lloyd George.

Under the Ministry of Munitions, the government took control of the manufacture of munitions in 'national factories', although private factories remained. Those who worked directly for the government were usually better off: 'official wage rates established for women were only enforceable in the specially built national factories; they were simply 'recommended' in the control factories.'[56]

Despite the increase in factories, there was still a lack of workers to make the munitions. Many male workers had enlisted with the armed forces, and the factories needed an extra 14,000 skilled workers to replace them in order to function. The Ministry actively recruited women to make munitions.

Lloyd George's demand for women workers received a quick response from the UK and across the Dominions of the Empire. Many were eager to leave behind their former work and were attracted by higher wages. Age and marital status were varied - some women were over 35.

According to the Defence of the Realm Act of 1914, it became lawful for the Admiralty or Army Council 'to take possession of, and use for the purpose of, His Majesty's naval or military service any such factory or workshop or plant thereof'. In this period, the Ministry of Munitions controlled 218 National Factories, included factories already owned by the government as well as those that were in private hands.

Although some factories were used exclusively for the manufacture of munitions others did not produce ammunition. The factory in Farnborough, Hampshire, for example, produced aircraft and related materials, and workers in Kentish Town made optical instruments.

The different types of national factory controlled by the Ministry of Munitions up to November 1918 were:

Aero Engine Factory
Anti Gas Factory
Balloon Factory
Box Repair Factory
Cylinder Depot
Chemical Shell Assembling Station
Chemical Warfare Factory
Casting Shop
Concrete Slab Factory
Government Cartridge Factory
Gun Carriage Repair Factory
Government Rolling Mills
HM Cotton Waste Mill
HM Explosive Factory
Machine Gun Factory
Mine Sinker Assembly
Manufacturing Warehouse
National Aircraft Factory
National Ball Bearing Factory
National Box Factory

National Cartridge and Box Repair
    Factory
National Cartridge Factory
National Components Factory
National Filling Factory
National Fuse Factory
National Fuse Rectification Factory
National Gauge Factory
National Ordnance Factory
National Projectile Factory
Non-Returnable Box Depot
National Rifle Factory
National Sawmill
National Small Arms Ammunition
    Factory
National Shell Factory
National Tool Factory
Optical Munitions Factory
Steel Billet Breaking Factory
Timber Drying Kiln
Trench Warfare Filling Factory.[57]

Some of the most dangerous munitions work took place in His Majesty's Explosive Factories (HMEF), which employed women at Gretna in Dumfriesshire, Bradley in Yorkshire, Pembrey in Carmarthenshire, Queen's Ferry in Flintshire, Greetland in West Yorkshire, Ellesmere Port in Cheshire, Coleford in Gloucestershire, Rainham in Essex, Oldbury in Worcestershire, Bideford in Devon, Gadbrook in Cheshire, Hackney Wick in London, Penrhyn Deudraeth in Merionethshire, Trafford Park in Lancashire, West Gorton in Lancashire, Langwith in Nottinghamshire, Sutton Oak in Lancashire, Victoria in London, Winsford in Cheshire, Litherland in Lancashire, King's Lynn in Norfolk, Craigleith in Edinburgh, Colnbrook in Middlesex, Avonmouth in Gloucestershire, Swindon in Wiltshire, Lytham in Lancashire, Irvine in Ayrshire, Longparish in Hampshire, Mid Lavant in Sussex, Ludlow in Shropshire, Sandycroft in Cheshire.[58]

Explosive substances, such as cordite, gunpowder, tetryl, guncotton and fuse powder were also used at the government's Royal Ordnance Factories, such as the Royal Arsenal at Woolwich and the Royal Gunpowder Factory at Waltham Abbey. The other Royal Ordnance Factory, the Royal Small Arms Factory in Enfield Lock, continued to produce rifles, machine guns and small arms.

By the end of the war, there were twelve National Filling Factories (NFF) belonging to the Ministry of the Munitions. These were identified by numbers: for example, Coventry (21), Gloucester (5), Hayes (7), Hereford (14) and Park Royal Willesden (3).

Government Controlled Establishments were privately owned factories, taken under control of the Ministry for the duration. These included Armstrong Whitworth & Co in Newcastle, WE Blake Explosives Co Ltd at Wood Lane, Leeds; George Kent Ltd at Chaul End Fuse Filling factory in Luton; King's Norton Metal Co Ltd at Abbey Wood; Prana Sparklets Co in Edmonton, Canada; Vandervell & Co in Acton; Vickery's Patents Ltd in the Old Kent Road; the National Projectile Factory in Sheffield and the Minerva Motor Works in London.

Pay and Conditions

Although many were attracted by higher wages than they had been receiving in domestic work, for example, female workers in the factories were not paid as much as men. Lack of experience was the official reason given for this. Of the 11,000 women employed in the national cordite factory in Gretna, more than a third had worked in domestic service before the war. However, some women were from the middle classes, who were more likely to be given skilled labour or advisory positions, where a more general education was needed[59].

Long hours, acrid fumes and low pay were among the negative features of the work, but the patriotic call for volunteers was as strong as it was for soldiers. During the war, women were attracted by the pay, particularly those who were placed or promoted to skilled or senior roles, which involved supervising the work rather than making munitions.

The munitionettes who replaced semi-skilled men were paid more, although the situation was skewed against women. The regulations stipulated that:

> 'A woman shall be considered as not employed on the work customarily done by fully skilled tradesmen, but a part only thereof, if she does not do the customary setting up or, where there is no setting up, if she require skilled supervision to a degree beyond that customarily required by fully skilled tradesmen undertaking the work in question.'[60]

However, women challenged this discrimination with several joining trades unions and other groups for support. By January 1916, just under 12% female munitions workers were members of the National Union of Railwaymen and the Amalgamated Association of Tramway and Vehicle Workers.

Training

Women who were not previously employed in munitions factories were considered unskilled. However, some educated women objected to this categorisation, for example, women working at Sir William Beardmore's Engineering Works in Glasgow were re-classified as skilled in June 1915. From November 1915, this factory established training of upper-class ladies for part-time employment[61].

From 1916, the Ministry of Munitions, in co-operation with the Board of Education arranged to use technical schools across the country for training munitions workers. Women in London could receive four weeks' munitions training at the London Society for Women's Suffrage. A technical schools course (6-8 weeks) began there in 1916. Training benefited women by providing both skills and income. Untrained women began on 15 shillings for four weeks; trained women on £1 for a 53 ½ hour week. The fact that women were paid less than men caused resentment, particularly when women became more skilled and experienced. Although set hours had been laid down for women in the Factory and Workshops Act, many were unaware of these and were vulnerable to exploitation. Full time workers typically worked six days a week, Monday to Friday from 7.30am-1.00pm, then 2.00-8.00pm; and on Saturday to 6.00pm.

From 1917, training was compulsory, although the length of training varied. Those who had honorary degrees tended to be employed in more difficult work or given more responsibility. Joan Birsting, for example, had an honorary degree from University College London, and was given the position of overseer at the new foundry in Western Park. Despite her seniority, she was required to undergo a training course at Machinist Ltd, in Birmingham[62].

Nature of Work

Munitions work involved numerous roles, often performed at different sites or huts in the arsenals. Some women may have performed the same task each working day of the war. Others may have taken on different roles throughout their time in the factories. Among the jobs, female munitions workers undertook were:

light labouring	slotting	assembling
turning	drawing	punching
shaping	grinding	shearing
machine riveting	filing	welding
gear-cutting	crane-driving	

To signify their status as women in military service, each munitionette wore a 'For War Service' badge. This was a metal triangle-shaped pin and can be seen in the photograph.

Workers in the danger buildings where metal was not allowed could not wear their badges. Here metal could produce a spark which could lead to an explosion, and even hairpins and corsets had to be removed. In these locations women were assigned a plain uniform of khaki or brown overalls, with a skirt and cap. In general, the munitionettes wore plain dresses of hard-wearing brown or beige cloth, some with an apron. A few wore trousers. Almost all wore caps.

3. Munitions worker: this photograph shows the munitions worker pin that demonstrated the wearer's war service.

Welfare of Workers

During the war, women (and girls aged over 10) were employed in huge numbers for industrial work. While women were an essential part in providing the necessary munitions of war, the dangers were ever-present. Tragically, insufficient safety measures were taken. Not only did these women risk the danger of explosions but several were permanently affected by the poisonous substances they handled.

The Lancet of 12 August 1916 published a report on the toxic effects of the explosive, Tri-Nitro-Toluene (TNT), on munitions workers by two Medical Officers in the Factories, Doctors Agnes Livingstone-Fairmont and Barbara Martin-Cunningham. These Officers recommended that, 'all women recruited for work on TNT should be very carefully selected with regard to their physical characteristics. none should be under 21 nor over 40. Factories should be adequately ventilated, and the women should be provided with good and adequate clothing. They should only work for short periods on TNT and be taken off regularly for other types of work'[63]. However, such recommendations were often ignored.

4. Welding school at Women's Service Bureau.

Sufferers of poisoning caused by the explosive TNT often experienced yellow-tinged skin from their exposure to sulphur. At the time, jokes were made on the street and in the press, referring to the women as 'canaries' or 'canary girls'. The reality of TNT poisoning was far from funny. Besides, the effects on their skin, munitionettes complained of bilious attacks, blurred vision, depression and jaundice[64]. By the end of the war, at least 109 women munitions workers had died of chemical poisoning caused by the chemicals and explosives they handled at work[65].

5. Munitions workers at the Works Marshall Sons & Co Ltd in Gainsborough.

The welfare of munitions workers was monitored by female factory inspectors and welfare supervisors. These supervisors also helped women who were mothers. In 1915 a group of suffragists, pacifists and trade union activists set up a Women's War Interest Committee in Manchester. This committee used their skills and experience to research conditions of women munitions workers and to lobby the government on their behalf. Some women found working and caring for a child too difficult. Unmarried women often had greater need to work in the factories as legal wives of those serving in the armed forces were eligible for a separation allowance. Many women were unmarried and often without extended family support, and there is evidence of some giving up their children to foster care during the war. For some, this was intended as a temporary measure. However, for others, this may have been the last time they saw their children. During this period the Home Children movement, which sent British youngsters to parts of the Empire, was particularly active.

Besides health and safety considerations, welfare at the factories was aided by a number of social activities including music, theatre and sports clubs. The leisure provision for munitionettes included the establishment of football teams often playing games for charity: 'In August 1917 the first football tournament was launched for the female munitions workers' teams of the north-east England.'[66] The Dick Kerr Ladies team from a munitions factory in Preston played the first international women's football match against a French XI in 1920.

Explosions

It is believed that more than 400 munitions workers were killed in accidental explosions during the war, although not all were women[67]. There are some known figures of casualties, such as one woman who was killed at the factory in Gretna, the 73 who died at Silvertown in East London, the 35 killed in an explosion at Barnbow in December 1916 and the 35 who were killed in July 1918 at Chilwell. However, the details of many of these explosions were kept quiet at the time under fears of national security. For this reason and the fact that many died of the effects of their injuries some years later, it is difficult to give an exact figure of casualties. Among the deaths of munitions workers, including men, were those in the explosion at a munitions factory at Faversham, Kent in April 1916, which killed 106 munitions workers. These figures do not include those who died after 1921 from long-term effects of the blasts, nor does it take into account the chronic disabilities, disfigurements and loss of earnings suffered by those who were injured. At Silvertown alone, more than 400 were injured in blasts.

The explosion at Silvertown on 19 January 1917 was caused by an accidental fire, which went on to ignite 50 tons of TNT. The subsequent blast devastated a square mile of London's East End, causing more destruction than all the First World War raids on the capital combined. Because the factory was owned by Brunner, Mond and Company, of German origin, xenophobic attacks on them increased. Sir Alfred Mond, however, remained a Liberal MP from 1906 to 1928 and after the war became Minister of Health 1921-22 and later 1st Baron Melchett.

Male and female munitions workers were killed, alongside others who lived or worked nearby. The women and girls killed in this explosion were[68]:

Ethel Elmer Betts, 4 months, West Ham Cemetery.
Mary Ann Betts, 58.
Ellen Boyce, 32.
E. Croft.
Lillian B. Davey, 15, Domestic servant, East London Cemetery.
Charlotte Hiscock, 76, East London Cemetery.
Catherine Elizabeth Hodge (also called Lizzie Lawrence), 16, Worker at Brunner Monds.
Agnes Jennings, 23, East London Cemetery.
May Gertrude Jennings, 20, East London Cemetery.
Eliza Lettson, East London Cemetery.
Ellen Frances Jane Noakes, 29, Cook, East London Cemetery.
Frances Oates, 20.
Rosa Patrick, 4, West Ham Cemetery.
Ruby Patrick, 6, West Ham Cemetery.
Elizabeth Priscilla Preston, 28.
Dorothy Preston, 11 months.
Hannah Preston, 68.
Winifred Sell, 15, Scholarship pupil at Central Secondary School, West Ham Cemetery.
Kathleen Smith, 16.
Sophia Jane Villiers, East London Cemetery.
Alice Wass, 10.
Elsie Wass, aged either 13 or 10, East London Cemetery.
Mary Wass, 32, East London Cemetery.

The Gretna explosion of 1917 occurred among the biggest single concentration of women workers in this war. When the vast HMEF Gretna was built in 1915, the shortage of housing in the area became evident. Consequently, a complete town for 20,000 women and men was built to house the new workforce. Around 11,000 women were to work at the cordite factory during its commission. On 9 August 1917, a building 'containing several tons of nitro-glycerine suddenly disappeared in a lightning sheet of flame, with a crash that could be heard far into the countryside'[69] An Australian woman, J Royal, was killed and is remembered at Gretna Cemetery[70]. On 22 December 1917, The Leader (Melbourne) published an article praising women munitions workers under the misleading heading, 'Great Sacrifices in England'. The article referred to a letter of October that year from Mr A E Leighton, general manager of a prospective Commonwealth arsenal, to the Imperial government stating, 'The women here are fine, and I do not know what we should have done without them. It would make you smile to see them pushing trucks about through the snow and slush at Gretna. Nothing seems to damp their ardour, not even the mixture of open-work stockings and snow.' Like many munitionettes, the workers at HM Factory Gretna had their own song:

Give honour to the Gretna girls,
Give honour where honour is due,
Don't forget the Gretna girls
Who are doing their duty for you.

And when they are in the factory
Midst the cordite and the smell,
We'll give three cheers for the Gretna girls
And the others can come as well.

Come boys and do your little bit,
We'll meet you by-and-by.

On 1 October 1917, 10 people - mainly firemen- were killed in a series of explosions at the National Filling Factory on White Lund, near Morecambe. The force of the blasts from thousands of shells was felt through the night and up to around 40 miles away in Burnley. Shop windows smashed in nearby Lancaster, with shrapnel travelling several miles into the surrounding hills and fields. The effects of the disaster would probably have been worse had the initial fire not broken out at 10.30pm while most of the workers were taking a break in the canteen. The damage was such that the factory was out of commission for the rest of the war. Today, unexploded shells are still being discovered near the site.[71]

240 women munitions workers who were killed in this war are commemorated at Screen Eleven in York Minster (see Appendices). The Five Sisters Window there was dedicated after restoration in 1924 as a memorial to the women of the British Empire. The munitions workers who are named on the CWGC website are those who deaths were recognised officially by the British government as war deaths. Their families should have received a death plaque, letter or scroll in honour of their sacrifice.

Case Study of a Bradford Munitions Worker: Martha Emma ORWIN

Reproduced by kind permission of Kathryn Hughes PhD of Bradford WWI: **www.bradfordww1.co.uk/tags/world-war-one**

Martha Emma Orwin was born in Whittington, Derbyshire, on November 1, 1895 to Thomas and Alice Orwin. The family moved to Bradford around 1906 and Alice found employment as a servant to the Jefferson family where she worked until the start of the First World War.

Her family uncovered a picture of Martha believed to be taken 1916-1917 in her blue munitions uniform. Although she has no visible badge, one of the girls (middle row with the curtain behind her) has the familiar munitions worker badge on her hat. This is triangular with three 'dots' in it, and the older woman at the end also had a similar badge in her collar. It is believed by her family that Martha took up work at the Phoenix munitions factory in Thornbury, Bradford, which during the war manufactured artillery shells and aircraft parts.

Bradford was home to several munitions factories including a National Shell factory as well as a wide range of over 80 other companies that were manufacturing a range of materials for the Ministry, from tanks to petrol bombs and shell cases to shrapnel sockets. Unfortunately Martha wasn't listed in the *National Roll of the Great War* for Bradford. The roll was compiled by families of those who served during the First World War at home or abroad and contains the names of some female munitions workers, but it is far from complete.

There are also no records of employees of the Phoenix Company that would confirm whether Martha was a worker there or at another factory. However there are documents about the works and newspaper reports and articles relating to the factory which give a good indication of what life was like for munitions workers.

The Phoenix Company introduced women within a few months of the outbreak of the war, and was at the forefront of creating a successful workplace. Lloyd George asked the managing director to write a book, 'Women on munitions of war.' The company created women's canteens, recreation, rest and dining halls they considered the social well-being of the workers resulted in happier and healthier employees.

The Bradford Royal Eye and Ear Hospital treated at least 5,000 cases of munitions workers with foreign objects in their eyes during WWI. However the only records that survive for the period were those for operations and not those of outpatients who are just having foreign objects removed. Martha does not appear to have been one of those requiring an operation.

In June 1918 King George V and Queen Mary visited the Phoenix works. After the war the company held a party for 5,000 workers to celebrate the armistice. They couldn't find a hall in Thornbury big enough so they held it in the factory. According to a contemporary report:

'One of the shell shops turned into a games and music room, the aviation metal shop becoming a ball room in which 1,500 dancers took to the floor, while the aviation erecting shop became a concert hall and picture palace. With the aid of a plentiful supply of bunting the great workshops were suitably camouflaged and a brave display of electric lights helped to make the place look like a fairy palace than a modern factory which has turned out 2 million shells, not to mention hundreds of seaplanes and other aircraft... all guests over 18 years of age (about 4,000) in number received a victory gift of a £1 treasury note, while those under 18 received 10s.[72]'

A search of the parish registers revealed banns were called for a marriage in October 1917 between Martha and Frederick Smith of Elland, but the marriage does not appear to have taken place. It is quite likely that Frederick died before the wedding could occur. After the war, in December 1918, Martha married Frank Spencer.

Although it may not be possible to find specific information about your ancestor's work at the munitions factory, there are other places where you might find information about them, e.g. local eye hospital records, National Roll of Honour. Furthermore, if your family know which factory they worked at you may be able to uncover even more information about their working conditions.

Notes On Researching Munitions Workers

Munitions workers are not easy to research, and finding a variety of sources with individual names may be difficult. There are no service records, but sources from factories may provide useful details on the nature of your ancestor's work. In order to explore existing records, it is important to identify the names of the factory or factories where your ancestor worked. Local studies and archives should contain directories, maps and other material identifying factories in the area where your ancestor lived. Further lists exist at TNA for 1916-1918 inclusive and for every type of factory.

When looking at records of government departments, note that women who worked in arsenals and dockyards worked in munitions, but so also did those who were described as working in the wood and aircraft trades.

In the IWM Explore History Centre, the open shelves hold *Notes on the Employment of Women on Munitions of War (London: Ministry of Munitions, 1916)*. This details how workers were trained and also contains many photographs of women at work, and women illustrating the nature of the work. The collections of audio, images, video and private papers can be searched online with terms 'industry', 'munition production', 'munitions', 'industrial relations', 'labour', 'female employment', 'female labour' 'women workers' and 'aeronautical engineering'. Searches can also be made using the name of your ancestor or the place where she worked. Results can be filtered by the subject period 'First World War'.

Details of munitions workers who were killed during the war may be found on the CWGC website. Not all workers who died are found here. Those that are include Australians and other imperial subject munitions workers who were buried in the UK, as well as British nationals.

Although there were some contemporary news reports on explosions at munitions factories, few details were revealed due to concerns about national security. Reports of deaths of munitions workers would have had a negative effect on recruitment and were thus avoided by patriotic publications. However, names or obituaries of those who died in the years following the war of injuries sustained in explosions may be found in local newspapers or on the BN Archive website. Some local newspapers have published features on these events in recent years.

Women factory workers who received the Order of the British Empire may be named in local newspapers, *London Gazette*, or *The Times.* These reports often give details of the ceremonies.

If your relative worked away from home, look into lodging options. Some may have lived with relatives, but many lived away from home in hostels, such as the Government Hostel in Coventry. Street directories can be used to identify them. Records of such establishments may be found in local record offices.

Some factories produced magazines or booklets as a souvenir of their war work: National Ordnance Factory No.1 Newlay, Leeds produced *The Shell Magazine: an original souvenir by employees of the National Ordnance Factory No.1*, which includes some photographs of those who worked there. Copies of this are held at the Imperial War Museum.

Conditions in the factories were monitored by a Women's War Interests Committee, which was formed in May 1915. Some records relating to this Committee can be found at TNA. In 1916, the Manchester, Salford and District Women's War Interests Committee published a pamphlet entitled 'Women in the Labour Market, Manchester and District, During the War'. A copy of this is held at the London School of Economics. Alison Ronan of Manchester Metropolitan University is researching this Committee.

Trades Union records can be found in the Modern Records Centre at the University of Warwick, the British Library, London School of Economics, the National Library of Scotland, the National Library of Wales and in some local archives.

Hospital records, particularly those of eye hospitals or in areas of known explosions, can also be useful to explore for munitions ancestors.

When women moved from one factory to another, they were awarded 'leaving certificates' which enabled them to take up their new employment. These certificates may be found in private collections, or may have been donated to archive collections.

Local newspapers often reported the sport, musical and theatrical activities of the munitionettes. Your ancestor may not be mentioned by name, but there may be a picture of her. Records of the membership of these clubs may survive in personal or private collections, and at local archives or football museums.

CHAPTER FIVE

Women Nurses, Doctors and Medical Services in the First World War

'She has taught the bravest man amongst us a supreme lesson of courage; and in this United Kingdom and through the Dominions of the Crown there are thousands of such women, but a year ago we did not know it.'

Prime Minister H. H. Asquith on Nurse Edith Cavell, 1915.

In many ways, British medical services seemed well prepared for war when it began in August 1914. Britain's role as leader of a great empire, and the complex treaties with which it was bound with other European nations, led to a sense of anticipation of the conflict. However, Britain's nurses, doctors and hospitals were not prepared for the enormous number of sick and injured men that the fighting would create.

In the British Empire of 1914, there were 297 professional Army nurses serving in the Queen Alexandra Imperial Military Nursing Service (QAIMNS). There were also civilian nurses and a number of reserves - some of whom were working in civilian hospitals - prepared to work caring for injured soldiers. Some were members of the Civil Hospital Reserve (CHR), which had been founded in 1911. Others joined the Territorial Force Reserve, formed in 1908 and supported by the TFNS. The British Red Cross Society (BRCS) along with the Order of St John of Jerusalem already

provided first aid, and were readied to assist with war, as required. Thousands of volunteers had joined before August 1914. And, since the Medical Act of 1876, there were also trained women doctors, although progress was slow and there were still only 200 female doctors in the whole of the UK in 1900.[73]

Initially, the War Office did not believe that non-military nurses should be sent to France. British allies on the Continent had different views, with the Belgian, French and Serbian Armies welcoming all women. The suffragist Mrs Mabel St Clair Stobart challenged the War Office's view by organising a group of nurses, the Women's Sick and Wounded Convoy Corps, who had previously worked in the Balkan War of 1912. In 1914, Stobart took her charges to Belgium, where she set up a field hospital, working with the Belgian Army. Stobart later commanded the Serbian Relief Fund's Front Line Field Hospital. This group were not the only nurses who defied the War Office: a small number of British women are known to have served as nurses with the Russian Army, too.

Away from the fighting, emergency and convalescent hospitals emerged in Britain to supplement the existing military hospitals. Military wings were also added to civilian hospitals. Many of the emergency hospitals were set up in private houses, under a scheme pioneered by the Director General of the Army Medical Service (AMS), Sir Alfred Keogh (1857-1936). As the crisis deepened, and thousands of wounded and

6. Hampstead War Hospital Supply Depot staff engaged in producing hospital supplies. Items made here included roller bandages, bed jackets, towels, splints, crutches, pyjamas and swabs.

sick soldiers arrived in Britain urgently needing medical attention, the government quickly realised that the country was suffering from a lack of trained nurses. Soon, therefore, British nurses were approved to work for the French or Belgian armies under the auspices of the British Red Cross.

Probably the most famous example of these is Edith Cavell, a Red Cross nurse who worked in German-occupied Belgium. The daughter of a Norfolk clergyman, Cavell guided some 200 Allied soldiers to safety from German-occupied Belgium in the First World War. On 12 October 1915, aged just 49, she was executed for treason by firing squad. She is remembered with a large statue in St Martin's Place in central London.

Nursing Volunteers: VADs

VAD (Voluntary Aid Detachment) nurses were often known as Red Cross nurses, and can be identified in photographs from the large cross they wore on their uniforms. They were volunteers and part of the general VAD, with their nursing work being overseen by the Red Cross. Besides VAD nurses there were other nurses who volunteered through and were supported by the Red Cross, such as those of the St John Ambulance Brigade Hospital and Friends' Ambulance Unit.

The Red Cross had been re-organised in 1905. This led to the War Office developing a scheme, to arrange voluntary aid across the country in the form of Voluntary Aid Detachments. In 1909 the Red Cross organised these VADs through their local Territorial Forces (TFs). In this way the VADs were to assist the TF Medical Services that had been created in 1908. VADs had a number of roles for both men and women, although the term is now most often used to describe nurses. General Service VADs worked as cooks, laundresses, clerks, typists, telephonists, drivers, and chauffeurs; they could also be employed by government departments other than the War Office, as required. When war began, a Joint War Committee (JWC) was created from the Red Cross and the Order of St John of Jerusalem. This committee would oversee relief work for the duration.

Of all the nurses who served in this war, most were VADs. By 1914 there were more than 6,000 members arranged in women-only detachments of 24. All were trained in first aid and nursing by the Red Cross. VADs assisted regular nurses in hospitals. They were not paid, but in 1915 the War Office was forced to introduce direct payment of £20 per year (£30 for those in military hospitals) to attract more nurses. Complications arose as this contradicted the voluntary status of the Red Cross VADs[74].

Like nurses of other organisations, VAD volunteers applied from all over the Empire. Volunteers from Canada arrived in Britain in 1916.

7. Nursing sisters and staff nurses of the Territorial Force Nursing Service with VADs.

8. Nursing sisters, VADs and patients at a section of No.2 Western General Hospital.

9. Mixed group of medical staff, nursing sisters and VADs, location unknown.

10. Mixed group of nurses with patients, location unknown.

VADs are usually easy to identify in photographs as they wore aprons with a large red cross and an armband. Each nurse was given a certificate of identity, which may survive in private collections. Volunteers, usually drawn from the upper-middle or upper classes, were recommended by a respected member of society, and had to be able to afford the cost of uniforms (at £1.19s.2½d each) and lectures. Those who worked part time in a local hospital were unpaid, but received expenses for board, lodging, laundry, and travel. A Compassionate Fund supported those who became sick or injured during their service.

VAD hospitals were local establishments (often large houses) usually staffed by local nurses, with the support of VADs. Officially termed Auxiliary War Hospitals, they were commonly known as Red Cross Hospitals. Examples of these are the No.2 Southern General Hospital (Territorial Force) in Southmead, Bristol and No.2 Western General Hospital, Manchester (see images).

VADs in Britain performed a number of nursing roles, including air raid duty. They worked in VAD hospitals, such as that for officers, which was set up in the private home of Viscountess Mountgarret in Cadogan Gardens, London. By September 1916, there were 8,000 VADs serving in military hospitals. VADs also worked shifts on ambulance duty in Manchester munitions factories, where the fires were never allowed to go out.[75]

Like military nurses, hundreds of VADs were sent abroad. Thekla Bowser, who had been a Sister of the Order of St John since 1902, served in France in the war until illness forced her to return home. In 1917, Bowser wrote a well-respected account of VAD work, *The Story of British VAD Work in the Great War*.

Life as a VAD was unpredictable, and women often found themselves in unusual circumstances. The VAD headquarters in France was a hotel in Boulogne. Some VAD nurses in France worked in monasteries or chateaux. Others were sent to Ireland to deal with the casualties of the Easter Rising in 1916.

Work on any of the overseas fronts was extremely dangerous for all, including nurses, and particularly for those based at casualty clearing stations. VAD nurse Gertrude Bytheway, for example, was killed on 31 December 1917 when *HMS Osmanieh* was sunk by a mine off Alexandria. She was 37 years old. Gertrude was the daughter of George and Lottie Bytheway, of Walsall in the West Midlands, and is remembered by the Commonwealth War Grave Commission on Women's Screen Five in York Minster and at grave B 42 in the Alexandra (Hadra) War Memorial Cemetery. In its report of the death of Gertrude and her colleagues, the Royal College of Nursing Journal wrote:

'The most distressing tragedy of these deaths emphasises the risks continually taken, with the utmost courage and coolness, by the members of the various Nursing Services, who well know that they go at the peril of their lives, whether on hospital ships or on transports in the seas sown with mines and infested with submarines. Nevertheless, not a Sister but thinks it an honour to brave the peril to place her skilled help at the service of our sick and wounded men, and when death confronts her she meets it with unflinching courage.'[76]

Nursing Volunteers: First Aid Nursing Yeomanry (FANY)

Despite their need for nurses, the British Army were at first unsympathetic to the mainly middle and upper class women of the First Aid Nursing Yeomanry (FANY). FANY had been formed in 1907 and was based in Westminster, London, where applicants over 23 years of age were interviewed. When war broke out, Grace Ashley-Smith and FANY's recent recruits attempted to travel to Belgium, whose Army was grateful for their efforts. This was delayed after Antwerp fell to the Germans. A small FANY troop eventually travelled to Calais on 27 October 1914 with only £12 of funds. Here they established a hospital for wounded Britons in a convent school. Besides nursing, FANY volunteers drove ambulances, transported food and clothes to the trenches, and ran canteens.

As the war progressed officials in the British Government and Army began to appreciate the efforts of these volunteers. Although still considering them inferior to the trained Red Cross nurses, they did allow them a base in the British Army hospital in a former casino in Calais.

By August 1918, there were 120 FANYs serving in France[77]. Those at the Front were in constant danger. FANY nurse Evelyn Fidgeon Shaw died there on 24 August 1918 and is buried in grave A. 40 in Sezanne Communal Cemetery in the Marne. For her bravery, Shaw was awarded the Croix de Guerre with Palm (France).

Military Nurses: QAIMNS, QAMNSI, QARNNS and the TFNS

The official Army nurses of the QAIMNS were mobilised immediately. The Directorate of the Army Medical Services (AMS), led by the Director General, Sir Alfred Keogh (1857-1936), oversaw the nursing of armed forces personnel, including members of the Territorial Force Nursing Service (TFNS), the Queen Alexandra's Imperial Military Nursing Service (QAIMNS), the QAIMNS Reserve (R), the Queen Alexandra's Military Nursing Service for India (QAMNSI), and the Queen Alexandra's Royal Naval Nursing Service (QARNNS). All of these services were called upon for war service, and many of their members were sent to areas of fighting across the globe.

11. A group of nursing sisters and staff nurses of Queen Alexandra's Imperial Military Nursing Service, Bristol.

QAIMNS remained small throughout the war, but its reserve saw over 10,000 recruits up to 1918.

12. Volta Billing, a Matron of the Territorial Force Nursing Service.

Nurses who served in India during the war often came from the United Kingdom. Papers of Nurses appointed to the Indian Nursing Service (INS) in reference IOR: L/MIL/7/11803 at the British Library reveal, for example, that Emily Frances Sarah Agnes Talbot[78], was born 25 December 1887 at Killart, Clonaslee, Queens County, Ireland. She was the daughter of a gentleman farmer and had been educated at Ladies School, Rutland Square, Dublin before training to become a nurse at Liverpool Royal Infirmary. She applied to nurse in India on 17 February 1916, and was interviewed at the India Office in 1917. Like many of the nurses in this war, she was unmarried.

Nurses in the INS (later the QAMNSI, and merged with QAIMNS in 1926) were sent wherever the Indian Army was posted. They included postings at the Western Front and Basra in Mesopotamia (now Iraq). Nursing Sister I M Kearney of the Queen Alexandra's

Imperial Military Nursing Service died there on 26 September 1916 and is buried in Basra War Cemetery in plot VR 14.

From across the Empire, nurses travelled to the Western Front to tend to men from their respective countries. However, where there were not enough women from one service to deal with the number of injured, nurses from another nation's service would be posted to assist. Imperial nursing services working in this war were the South African Military Nursing Service (SAMNS), the Australian Army Nursing Service (AANS), the Canadian Army Medical Corps Nursing Service (CAMCNS), the New Zealand Army Nursing Service (NZANS), and QAIMNS for India (QAMNSI).

Territorial Force Nursing Service

The Territorial Force Nursing Service (TFNS) was created in 1908 to nurse members of the Territorial Force.

Standing Orders for the Territorial Force Nursing Service (1912: reprinted 1914; HMSO - copy in IWM Research Room) gives the following details on the organisation:

'The TFNS is formed for the purpose of maintaining an establishment of nurses willing to serve in general hospitals in the event of the mobilization of the Territorial Force ... The establishment consists of a matron-in-chief, principal matrons, matrons, sisters, and nurses. The TFNS is required for 23 general hospitals, located as follows: 4 in London, 2 in Glasgow, and 1 at Aberdeen, Edinburgh, Newcastle-on-Tyne, Leeds, Sheffield, Manchester, Liverpool, Lincoln, Leicester, Birmingham, Oxford, Cambridge, Cardiff, Bristol, Portsmouth, Plymouth, and Brighton.'

There were 520 beds per establishment. Uniforms had to be bought but wearing was optional in peacetime. All nurses were to be paid on mobilisation: wages ranged from £40 per annum for nurses to £305 per annum for Matrons-in-Chief.

A typical day for a TFNS nurse is described in the *Standing Orders:*

Appendix E: Sisters' Time Table

7am	Called	4 or 5pm	Tea
7.30am	Prayers	5pm	Wards
7.35am	Breakfast	8pm	Dinner
8.15	Wards	10.30pm	Bedrooms.
1.30pm	Lunch	11pm	Lights out.
2pm	Wards		

13. Two nurses of the Territorial Force Nursing Service with a VAD, location unknown.

14. Matron, nursing sisters and VADs of No.2 Southern General Hospital (Territorial Force), Southmead, Bristol.

QARNNS and QARNNS Reserve

In 1902, the Naval Nursing Service had been renamed the Queen Alexandra's Royal Naval Nursing Service (QARNNS). This service was administered by the Royal Navy. A Reserve was set up in 1910 of civilian nurses who would supplement the regular Service in case of war.

PMRAFNS

The Royal Air Force Nursing Service was formed in June 1918 under the precepts of the RAF. Despite its title, the RAF Nursing Service cared for men of the Army, Navy and Air Force. In 1923, the organisation was renamed the Princess Mary's Royal Air Force Nursing Service (PMRAFNS).

Professional Civilian Doctors and Nurses

Some female doctors were given temporary commissions as officers in the RAMC. More medical schools allowed women to train as doctors for the duration. Civilian nurses worked alongside newly trained army nurses in this war.

Women's Hospital Corps (WHC)

The WHC established military hospitals for the French Army in Paris and Wimereux. A military hospital was created in the Women's Hospital in Endell Street, London. This hospital had an all-women staff overseen by Dr Flora Murray. Records can be harder to find on this hospital, as Dr Murray considered it a military hospital not women's war work. For this reason she refused to contribute to the IWM collection after the war. This collection was the basis for Women, Work, and Society Collection in the IWM today.

Scottish Women's Hospital

The Scottish Women's Hospital (SWH) was founded by Dr Elsie Maud Inglis at the outbreak of war to provide assistance to the Royal Army Medical Corps by female doctors. As with many of the women's organisations, the War Office had been unsupportive. Dr Inglis eventually opened a hospital at Abbaye de Royaumont in France. The SWH broadened its original remit to include cooks, nurses, drivers and orderlies. The SWH accounts were supported by the NUWSS and the American Red Cross.

Other SWH were established in Corsica, Malta, Romania, Russia, Salonika and Serbia. Dr Inglis was taken prisoner while serving in Serbia in 1915 and in 1916 she travelled to Russia. Conditions of hygiene at the auxiliary hospitals in Serbia and Russia were poor. Dr Inglis became ill and was forced to return to England in 1917. She died of gastro-enteritis and perforation of the bowel in Newcastle-upon-Tyne on 26 November 1917.

15. Matron, nursing sisters and members of the Royal Army Medical Corps.

Other Wartime Medical Services

Military Massage Service
The Military Massage Service / Almeric Paget Military Massage Corps (APMMC) was accepted in 1914. In Britain, they provided 50 trained masseuses.

This Corps was founded by Mr and Mrs Almeric Paget who had formerly lived in India where they had learned of the benefits of massage. They approached the War Office offering to run a Corps of fully trained masseuses for work among the wounded. A separate detachment was sent to France in 1917. By January 1916, there were 900 masseuses, by January 1917 there were 1,200 and by Armistice Day 1918 the number had reached 2,000[79].

Flying Ambulance Corps

Dr Hector Munro established a small flying ambulance corps, which included four women: Mairi Chisholm, Lady Dorothy Fielding, Elsie Knocker and American Mrs Helen Gleason. Elsie and Mairi became known as the Women of Pervyse.

Casualties

Casualties were heavy amongst nurses, particularly those serving at the Western Front or other areas of conflict. Sister Baines was killed alongside four orderlies and 11 patients in an air raid on 31 May 1918 in Etaples.

Nursing Sister Esther Louise Hammell

Besides tending to the sick, nurses tended to necessary tasks of welfare and assistance. This could include writing letters of sympathy, particularly where they were with the soldier when he died. Your nurse ancestor's letter may be with the family of the man she wrote about, or in a local archive. Camden Local Studies, for example, has letters that were found in the effects of a Kentish Town resident who died in 1978. They were the official Army notification of the death of her husband, Gunner Edwin Prosser, and the letter of sympathy from the nurse who had been with him when he died (see pages 72 and 73).

The problem for researchers is that even though an ancestor's name may be found in the letter or other document, her name will not always be listed in a library's catalogue. These items can be difficult to find.

The nurse in this specific case was Sister E. L. Hammell of No.2 Canadian General Hospital, B.E.F., France. The list of Base Hospitals in France and Flanders on the Long, Long Trail website: **www.1914-1918.net/hospitals.htm** shows that this hospital was based at Le Treport. Gunner Edwin Prosser, number 1809 of the Royal Field Artillery, died on 3 November 1918, aged 36. Strangely this date does not correspond with that on the letter. The letter appears to have been written on 2 November, but the nurse writes that death took place 'last Sunday evening'. He was serving with 'B' Battery. 161st Brigade. He is buried at the Mont Huon Military Cemetery, Le Treport. His casualty details on: **www.cwgc.org** state that he was the 'Son of Edwin and Ann Prosser, of London; husband of J. Prosser, of IS, Regent St., City Rd, London.' Edwin had married Josephine Spiecker in Holborn in 1911.

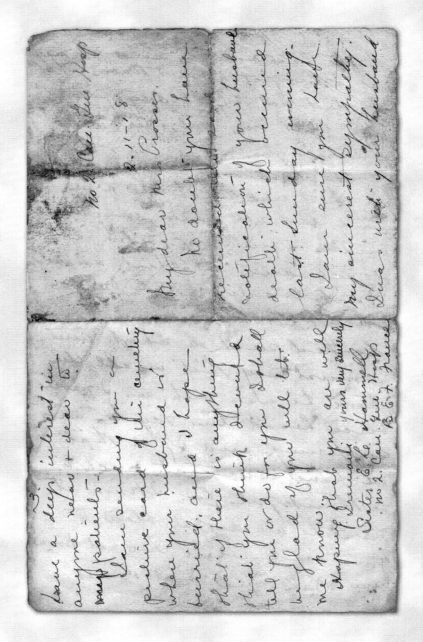

16. Letter written by Nursing Sister Esther Louise Hammell to of the widow of Gunner Edwin Prosser. (Josephine Crawley ephemera file '75.1 Crawley, Josephine'.) (*Continues opposite.*)

to the last moment, and it may
be a comfort to you to know that
he did not suffer any pain.
his last moments were most
peaceful.

He had a very bad wound
in chest and under the arm,
but did not seem any worse
until a few days before his
death, and the chest wound
just lead on to a bad
lung condition and he
lasted such a short time
I must say that in all the
time he was with us I never
once heard him say he was
suffering - and I feel that
we have even that much to
be thankful for. I know it
must be an awful blow to
you - and while I do not know
you I feel real sad at least

There is an entry for Sister Hammell in the Military Nurses 1856-1994 section on Findmypast. The entry is a transcription of an entry in the Royal Red Cross Register and was transcribed by Sue Light. It reads:

'First Name(s): Esther Louise Last Name: Hammell Service: CANADIAN ARMY MEDICAL CORPS Initials: E L Title: Miss Position: Nursing Sister, No.16 Canadian General Hospital, Orpington Class of 1st award: Second Volume 1:145/2 Page 1:345.'

London Gazette Date 1: Fri Dec 12 1919 1st Award.
Notes: RRC sent to Colonial Office, 8 January 1921.

There is also a less detailed entry for Sister Hammell on the Canadian Great War Project website: **www.canadiangreatwarproject.com/searches/soldierDetail.asp?ID=85650**

Lily Harris (1891-1982)

Harris's QAIMNSR service record is one of those that survives and is held at TNA in reference WO 399/358. Both Harris's service card and her medal card can be found on Documents Online. Hers is the 'Lily Harris' card on the bottom row in the example (pictured opposite). The card shows that she began her war service as a staff nurse aboard His Majesty's Hospital Ship (HMHS) *Letitia*. This former passenger vessel had been commandeered by the British Admiralty and was used to transport wounded soldiers from Europe to Canada. The *Letitia* ran aground on 1 August 1917 at Chebucto Head, Halifax, Novia Scotia[80].

17. Lily Harris (seated).

The second row of the medal card for the Corps states 'Q. A. I. M. N. S. R.', indicating that Harris had served in the Reserve of the QAIMNS. She was promoted to Sister. For her service she received the QAIMNS and the 1915 Star. After working on the hospital ship, Harris served in Alexandria and the Balkans from 13 November 1915 to 22 August 1916.

Although much of Harris's service record survives, a page in her file reveals that it was weeded in 1936, with parts destroyed. A letter from her to the War Office confirms that she joined the QAIMNSR in May 1915. She was sent to Malta on the 12th May. She remained with the service until January 1920 when, as a temporary member of the QAIMNS she was 'demobilized as surplus to establishment'. The reason given in the second part of her record was that following an 'examination by a Medical Board', she was 'found permanently unfit for further Military Nursing Service'. However, in June that year, Harris wrote asking to be allowed to return home as she had been abroad for four years. In 1919, Harris was still working abroad - at the Station in Suez. She sailed back to the UK on 8 October that year.

Unlike the Red Cross nurses, or even many of her fellow military nurses, Harris came from an industrial working-class family in West Yorkshire. However, her service record shows that like many in the Reserve, Harris had worked as a civilian nurse before the war. She trained at the Township of Leeds Infirmary from 30 December 1911 to 30 December 1914. She was still working there when she applied to the Reserve.

Harris's family retain her diaries of the war, which were written in pencil in an exercise book. These give an indication of how hard life was for members of the Reserve serving overseas. She writes of suffering a boil on her face, and complains that it is not 'a nice thing being sick here. Could die for all the Matron or her assistant care.' The diary includes names of her colleagues and some reference to the fighting: 'rumours of Jerusalem having fallen'. Lily Harris also names patients, including a Corporal Aitchison' whom she describes as 'a dear, patient, boy'.

18. Medal card of Lily Harris.

19. 11. 17.

We are again in the midst of war
& victorys gained Gaza Beersheba & Jaffa taken
& rumors of Jerusalem having fallen

First wounded arrived here. 15 days ago. the 4th
we have been frony busy since then. Though I
feel much out of it. am in Ward 2 doing medical
have had some very bad cases, there 2 death last
week Pt Boose Fract Spine & Cpl Murphy. Empyema
Have another Fract Spine case Cpl Aitchison. such
a dear, patient, boy. have a few other such ones to.
Today are admitted 20 Surgical walkers & 4
Medical cots. A Conway went to Alex the
morning We were so quiet, I went to help
Miss Holmes

Habe not heard from Sgt newinder since he
left Kantara A letter from Mr Dawson a week ago
They are still advancing, Also 2 letters from
Davies.

Letter from home. Aunt Ellen Barron died

19. Diary entry of Lily Harris. (*Continues opposite.*)

one today from Copley. He has left Moascar
is now beyond Eberash.

My dress is finished, so can get to bed
early.

April 14th

At last I am writing in diary again
This is the end of my 3rd days C. B
with a boil on my face. Not at all
a nice thing being sick here. Could die
for all the Matron or her assistant care
But I'm better with the assistance of

Misses Sommerville & Addison

I came off duty Thursday morning with a
boil on my cheek. had three previously the
worst on my arm. very sore but was able to
keep it covered. But Thursday morning
my face was so swollen. I could not see
out of my left eye. & to think of doing
dirty dressing with numerous flies about, it
was too risky to stay on duty longer.

Notes on Researching Women Nurses, Doctors and Medical Services in the First World War

Some service records can be found on the internet at Findmypast and DocumentsOnline.

Arguably the best online resource for researching nurses at war is the Scarletfinders website: **www.scarletfinders.co.uk**

Service records do survive for some nurses. If a nurse continued to serve into the Second World War, her file will be retained by the Ministry of Defence.

QAIMNS
Most service records have survived, and are retained at TNA. These can be downloaded at Documents Online. Many QAIMNS (R) files do not survive or are not intact. Those that do are held at TNA and can be downloaded at Documents Online.

Other imperial nursing service records can be found at TNA. Sue Light has transcribed some material relating to them onto the Scarletfinders website.

TFNS & QARNNS
Surviving records are held at TNA and have been digitised on Documents Online. All QARNNS records survive and are held at TNA in ref. ADM 104. They can be read online.

VADs
VAD records are retained by the BRCS. Original card index detailing service with the VADs 1914-1919 is held at the British Red Cross Museum and Archives at 44 Moorfields, London EC2Y 9AS. They also hold the Trained Nurses Index which names those who served with the Joint War Committee: 'A sub-index of VADs who worked in military hospitals at home and overseas.' There is some information on auxiliary hospitals. Other useful sources can be found at LMA, in local archives, at TNA and in newspapers. VAD hospital records may be found in local archives. Thekla Bowser's history is on open access shelves in the Explore History Centre and can be read online at **http://archive.org/details/britainscivilian00bowsuoft**.

Well-known writers who served as VADs in the war, and whose biographies, memoirs, letters and diaries provide further detail, include Vera Brittain, Agatha Christie and Naomi Mitchison. Recollections of serving as a VAD can be found in the Liddle Collection, including the Ada Clarke papers. A memoir by VAD, Olive Dent, *A VAD in France* can be read online at **http://archive.org/details/vadinfrance00dentrich**

VADs who died in service can be found in IWM ref. BRCS 25/5.6/2. An envelope of photographs of those who died can be seen in ref. DEC 8/175, which has to be ordered up to the research room.

A few women served with the Russian Army and their records can be found with the Russian Red Cross Society.

FANY

The records of those who served in the First Aid Nursing Yeomanry (FANY) are held at FANY headquarters. Copies of the FANY gazette are held at the British Library and copies of *Women and war: Official Gazette of the 1st Aid NYC and Cadet Yeomanry* can be found at IWM.

APMMC & RAMC

APMMC records can be found at LMA, the Wellcome Library, TNA, IWM and in local newspapers. WHC sources are held at TNA, IWM, and The Women's Library @ LSE. The RAMC auxiliary section attended WAACs and can be researched at TNA, IWM, in newspapers, at the Army Medical Services Museum, in war diaries and at the Wellcome Library.

QAMNSI

QAMNSI records are held at the British Library in the India Office Records. Further information can be found at TNA, in newspapers and in the *Indian Army List.* Postings of the INS can be traced through the *Indian Army List.*

Civilian Nurses

Records of civilian nurses who were trained before 1919 may survive in hospital records. These can be located via the Hospital Records Database (HOSPREC) at **www.nationalarchives.gov.uk/hospitalrecords** - a joint project of the Wellcome Library and The National Archives (TNA). The database includes links and details of administrative records, as well as online hospital catalogues and finding aids.

More than 15,000 nursing service records for 1902-1922 can be found at: **www.nationalarchives.gov.uk/documentsonline/nursing.asp**. Other information may be found with the Royal College of Nursing at: **www.rcn.org.uk/development/ rcn_archives** Copies of the British Journal of Nursing, 'Nursing Record', 1888-1956 can also be accessed through this site. Records of district nurses are held within the records of the Queen's Nursing Institute at the Wellcome Trust archives department.

The Royal College of Nursing (RCN) has a genealogy webpage at: **www.rcn.org.uk/ development/rcn_archives/research_advice_-_tracing_nurses**. The RCN also holds a useful collection of oral recordings at: **www.rcn.org.uk/development/rcn_archives/ oral_history_collection**

Among its archived collections are copies of nursing journals, which feature many nurses' names. One of the oldest journals in their collection, the *British Journal of Nursing/Nursing Record* (1888-1956) can be browsed online at: **http:// rcnarchive.rcn.org.uk/** Also at this website is the archive of the Royal College of Nursing Journal, which regularly reported events concerning its members, including deaths. The Journal had a regular Roll of Honour which included VAD members in its Officers' Casualty Lists.

The Royal College of Midwive's collections are now held by the Royal College of Obstetricians and Gynaecologists (RCOG). Details of the library are held at: **www.rcog.org.uk/what-we-do/information-services/archives**

Less formal records can be found through the various nurses' leagues, which began in 1899 as associations for trained nurses. Those that remain publish regular magazines, hold reunions, or maintain websites for alumni to keep in touch.

QARNNS
The service still exists and has its own archive in Gosport. The website of the Service is: **www.qarnns.co.uk**

PMRAFNS
The service records of RAF nurses are retained by the Ministry of Defence and can be accessed via the Service Personnel & Veteran's Agency. The PMRAFNS has a website within the RAF's main website. Details of its history can be read at: **www.raf.mod. uk/PMRAFNS/history/princessmary.cfm**

Miscellaneous
The crucifix, last letter and the prison cell door number of Edith Cavell are on permanent display at Imperial War Museum North. Cavell is remembered on the war memorial of nearby Sacred Trinity Church in Chapel Street, Salford and in York Minster.

IWM's Explore History Centre holds a number of personal papers belonging to first world war nurses. For example, you can find there the papers of Lily Gunn (1887-1970) from her career in nursing. Gunn was from Kirkwall, and her collection includes, photographs, drawings, letters, handmade Christmas cards, newspaper clippings, reference to the British Farmers Hospital, no.2 Anglo-Belgian, Calais, France, her marriage certificate and a War Office letter about her British War Medal 4 Dec 1919.

War Diaries

War diaries survive for some nursing units in WO95 at TNA. War diaries of regiments serving near where your ancestor was based may name nurses or simply provide a detailed insight into the area of war where she was based. Some can be accessed via Documents Online. The War Diary of the Matron-In-Chief, British Expeditionary Force, France and Flanders has been transcribed and can be read online at: **www.scarletfinders.co.uk/110.html**

Scottish Women's Hospitals

Glasgow and West of Scotland NUWSS joint committee of the Scottish Women's Hospitals for Foreign Service (Scotland) 1916 *The Thistle: Souvenir Book in aid of Scottish Women's Hospitals for Foreign Service. France - Serbia-Salonika-Corsica-Roumania.* (With illustrations.] P.P.4039.wbp.(2) is in a bound volume with the trench journal, *Another Garland From The Front 1916-1919.* This is a solid hardback compilation found in the BL and other archives. The two volumes for 1916 and 1917 are thick, at around 100 pages long and sold for 1/6d. Jane Hamilton M'Ilroy, the editor, wrote the introduction to the 1916 volume, saying, 'The excellence of the work carried on amongst the sick and wounded of our allies by this Voluntary Organisation has been warmly acknowledged by high officials of the French and Serbian Governments.' The issue included poems, stories, plays and drawings. Some were by women, including May Sinclair, Josephine Calina, Edith F B McAlister, Jessie M King, Helen McKie, Maude G M'Ilroy, the Hon. Mrs Dowdall, Cicely Hamilton, Constance Ray and Wilma Hickson. Lady Skerrington wrote 'A True Story' of an officer in India. There is 'A Short Account of the Scottish Women's Hospitals'. The committee included a secretary for the headquarters Committee, Miss Edith May, and a Personnel Secretary, London Units, Miss Willis.

Medals

Nurses were mentioned in despatches and can be found in the *London Gazette*. FANY volunteers were awarded 17 Military Medals, 27 Croix de Guerre and 1 Legion d'Honneur. Royal Red Cross and Associate Royal Red Cross medal registers are held at TNA in reference WO 145. Transcriptions of the registers 1883-1994 have been uploaded to Findmypast.

Nurses who were awarded the Silver War Badge or the Territorial Force Medal can be found in the medal index cards at TNA that have been digitised on Ancestry. Records of the Military Medal, Albert Medal (a civilian gallantry award) and the Florence Nightingale Medal can be found at TNA.

Pensions

Pensions were awarded to nurses disabled through illness or injury sustained in war. Pensions are held at TNA in ref. PMG 42/1-12 and PIN 26/19985-20826.

The Western Front Association (WFA) now holds 6 million Great War Pension Record Cards, previously held by the Ministry of Defence. Although most cards are for male casualties, there are cards for each nurse (who was entitled to a pension) who was killed, injured or otherwise incapacitated. The cards provide the names of the nurses' dependants, as well as their addresses and dates of birth. The WFA plans to digitise the cards and make them available for the public. More details can be found at their website: **www.westernfrontassociation.com**

Memorials, Obituaries and Biographies

Women killed in the First World War are named in the Women's National Memorial in York Minster. Some women appear on the Commonwealth War Graves Commission's Register of Honour war dead VAD (panel 5 York Minster) - many not on CWGC. Women from the Dominions were also remembered on the panels. Fourteen Canadian nursing sisters were drowned when the hospital ship *Llandovery Castle* was sunk by enemy action on 27 June 1918.

The CWGC lists at least 72 VAD members at: **www.cwgc.org**

In York Minster members of the QARNNS are remembered on Screen 1, the QAIMNS and QAMNSI are on Screen 2, the Order of St John & the British Red Cross, as well as 'Members of the Voluntary Aid Detachments who lost their lives on Active Service' are on Screen 5. Screen 6 bears the names of 'Medical Women', Scottish Women's Hospitals, Endell Street Women's Hospital, the British Committee of the French Red Cross and Auxiliary Hospitals. Screen 7 remembers members of the Canadian Nursing Service, while members of the Australian Army Nursing Service are on Screen 7. The Union of South Africa Army Nursing Service and the Colonial Nursing Association are on Screen 10.

Local newspapers often produced a Roll of Honour in each edition. These include soldiers and nurses. The length of the entries varies from one line to a full biography.

Local memorials may provide further details on your ancestor, as may local projects taking place across the country to mark the centenary of the conflict.

General reading of military histories concerning the areas where your ancestor, served or the regiments of the soldiers she cared for, will provide useful insight into her war service and experiences.

Details of extant notebooks, diaries, letters and memoirs written by women, including nurses and doctors in this period, can be found in Sharon Ouditt's *Women Writers of the First World War: An Annotated Bibliography*. Ouditt includes names of corps, as well as the dates of sea passages and dates of commencement of service of some of the writers. These can be corresponded with the known dates and corps of your ancestor in order to help you find a written record of a relative's former colleague or passenger.

An index of male and female doctors in Scotland during the war, enrolled under the auspices of the Scottish Medical Service Emergency Committee, can be found online at http://smsec.rcpe.ac.uk/. The index was compiled by volunteers from Edinburgh University and the Scottish Genealogical Society.

20. Nurses marching at the Victory Parade, London, 19 July 1919.

The Women's Royal Air Force during the First World War. Members of the Women's Royal Air Force (WRAF) on board an RAF lorry circa 1918. Public domain image.

CHAPTER SIX
Women's Auxiliary Services of the First World War

'In the WAAC women do all kinds of work which a woman can do as well as a man, and some which she can do better.'

WAAC Publicity Material.

From 1917, three new auxiliary forces were created specifically for women. These forces were attached to the Army, Navy and (from 1918) the newly-established Royal Air Force. Auxiliaries were required to perform non-combatant roles such as catering, store-keeping, administrative work and mechanics. The War Office was keen to organise women's war work more efficiently and to recruit female auxiliaries, thus freeing thousands of soldiers for the fighting. Women's service in this context was fully approved by the government and the Army: the commander in the field, General Sir Douglas Haig, being consulted over the specifics of their role.

In December 1916, the War Office ordered a report on 'the number and physical categories of men employed out of the fighting area in France'. On 16 January 1917, General Lawson responded by recommending the army employ women to work in France.

The auxiliary services were distinct from women's volunteer groups, such as the Women's Emergency Corps, Women's Volunteer Reserve, Army Service Corps, and Women's Legion, that had been formed earlier in the war. One of the most controversial distinctions was that, even though most of the women who served with the Women's Army Auxiliary Corps (WAAC) for example, were middle class, they received payment for their work. This led to some discrimination and negative feeling towards WAAC members, who were sometimes considered less patriotic than women who had volunteered, particularly those who were risking their lives overseas, like some VAD nurses. However, other members of women's volunteer groups later served with the WAACs, particularly those of the Women's Legion. The work of volunteers in the Women's Legion had inspired the creation of WAAC and in 1918 some wanted to see the two organisations merged.

Another key difference was that, in contrast to the dismissive attitude shown by the War Office towards the early voluntary organisations, it regarded the auxiliaries as service personnel. The respect and seriousness that the government showed towards the auxiliaries was evident in 1921 when former members of WRNS were allowed to wear their uniforms while selling poppies in London's Trafalgar Square[81].

Significantly, members of the auxiliary services did not fight, although thousands were at risk of injury, illness or death while working near the front line or travelling at sea. The only British woman who enlisted officially as a soldier in this war was a nurse, Flora Sandes, who became a Sergeant Major in the Serbian Army. This contrasted with the Russian Maria Bochkareva (1889-1920) who led over 250 female soldiers (out of an initial 2,000 volunteers) in the 1st Russian Women's Battalion of Death. Unofficially, an aspirational war correspondent, Dorothy Lawrence (1896-1964), managed to disguise herself as a man and enlist as a private (later sapper) under the name of Denis Smith.

Women's Army Auxiliary Corps (WAAC)

The first auxiliary service to be created in Britain was the Women's Army Auxiliary Corps (WAAC). Founded in March 1917, the WAAC was governed by the Adjutant-General's Department. It was formally established by an Army Council instruction No.1069, dated 7 July 1917. Although the service functioned within the British Army, women would not receive a commission and there would be no ranks as such. Those of officer status were to be known as 'officials'. However, WAAC would be recognised as an armed service as opposed to war work. Women would wear an official uniform with a distinctive cap badge, which would be provided free.

Women were enrolled for work in Britain and on the Western Front within one of four sections: Cookery, Mechanical, Clerical and Miscellaneous. Cooks could work in hospitals or at the Field Bakery (cooking away from the troops). Those in clerical positions may have worked as typists, clerks or telephonists. While there were no officers, women in charge of the 'Workers' were known as 'controller' and 'administrator'. Several WAACs (Immobiles) lived at home, but not the cooks - due to fears they may have stolen the food. For the full-time women who lived at camp or in local accommodation (Mobiles), board and laundry were 14/- and rations of 12/6 were deducted from their wages.

Many women were unclear as for what exactly they were enrolling. Nevertheless, thousands applied to the Recruiting Headquarters. Women were required to have two references and received checks by a Selection Board and a Medical Board via the offices of the Director General of National Service. They had to be over 21 years of age and applied for service at home and abroad. WAACs who were sent to France were vaccinated and based in camps. They worked at Regimental Base Depots. Some met their future husbands there.

Marwick gives details of Circular 30 from WAAC Headquarters 22 January 1918 (Wom. Coll[82]. Army 3.14) stating that, 'no discharges on compassionate grounds can be given for: enrolling in a fit of temper; enrolling without taking into due consideration the fact that the member has enrolled for the duration of the war; enrolling without parents' knowledge'[83] This indicates how some parents may have felt about the actions of their daughters. Welfare and the image of the WAAC were important to the War Office: women would be discharged from the service 'on medical grounds' if they were discovered to be pregnant.

Mrs Furse (see page 92) argued that women 'should, as far as possible, be drawn from the upper middle and middle classes'. Despite this, many working class women applied, possibly realising Mrs Furse's worst fears when many turned out to be lice-ridden and thinly-clad[84]. Some working class women were, however, accepted into the service, being taken on as unskilled workers for a minimum of 24/- a week. This small sum contrasts with that of skilled workers, such as shorthand typists, who could earn 45/- a week.

All recruits received training. This was based at training headquarters, such as the one at a large country house in Farnborough, near a Royal Flying Corps Camp. In 1917, 200 girls trained here at any one time.

To prevent further problems, the Chief Controller issued, via a WAAC Headquarter's circular 37. Wom. Coll. Army 3.13, the following list of essential items for an enlisting WAAC[85]:

1 pair strong shoes or boots

1 pr low-heeled shoes for housewear

2 prs khaki stockings

2 prs at least warm Combinations

2 prs dark coloured Knickers with washable linings

2 warm Vests of loosely woven Shetland wool

1 doz khaki Handkerchiefs

2 prs Pyjamas or 2 Strong Nightdresses

Burning Sanitary Towels

It is advisable to bring as well, a jersey or Golf Jacket which should be worn under the frock coat in cold weather

For those at the Western Front, war service was dangerous, as the casualties on the Panels at York Minster testify. Air raids were a particular problem. One German attack on a railway bridge in Etaples in May 1918 led to the deaths of nine WAACs. Three WAACs received the Military Medal for bravery during enemy air raids: Dr. Phoebe Chapple RAMC, attd. QMAAC, Asst. Adminr. Elizabeth Sophy Cross, QMAAC and 18659 Forewoman Clerk Ethel Grace Cartledge, QMAAC.

The WAAC was renamed the Queen Mary's Army Auxiliary Corps (QMAAC) in April 1918 and disbanded in 1921.

Gladys L Lowe

A number of photographs survive for the former WAAC Worker No 2614, Gladys L Lowe, one of which shows her with fellow members. Another shows her as a child, and a further two in fancy dress, possibly as part of an entertainment party at the Front.

Lowe's service record is one of the many that do not survive but her medal card reveals that she enrolled as a Worker in WAAC and was awarded the British War Medal for her service overseas (see image).

Women's Royal Naval Service (WRNS)

The Women's Royal Naval Service (WRNS) was formed in November 1917 to provide cooks, clerks, electricians, signallers, storekeepers and telegraphists for the Royal Navy. The early members were based at shore bases or Royal Navy Air Service stations, including those at Gibraltar, Malta and Genoa. Their motto was 'Never at Sea'.

21. Medal Information Card (MIC) of Wkr Gladys Lowe
2614 showing her entitlement to the British War Medal and
the Victory Medal. These medals signify overseas service.

22. British War Medal to Wkr Gladys Lowe QMAAC.

23. Gladys Lowe as a child seated right.

24. Two pictures of Wkr Gladys Lowe presumably dressed up as part of an entertainment party.

25. Group picture showing Gladys Lowe 2614 QMAAC standing 4th right with two very early wooden barrack blocks visible. This may have been in France.

26. Family pictures of Gladys Lowe.

Not all WRNS members, known as Wrens, wore uniforms: 'The first Wrens to appear in uniform were enrolled at the Royal Navy Depot, Crystal Palace in 1918. Most 'Wrens' were give a trade category denoted by blue non-substantive trade badges worn on the right arm'[86].

As with the other auxiliary services, work done was varied. Florence Allum, a rating in the WRNS, served as a Marion Gas Mask Worker from 10 July 1918. Her record can be found in the WRNS Service Register at TNA and on Documents Online in reference ADM 336/26/23.

One of the most significant officers in the WRNS was Mrs (later Dame) Katharine Furse (1875-1952), who had led the first Voluntary Aid Detachment to be sent to France. After her resignation at the end of 1917, Mrs Furse was made Commandant-in-Chief of the WRNS.

During the war, at least 23 Wrens died in service; the 23 are commemorated on Screen One in York Minster (see Appendices). One of these is Phyllis Annie Skinner, Chief Section Leader Steward, service number G6776, who enrolled on 6 May 1918. She died, aged 23, on 5 November 1918 - 6 days before the Armistice. She was the daughter of Philip W. and Annie Skinner of 108 Langney Road, Eastbourne and is remembered at Ocklynge Cemetery in Eastbourne. Her service record can be accessed via Documents Online in reference ADM 336/29/764.

By October 1919, when the organisation was wound up, there were more than 6,000 Wrens, of whom 5,054 were ratings and 438 were officers.

Mercantile Marine

Women had been working as stewardesses with the Mercantile Marine before the war but enrolled in greater numbers to free male stewards for the front. Mercantile Marine Stewardesses were in great danger from mines, aerial bombing and enemy shipping. 50 stewardesses are commemorated on Women's Screen Eleven at York Minster (see Appendices).

Women's Royal Air Force (WRAF)

The Royal Air Force was founded on 1 April 1918, out of a merger of the Royal Flying Corps (RFC) and the Royal Naval Air Service (RNAS). Women who had been serving as auxiliaries in the RFC and RNAS thus found themselves in the newly-formed *Women's Royal Air Force* (WRAF). Its Chief Superintendent was Lady Gertrude Crawford.

The WRAF was established as distinct from the WAAC, although many of its members came from there. Helen Gwynne-Vaughan (1879-1967), the Commandant of the WRAF from September 1918 to December 1919, had previously served as Controller of the WAAC in France. For this, Gwynne-Vaughan was awarded the military CBE - becoming the first female recipient. After the war she became Dame Commander of the Order of the British Empire (DBE) and later, in the Second World War, she was appointed Chief Controller of the Auxiliary Territorial Service (ATS).

The first Commandant of the WRAF was the philanthropist, the Hon. Violet Douglas-Pennant. Controversy surrounded the termination of her appointment in 1918 and eventually led to her being sued for libel. Details on this can be found at TNA in AIR 1/2313/221/49 and AIR 2/11889-908. A House of Lords Select Committee investigated Douglas-Pennant and its report, along with papers on the WRAF 1919-20, is held in reference TS 28/3.

Unlike the WAACs, WRAFs received no training. They were asked to perform a wide range of tasks, from waitressing to sailmaking to fitting engines. Women electricians maintained the lights at Blandford Camp in Dorset, at the time the base of the Royal Naval Division and now the home of the Royal Signals. Roughly 10,000 WAACs served as mechanics, drivers and in other roles at RFC airfields. Women clerical workers took over the roles of male civilian subordinates in Army Pay Offices and other areas.

However, like other auxiliary service members, the WRAFs were given a uniform. This was in the shade of 'air force blue'.

By December 1918, there were 24,659 officers and airwomen, with over 1,000 serving in Germany and France in 1919[87]. The WRAF was disbanded on 1 April 1920 for reasons of national economy.

Florence Beatrice Green (nee Patterson: 1901-2012)

The last known surviving veteran of the First World War, Florence Green, served with the WRAF as a waitress. Her service number was 22360 and she enrolled in September 1918 under her then (maiden) name, Florence Beatrice Patterson. Florence had been born in Edmonton, but later moved to Norfolk. Aged 17, Florence started work with the WRAF on 13 September 1918 at the local Norfolk aerodrome of Narborough (later known as Marham). She was demobilised on 18 July 1919. Her service record survives at TNA in reference AIR 80/185/74 and can be downloaded via Documents Online.

At the time of her 110th birthday, Florence spoke of her war service:

'I enjoyed my time in the WRAF. There were plenty of people at the airfields where I worked and they were all very good company. I would work every hour God sent but I had dozens of friends on the base and we had a great deal of fun in our spare time. In many ways I had the time of my life.'[88]

Casualties

Members of the Auxiliary Services who were killed during the First World War are named in the Women's National Memorial in York Minster. These include members of the WRNS on Screen 1, QMAAC (formerly WAAC) on Screen 2, the WRAF on Screen 4 and Mercantile Marine Stewardesses on Screen 11. Some women also appear on the Commonwealth War Grave Commission's Register of Honour.

Among those recorded on York Minster Women's Screen 3 is Frances Mary Tooby (1894-1918), who served as a Forewoman (Cook) in the WAAC (Service No: 12988). She died a few days after the Armistice on 14 November 1918, aged 25. She died in Woolwich, but is remembered in Bicknor St Mary churchyard in Gloucestershire.

29 year old Gertrude Mayne (nee Sadler: 1888-1918), Service Number 27339, was serving as a Worker in WAAC when she died on 9 April 1918. Her record in the CWGC Register of Honour reveals that she was the daughter of John Thomas and Elizabeth Sadler of 14 Strawberry Place, Armley. She is buried at Armley St Bartholomew churchyard in Yorkshire.

Casualties are recorded for those who served up to 1920, such as L Speight, QMAAC Worker Number 33966. She was based at the Hostel in Dublin and died on 8 January 1920. She is remembered at Sowerby Bridge Cemetery in Yorkshire.

Notes on Researching Members of the Auxiliary Services

Only 7,000 WAAC records survived the burnt records after the Blitz out of 57,000. These are retained at TNA in series WO 398 and can be explored there or on Documents Online. SoG holds a microfilm copy of these records in the Lower Library. No records survive for senior ranks. Service records that were retained by individuals may have been passed on to the Women, Work and Society collection at IWM. It is worth checking their catalogue for the name of your ancestor, particularly if you can find her name nowhere else.

Other useful records for researching WAAC ancestors are the campaign medal records which can be searched on Documents Online. The Medal Index Cards online also have details on recipients of the Women's Service Medal, awarded for exceptional duty of care.

At TNA, you can look through selected medical records of WAAC members in series MH 106. Women who were awarded OBE, CBE, MBE, DBE or were Mentioned in Despatches (MID) can be seen in file WO 162/65.

Thousands of WAACs transferred to WRAF and their records may thus be found at TNA in the AIR 80 series. Also included in these records are some Women's Legion Drivers and the Women's Civilian Subordinates (directly employed and paid by the War Department). All WRNS who were still serving with the RNAS in April 1918 transferred to WRAF, but their records are held in ADM. Around 30,000 WRAF airwomen's records are held at TNA. They include an enrolment form, a certificate of discharge and a casualty form for active service.

WRAF Officers' records have not survived.

The unit war diaries of the WAAC/QMAAC attached to the BEF in France are located in WO 95/84-5. These can reveal more detail on your ancestor's service and can be downloaded at Documents Online.

Some women may be found on the Medal index on Ancestry. Women may have been awarded the Silver War Badge. However, they were only entitled to one gallantry award and this was the Military Medal (MM). Those who were awarded the MM are named in the *London Gazette*. The medal details and some photographs of those awarded may be found in the IWM's Women's Work Collection.

In 1994, the National Army Museum (NAM) inherited WAAC/QMAAC records from the former WRAC Museum at Queen Elizabeth Barracks in Guildford. This collection includes records, pictures, reports, and journals. The Templer Study Centre at the NAM holds hundreds of official documents, private papers, images and ephemera relating to WAAC and its members. These include personal memoirs, British Empire certificates of identity and discharge certificates. The online catalogue, Inventory: **www.nam.ac.uk/inventory/objects/** can be searched by regiment or by name of the person you are researching.

Further WAAC material from the Museum can be found at the AGC Museum archive at Winchester.

WRNS officer and ratings records can be searched at Documents Online. The originals are held at TNA. Naval medal records are held at TNA in ADM 171/133.

Photographs of WRNS members who were awarded medals may be found in the Women's Work & Society Collection at IWM. Other interesting material is held at the Royal Naval Museum and the National Maritime Museum.

Women of officer status in the auxiliary services are named in the *Navy Lists* and *Army Lists.*

Names of casualties may be found in local archives and on local memorials. Names of WAAC official casualties can be found in *Officers Died in the Great War* (HMSO, 1919) and names of members are found in *Soldiers Died in the Great War: Part 80* (HMSO, 1921).

CHAPTER SEVEN
Between the Wars

'Between the firing, you could hear the wind going through the trees, peaceful as hell.'

Felicia Mary Browne at the Spanish Civil War, July 1936.

Ireland

During the Great War, Britain experienced attacks not only from Germany, but from a separate front nearer to home. Ireland had long been a land of conflict and anti-British feeling, and many women were again willingly or unwillingly caught up in the battles.

In April 1916, women played an active role in the Easter Rising, where Irish insurgents rose up against the British rulers, declaring Ireland independent. The uprising ended in failure with the insurgents surrendering and the eventual execution of their leaders. Many were members of independence groups such as the Irish Volunteers and subsequently the IRA, Cumann na mBan, the IRB, Sinn Féin and the Irish Citizen Army. One important source of information is the Bureau of Military History, which was established in January 1947 by Oscar Traynor TD. Traynor was Eire's longest serving Minister for Defence and had formerly been Brigade Commandant of the Dublin Brigade after the death of Richard McKee. The objective of the Bureau was 'to assemble and co-ordinate material to form the basis for the

compilation of the history of the movement for Independence from the formation of the Irish Volunteers on 25 November 1913, to 11 July 1921.'[89]. Witness statements survive and can be useful for family historians.

Ministry of Reconstruction

In 1917, a Ministry of Reconstruction was established in the United Kingdom with the purpose of easing the nation back to peacetime existence. One aspect of its mission was to look at the role of women in society. John Waller Hills produced the *Report of the Women's Employment Committee in 1918* (Volume XIV, p.783). The Women's Advisory Committee of the Ministry of Reconstruction set up subcommittees on specific topics, such as housing, adult education, emigration to the Dominions and employment of voluntary workers. These papers are in TNA series RECO.

Continuation of Women's Services

Although fighting ended officially with the Armistice on the 11 November 1918, Britain continued to maintain a military presence at the former frontlines. The Great War had been a war of empires and Britain was keen to ensure her imperial interests were bolstered in the aftermath.

Many of the women's volunteer and auxiliary services continued to function after 1918. Women VADs were working in Belgium, and QAIMNS nurses like Lily Harris were still serving in areas of diplomatic concern, such as Egypt. Members of the Women's Royal Air Force served in France and Germany through 1919. Within a few years, however, the government's need to reduce defence spending led to the end of the auxiliary services. The Women's Royal Naval Service disbanded on 1 October 1919, the WRAF on 1 April 1920 and the Women's Army Auxiliary Corps on 27 September 1921.

TFNS became TANS after the Territorial Force became the Territorial Army in 1920.

The Navy and Army Canteen Board (NACB) had been formed in 1917 out of the Army Canteen Committee, the Canteen and Mess Society and private Army food suppliers to the Army. NACB worked alongside the Expeditionary Force Canteens, which were set up to avoid the need for private caterers and suppliers. Women were employed by NACB in large numbers from March 1917. The NACB became the central provider of food to the Armed Forces. After the war, NACB continued to serve in France as British troops were demobilised and replaced the Expeditionary Force Canteens. Eight officers and 500 members of QMAAC were transferred to NACB to support this. In 1921, the NACB became part of the newly established Navy, Army and Air Forces Institutes (NAAFI), which continued to feed and supply troops.

Also, in 1921 the Queen Alexandra's Military Families Nursing Service - nursing and midwifery for military families (wives and children) - became part of the QAIMNS in 1926, as did the Queen Alexandra's Military Nursing Service for India. Interestingly, the QAIMNS also functioned in India from 1927, as did the Nursing Service for Indian Troops' Hospitals (later called the Indian Military Nursing Service).

In 1923, the RAF Nursing Service was renamed Princess Mary's Royal Air Force Nursing Service and established as a permanent branch of the RAF.

QARNSS continued to function. The rank of Head Sister-in-Chief was created in 1927. This was later altered to Matron-in-Chief.

The Colonial Nursing Association was renamed the Overseas Nursing Association (ONA).

Many voluntary organisations ceased to exist during the war as their roles were absorbed into those of the auxiliary forces. Others folded in the years following the war. The Women's Land Army disbanded in 1919.

One voluntary group that did continue, albeit in a slightly different profile, was the Women's Police Volunteers. In 1921, the organisation was renamed the Women's Auxiliary Service (WAS). Six women under Mary Sophia Allen were sent to patrol Cologne in Germany in 1923.

The Women's Legion also continued, with a strong focus on its transport role. The Legion would go on to be central to the creation of the Auxiliary Transport Service.

Peacetime Roles

After the war an Officers Association was formed and included wartime commissioned women. For many women, however, war service was soon forgotten. Most raised children and focused on peace time roles.

Many nurses returned to, or retrained as, civilian nurses and midwives. However, opportunities became more restricted for women to train as doctors as many of the medical schools who had allowed women to train for the war effort, now refused entry. Their struggle was taken up by the Medical Women's Federation.

Passage to the Dominions

At the end of the war, ex-service men and women, including Women's Land Army members, were offered free passage to the Dominions. This scheme was created to relieve the financial hardship suffered by those who found themselves unemployed in peacetime. If your ancestor arrived in Canada, Australia or New Zealand between the wars it may be worth checking if their passage was paid for as a result of their war service. This scheme was overseen by the Society for the Overseas Settlement of British Women. This Society worked with the Joint Council of Women's Emigration Societies (1917-1919), which was connected to the Colonial Intelligence League, the British Women's Emigration Association and the South African Colonisation Society.

Many ex-servicewomen were keen to take advantage of the free emigration passages. This can explain why some women appear to disappear from genealogical sources in this period.

Pioneers of Aviation

Beyond the WRAF, women were learning to fly aeroplanes. Pioneering British aviatrixes include Amy Johnson, who learned to fly in 1928 with the London Aeroplane Club at Stag Lane, Mrs Winifred Buller, who worked as a test pilot for the British Caudron Company based in Cricklewood and Harriet Quimby, who became the first woman to fly across the English Channel. These skills were to prove useful when Britain next found herself engaged in total war.

Spanish Civil War 1936-1939

After the Great War, and the introduction of female suffrage, an increasing number of British women became politically active. The interwar years experienced the political extremes of fascism and communism, fuelled by a global economic depression and evident social division. Communism was particularly popular among university students and other intellectuals, several of whom joined the Communist Party of Great Britain (CPGB) or its youth section, the Young Communist League (YCL).

Not all anti-fascists in the period supported communism, however. An illustration of this was 4 October 1936, when Oswald Mosley, the leader of the British Union of Fascists, led an anti-Jewish march through the streets of Stepney in the East End of London, people of all backgrounds joined the protest. Over 100,000 people had signed a petition against the march and the streets filled with anti-fascists. The march ended in what became known as the Battle of Cable Street, after protesters formed a barricade, threw fruit, bottles and other debris at the marchers and police were compelled to order Mosley to retreat.

Anti-fascist protesters were similarly passionate in their feelings towards General Franco of Spain. Franco's rebellion against the democratically elected Second Spanish Republic led to the Spanish Civil War. Beginning in July 1936, the war attracted volunteers from across the world, who fought in International Brigades. Female volunteers tended to travel to Spain as nurses, journalists, photographers or for clerical roles. Women in the UK raised money and food, and looked after refugees, particularly children from the Basque region[90].

While many of these women were politically motivated, others, particularly among the nurses, were driven by a duty of care. This sometimes had unintended consequences: as a result of her lack of Communist belief, the 'politically disinterested' nurse, Lillian Urmston, was accused of being a spy.

Sculptress and Communist activist Felicia Mary Browne (1904-1936) was the first British volunteer to die in Spain. Browne was there on holiday but had refused to leave when fighting began, instead joining a worker's militia. Her file in KV 2/1560 at TNA includes Secret Service reports, letters (some from Browne) and her photograph. It is claimed that Browne was the only British woman to fight in this war. Other women contributed in non-combative roles.

Pre-WWII Services

Other services were established in the lead up to WWII. In 1935, the War Office remained unenthusiastic about spending on women's services. Suggestions had been made for official support of the Women's Legion, but the War Office saw no need for an official role, arguing instead that in war women would simply take on non-combative roles like 'ambulance drivers, waitresses, cooks, domestic workers ... telegraphists, wireless operators, telephone operators, clerks and anti-gas personnel'[91]. The former WRAF Commandant, Dame Helen Gwynne-Vaughan was determined to create a peacetime women's auxiliary force, specifically to train officers. Out of the 1934 version of the Women's Legion, then, came the Emergency Service, renamed in October 1936 and commanded by Gwynne-Vaughan. Members trained weekly, attended summer camps, and received a payment of 10 shillings per year. On 23 June 1938, the Military Transport Section of the Women's Legion, the Emergency Service and the Women's Transport Service FANY combined to create the Women's Auxiliary Defence Service.

In September 1938, the Munich Crisis hastened the need for an official auxiliary force linked to the Territorial Army. QMAAC had been disbanded, but on 9 September 1938, the Women's Auxiliary Defence Service was renamed the Auxiliary Territorial Service (ATS). At this date, there was also a separate Royal Air Force ATS Company, which later affiliated to an Auxiliary Air Force (AuxAF) unit. This was not to last, and a new incarnation of the WRAF, known as the Women's Auxiliary Air Force, or WAAF, was formed on 28 June 1939.[92]

Finally, the Women's Royal Naval Service (WRNS) was reformed on 3 April 1939.

Notes on Researching Servicewomen, Ex-Servicewomen or Future Servicewomen between the Wars

Service records for women from this period are retained by the Ministry of Defence. Other useful records, such as personal papers and reports can be found at IWM and in the Liddle Collection.

The website **www.bureauofmilitaryhistory.ie** plans to upload all 1,773 witness statements of the Bureau of Military History regarding the Easter Rising in Ireland.

Recognition of the Great War service of thousands of women, resulted in women over the age of 30 and satisfying one of three qualifying requirements, receiving the vote in national elections in 1918. Their records may be found on electoral registers from that date. Ancestry has digitised some electoral registers for London and Warwickshire, but the indices are incomplete. From 1928, all women aged 21 and over received the franchise on the same terms as men. It is possible, therefore, for you to find your female householder ancestors, who were born before 1907, in their local electoral rolls.

Women who took advantage of a passage to Canada may be found on the 1921 Canadian census. This can be searched on Ancestry (worldwide subscription) and will eventually be uploaded to the website of the Library and Archives Canada.

Records of the Society for the Overseas Settlement of British Women are retained by The Women's Library @ LSE.

Members of the NACB who received medals in the First World War can be found in the WO 372 index via Discovery.

More details of the history of women in medicine can be found with the Medical Women's Federation.

A list of those who fought in Spain from the International Brigade Association and Friends of Republican Spain can be searched on Documents Online. More on the International Brigades of the Spanish Civil War can be read at: **www.internationalbrigades.org.uk/** Records of suspected Communists are held in the KV 2 series at TNA. The International Brigade Archive is held at the Marx Memorial Library in London.

CHAPTER EIGHT

The Second World War and the Emergence of New Roles

'Back to the Land, we must all lend a hand,
To the farms and the fields we must go,
There's a job to be done, Though we can't fire a gun,
We can still do our bit with the hoe.'

Song of the Women's Land Army.

As the failure of the September 1938 Munich Agreement became apparent, the British government took steps to prepare for a new war with Germany. With women already serving in auxiliary forces and military nursing roles, it appeared that they would be asked to play a major part in the future conflict.

A year later, on 3 September 1939, Britain declared war on Germany. Almost immediately, men aged 18-41 who were not in reserved occupations became subject to conscription. In October 1939 males aged 20-23 had to register for one of the armed forces. It was not until the enactment of the National Service (No.2) Act 1941, when greater numbers of men were required to fight, that women aged 20-24 were conscripted into the services, factories and farms. The Minister for Labour, Ernest Bevin, made a speech in March 1941, calling for women to volunteer for war work, particularly in munitions factories. From this date, all women aged 19 to 41 had to register at employment

exchanges. Women workers would be supported by a government programme of child minders. Unlike later posters for the Land Army or the services, Bevin did not glamorise war work: 'I have to tell women that I cannot offer them a delightful life. They will have to suffer some inconveniences. But I want them to come forward in the spirit of determination to help us through.'[93] The age of conscription was later extended to include women, single or widowed, of between 20 and 30 years. Those with children under the age of 14 could request exemption and women in socially useful work such as nursing or teaching were usually allowed to remain civilians.

27. St Pancras Air Raid Precautions Department Enrolment Form.

The Second World War is known for extensive of use of propaganda by both allied and enemy forces. This took place through the media of newspapers and posters, and the more modern wireless and cinema. A 1940 British Council film on women's contribution to the war effort can be watched at **http://film.britishcouncil. org/women-in-war-time**. The 1943 feature film, *Millions Like Us*, promoted the comradeship of young women who left home to work in factories and lived together in hostels. The film portrayed women from a range of social backgrounds living and working well alongside each other. In reality, life away from home and the mixing of social classes could prove very difficult, and homesickness was common.

Throughout the six long years of war, women served their country in greater numbers than ever before. By 1943, women formed 9.6% of the armed forces (450,000 women). Outside of the services, new roles included organising the Evacuation (particularly those in the Women's Volunteer Service), acting as Air Raid Precautions (ARP) wardens and taking on clerical positions, such as the typists in the Cabinet War Rooms (and other civil service posts) in London. Women were also subject to the dangers of war - at home, while travelling and when posted overseas.

The Luftwaffe's aerial raids on London began on 7 September 1940. These raids, or 'Blitz', brought death and destruction to the city. As the raids spread to other parts of Britain, civilians and service personnel lost their possessions, homes, family members and lives.

Air Raid Precautions (ARP) and Civil Defence

An Air Raid Wardens' Service was set up by the government in 1937 as part of its strategy for dealing with potential aerial attacks on Britain. In 1938, around 200,000 men and women volunteered for the scheme. These volunteers or Air Raid Precautions (ARP) Wardens began the war checking that the blackout was properly observed so that no light could be seen from homes, cars, street lights, or even cigarettes by enemy bombers. Once air raids began, the work became demanding, with wardens responsible for overseeing all aspects of life relating to the raids. This included handing out gas masks, monitoring air raid shelters (included the prefabricated Anderson shelters in private gardens), reporting on bomb damage, locating lost children and assisting emergency services. Some ARP were assigned to committees with specific roles, such as the National Air Raid Precautions Animal Committee. This committee or 'Animal Guard' was made up mainly of women and were responsible for the welfare of local pets. Most of Britain's 1.4 million ARP wardens volunteered outside of their day job. Your ancestor may thus have done war work by day and ARP work at night.

Where residents were made permanently or temporarily homeless by an air raid or where they were in need of hot food, civil defence organisations such as the Emergency Food Service and the London Meals Service provided necessary relief. Other vital post raid services included the Administrative and Information Centres, Emergency Information Rest Centres, the Mortuary Service, Inter-Hospital Transport and the Billetting Services.

North London resident Elizabeth Sadler[94] had been working as a hospital nurse when she became ill. After recovering, she was advised to give up full-time nursing and find less arduous war work:

'... so I joined the St. Pancras Civil Defence for the remainder of the war. At first I had tried to find gainful employment in Hampstead Civil Defence, but just then there had been a brief lull in enemy action and they had no vacancies for me. To begin with I helped staff the Medical Aid Posts in the Underground stations and other shelters in the Borough. For a while I was sent to a shelter under the Coach Station at King's Cross. I remember there were large pipes running along the walls at ceiling level and above the camp bed where I sometimes rested. These pipes were warm and at quiet moments around 4 a.m. big rats would creep along them doing a sort of trapeze act above me; while below I grew pale with suspense as to whether or not they'd make it or land on my head.

When there were no incidents to cause a rush, shelter nursing was a fairly routine job. Mostly doling out Brompton cough lozenges or aspirins for headaches, looking for spotty-faced children with infectious rashes and dealing with minor complaints. The doctor visited us at 10.30: there was tea, then a check on the drug-cupboard and look at anyone who needed the doctor's attention. Later when the pubs were all closed things began to get lively. The shelter marshals struggled valiantly with drunks, settled squabbles among the shelterers and kept a lookout for verminous or dirty bedding.'

Police

300 women were serving as police officers at the beginning of the Second World War. This was a tiny proportion of the full complement of 60,000 and grew to just 385 in 1944. Women's role in the police during the war was centred on domestic issues, particularly concerning women and children.

Women's (Royal) Voluntary Service (WVS/WRVS)

One of the most popular voluntary positions was working with the fairly middle-class organisation, the Women's Voluntary Service for Air Raid Precautions which had been established in June 1938. In February 1939, this became the Women's Voluntary Service for Civil Defence, known popularly as the Women's Voluntary Service

ST. PANCRAS A.R.P. DEPARTMENT

EQUIPMENT (Returnable).		
Item.	Date Issued.	Date Returned.
SILVER BADGE	/	
MANDATE CARD		
C.D. ARMLET	/	
REGISTRATION CARD (Signed)		
DOORPLATE		
STEEL HELMET	/	
C.D. RESPIRATOR	/	
WHISTLE	/	
EYESHIELD	/	
GENTS' UNIFORM SUIT		
LADIES' UNIFORM COAT		
" FELT HAT		
RAINCOAT		
SHELTER MARSHAL ARMLET		
GUM BOOTS		
ANTI-GAS SUIT		
" " GLOVES		
Warden's Torch	28/5/41	

NAME CLEMENTS Hilda (Miss)
ADDRESS 44 Warden Road
RANK N.W.5

DATE ENROLLED 11 - 10 - 38 AGE 41
COURSE NO. DATE OF EXAM.
CERTIFICATE NO. 1228 DATE 16 - 12 - 38
MANDATE CARD 7.9.3 DATE
SILVER BADGE ISSUED (DATE) 16 - 12 - 38
ENROLMENT FORM yes E.D.60.
CONDITIONS OF SERVICE FORM IDENTIFICATION CARD NO.
MARRIED OR SINGLE Single NO. IN FAMILY
NEXT OF KIN
USUAL OCCUPATION Storekeeper

A.R.P. HISTORY.				
Date.	Post or Shelter.	F.T. or P.T.	Date.	Transfer or Resignation.
	No. 11	PT		

28. ARP card of Miss Hilda Clements of London NW5.

(WVS) reflecting its work organising the mass evacuation and preparing for possible air raids. It was to become Women's Royal Voluntary Service (WRVS) in 1966. Over the course of the war, the WVS, led by Lady Reading, would contribute to the war effort in whatever way was needed. Its roles included collecting salvage, recycling clothing or toys, re-housing and acting as Civil Defence Support for (among others) Air Raid Precaution wardens, ambulance drivers, the Home Guard and fire brigades.

WVS members could be identified by their badges. Some wore badges of the WVS Housewives Services Identification. Other badges include a simple monogram bearing the letters 'WVS'. One WVS member, Nella Last, reported many of her wartime activities to the Mass Observation Archives. Her memoirs have since appeared in book form.

There was a related branch in India, known as WVS India.

Evacuation

Amidst the preparations for war, one of the greatest fears was that of gas attacks particularly from the air. Many remembered the Zeppelin attacks of the First World War when, during 51 raids, 5,806 bombs were dropped resulting in 557 deaths and

1,358 injured. In 1937, the Guernica air attack in the Spanish Civil War had prompted ideas of a mass evacuation of children in the event of such an attack here.

Operation Pied Piper was the government's codename for the evacuation of millions during the Second World War. From 1 September 1939 to the end of the war in 1945, almost a million and a quarter people were moved from London and from areas such as Middlesbrough, Leeds, Portsmouth, Manchester, Liverpool, Coventry, Plymouth, Birmingham and Southampton. Some children were evacuated overseas - most memorably to Canada. The operation required planners, administrators in both the cities or coastal towns and the reception areas, and travel companions for the children. All school-age children in the danger areas could be sent away to the countryside. Some were sent in school groups, with their teachers whose roles developed into a form of social worker, giving emotional and practical support. Most of those working in the evacuation were women.

Not everyone was evacuated at the same time: from very early on in the war, several evacuees returned to their home cities - often unofficially - and even went to school again. Some of these returned or were re-evacuated in the second wave of evacuation, which took place from 13 June to 18 June 1940. Most only began to return in July 1945 but by August 1945, 76,000 evacuees remained with their hosts. The evacuation ended officially in March 1946.

Women's Home Guard Auxiliaries

A little-known area of women's work in this war was their involvement in the Local Defence Volunteers (LDV). This functioned as a forerunner of the Home Guard, a civilian force set up to resist an enemy invasion. Some trained the men to shoot, although no woman in this war was compelled to use a lethal weapon. All women who used guns were required to sign their consent. Other volunteers became mechanics and radar operatives.

Women were never official members of the Home Guard. However, some did work alongside them, aiding with administration, cooking and operating telephones. Others set up their own illegal Women's Home Defence groups, including the London-based Amazon Defence Corps[95]. These groups of women practised shooting and prepared to tackle invading forces. The service performed by those in supportive roles led to the creation of the Women's Home Guard Auxiliaries. This Home Front Invasion Defence is one of the least celebrated areas of women's war work and can be difficult to identify, but members did wear their own blue badges with the letters HG in the centre, topped by a red enamel crown.

Women's Land Army (WLA)

The Women's Land Army (WLA) was revived on 1 July 1939. By this date, Britain was importing around 70% of its food. With merchant shipping under attack from enemy surface raiders and submarines, Britain needed to reduce the threat by producing more of its own foodstuffs. The government also feared a German U-boat siege and the risks of British starvation. As in the First World War, the WLA provided replacement agricultural labour for men fighting in the services. Their work reduced the pressure on merchant shipping and made a significant contribution to keeping Britons fed throughout the war. Their work was supported by the domestic Dig For Victory campaign, encouraging householders to grow food in their gardens and for public spaces to be converted into allotments. Where food was particularly difficult to obtain, such as sugar, it had to be rationed. Bacon, butter and sugar were rationed from 8 January 1940. Later restrictions were imposed on meat, cheese, eggs, lard, milk, tea, biscuits and processed fruit. Some tropical foods, like bananas, almost completely disappeared from British tables until 1945.

Most recruits, known as 'Land Girls', came from the countryside. Just over a third of the membership came from London and industrial cities of the North[96]. The need for Land Girls varied across the country. The highest number of land girls was in North and West Yorkshire (4,088 by the end of December 1943)[97] and the lowest was in Montgomeryshire (211 by end Dec 1943). At its peak, the WLA had over 80,000 members.

Although the WLA was not a service, it was subject to conscription and women were proud to enlist. Not all members wore the uniform of green jerseys and brown breeches, but others liked being identified with this essential wartime organisation. Its patron was Queen Elizabeth (later the Queen Mother). However, formal recognition was slow to appear and WLA members only received an official service badge in 2007.

Amelia King, a black British woman from Stepney in east London, was the daughter of a merchant seaman and the sister of a sailor in the Royal Navy. Keen to follow in their footsteps she volunteered in 1943, but was rejected because of her skin colour. King protested, leading the Member of Parliament for Dewsbury, Ben Riley to enquire in the House of Commons of Tom Williams, the Minister of Agriculture whether King 'has now been accepted into the W.L.A.; and whether she will be entitled to receive and wear the land army uniform?' Williams replied that he was, 'expecting that the enrolment of Miss Amelia King in the Women's Land Army will be effected this week, and as soon as she is drafted to employment she will receive and be entitled to wear the Women's Land Army uniform.'[98] The case came to the attention of interested groups such as the Holborn Trades Council, who created a leaflet in 1943 with King's photograph, headed with the words 'They tried putting a colour ban on the harvests' and asking for the public to 'add YOUR protest to the growing demand that racial discrimination be ended for ever'.

By 1943, the WLA had helped to increase the percentage of home-produced food to 70%, with imports down to 30%.

In April 1942, the Ministry of Supply (Home Grown Timber Department) formed the Women's Timber Corps (WTC), a revival of the Women's Timber Service of the First World War. Scotland set up its own WTC in May 1942 within the WLA. WTC members were known as 'Lumber Jills'. The work of the Corps involved felling trees, running sawmills, and loading timber. At its peak, there were 6,000 members of the WLA.

It was not just formal members of the WLA who worked on the land during the war. The young Margaret Webb (later Harriman) laboured hard on Troy Farm in Monmouthshire. Margaret had been born 27 April 1928, near Luton. In 1941, she and her family moved to the remote Welsh farm, where they rented rooms from the farmer. Margaret attended the local school but spent the rest of her time doing stable work, locating lost sheep and milking cows. After the farm was sold to more 'efficient farmers' who would help the war effort by increasing food production, Margaret stayed on as their tenant.

'This is the life for me,' I thought, 'high up on the hills or by the sparkling rivers with powerful machinery under my control. Learning the feel and characteristics of the soil until it becomes part of the soul, and the one gives to the other, as the rich crops rise after the touch of man's hands and minds upon the land.'[99]

When war ended, she and her friend were turned away from the local pub on Victory over Japan (VJ) night for being 'too young to join them.' However, this was not the end for Margaret's agricultural career: she passed the county scholarship examination for the Monmouthshire Institute of Agriculture and planned to become an agricultural engineering contractor. In the meantime, work on the farm continued, with Margaret working closely with Walter Wilski, a German prisoner of war. She was with Walter on 6 October 1947 when she was struck accidentally by a tractor. Margaret's spine was fractured: she was to be disabled for life.

In March 1948, she was admitted to Stoke Mandeville Spinal Injuries Centre. Seeing successful disabled athletes such as the wheelchair archers, Robin Imray and Sheila Perrin, proved an inspiration to Margaret. During this period, she met other girls who had been disabled in the war, such as, '[J.] Bunty Noon; a W.R.A.F. (WAAF) who had been knocked down by a Lancaster bomber; Pat Theobald from the Army; Robin Imray, Air Force; Beryl Bell, a civilian, 15 and the baby of the war. She had had thirty-odd bones broken in a motorcycle accident and was determined to become an artist.'[100]

Margaret was taught archery by 'Q', an ex-quarter-master, and she went on to participate in the second Stoke Mandeville Games of 1949. This was the brainchild of Dr L Guttman, head of the hospital's spinal injuries unit. The first archery tournament had taken place on 27 July 1947[101]. After marrying, Margaret and her husband migrated to Rhodesia in June 1957. As a Rhodesian archer, Margaret Harriman went on to become one of the first and finest athletes of the Paralympic Games.

NAAFI

Whereas in the First World War, canteens had at first been organised by private and voluntary organisations, by 1939 the Navy Army and Air Forces Institutes (NAAFI) was well-established. This was the central canteen supplier to the armed forces.

War Work: Factories

Beyond volunteer roles, many more women were employed in clerical roles with the civil service or making ammunition, aircraft or uniforms in factories - particularly after a factory-recruiting drive was initiated in 1943. Once again, women's work in factories kept the armed forces in weapons. And again, women workers were often under-valued, being forced to endure low pay, long hours and unpleasant conditions. In this area, social divisions were more evident than in the voluntary positions. Factory work did not appeal to middle or upper class women, who usually preferred to volunteer for the auxiliary services or the WLA.

Eileen Piggott (born 1921; nee Ball) worked in the Ediswan lamp factory at Ponder's End, Enfield. This factory produced lighting for mines, searchlights, and signal lamps, and had produced the receivers for the world's first public television service from BBC Alexandra Palace. During the war, manufacture concentrated on types of radar and sonar that were essential to the war effort, as well as later producing powerful signalling lamps for use by tanks in the deserts of North Africa. These new electronic detection systems were all top secret. For this reason, data sheets were never openly published and extant records can be hard to find.

Originally, Eileen joined the factory as her father worked there. When war broke out all staff received perfunctory Red Cross lessons. Despite working in a clerical position, Eileen worked long hours:

29. Eileen Ball around the time that she worked at Ediswan.

'Those of us who worked in an office were told, quite fairly, that we had to work 7.30am until 7.30pm, the same hours as those working in the factory. Also, we were put on fire watch duty, once a week, all night, sleeping on stretchers in a wooden hut. The first time I went, I was allocated the stretcher nearest the phone and heard a remark from an older woman (I was the youngest there), 'Oh, that's because she is an office 'tart' and will be used to a 'phone.' For this duty, we were given a free breakfast in the canteen, next morning, before going back to our work places. Actually, I became quite friendly with the women I was on duty with and we had many laughs, also learned many aspects about sex that I wasn't aware of!'

Eileen married in November 1940 and moved to Kent, but by the time conscription for women was introduced, her husband had been posted elsewhere. Eileen signed up for war work and returned to Ediswan, this time working on a machine, feeding in filaments on special bulbs. Work at the factory was skilled and demanding: it was not unknown for fragments of a captured lamp to arrive and for workers to be expected to create a reconstruction of the original.

Like factory workers in the First World War, women in this war were exposed to dangers at work. In the 1940s, the risk of factories being bombed was high, particularly when enemy aircraft targeted industrial areas. Ediswan escaped serious damage from the many air raids over the Lea Valley, but Eileen Piggot remembers another factory in the area being hit by a V2 rocket:

30. Wedding of Eileen Ball.

'I recall, the Chadwick Brush Factory [Chadwick's & Shapcott's Acorn Works on Waltham Cross High Street] heavily bombed one day, this was in Waltham Cross and the workers were there. One girl we knew slightly was one of those killed. Then we learned that some weeks later her parents on their way to her grave with flowers were caught by a bomb at the corner of Bury Green Road (where there are now flats) and they were killed!'

Women in factories worked on a variety of essential war products, including gas masks. Just as munitions workers in the First World War suffered ill health or death from exposure to toxins, so gas mask workers of the late 1930s onwards have suffered from the ill-effects of asbestos, which was used in the filters of the

31. Eileen Ball today.

masks. There were no health and safety warnings or masks for those who assembled the gas mask canisters. Since the war, women who worked at the J. E. Baxter factories at Blackburn and Leyland, the Bournville Utilities factory in Birmingham and the Boots factory in Nottingham have suffered breathing difficulties and in some cases died from diseases, such as mesothelioma, caused by their war work.[102]

Auxiliary Fire Service (AFS)

The Auxiliary Fire Service (AFS) was formed in the lead up to the war, after the government ordered all fire authorities to establish auxiliaries which would be used in the eventuality of war and air raids. At first, the AFS worked out of local buildings, such as schools and garages, and a shortage of uniforms led many to wear those of postmen. In August 1941, an amalgamation of the AFS and local authority fire brigades created the National Fire Service (NFS). NFS (Northern Ireland) was created in 1942.

The official AFS women's uniform was a navy woollen suit with a steel helmet for outdoor work and a peak cap for indoors. Either skirts or trousers could be worn. Like the ARP, the AFS recruited women full-time and part-time for driving, fire-watching and telephonist duties. Many of the recruits had to be taught to drive after enlisting. They also worked in mobile canteen vans.

Women could enlist for duty at any fire station. Telephonists passed on details from wardens and fire watchers of the whereabouts of fallen bombs and of subsequent fires. They contacted fire stations and co-ordinated where engines and fire fighters should be sent. They worked long hours, in shifts, with many operating the lines through the night. At its height, the NFS comprised 370,000 members, of which around 80,000 were women.

There were 40 Fire Forces, each divided into divisions with two columns and five companies.

Ranks in the Fire Service included:

Firewoman	Leading Firewoman
Senior Leading Firewoman	Assistant Group Office
Group Officer	Assistant Area Officer
Area Officer	Regional Woman Fire Officer

Some members of the NFS who later became well-known include Phyllis Stedman (1916-1996: Baroness Stedman), who was a Group Officer in Derbyshire and the radio personality Irene Thomas (1919-2001).

Dangers were rife. Members of the AFS worked around fire, rubble, destruction and unexploded bombs, even while raids were taking place. Londoner Albert Moody remembered a particularly dedicated AFS telephonist in the Gospel Oak area of Camden: 'This brave young lady, on duty at her post in Mansfield Road School, tracked a flying bomb all the way across London from South to North, its course in direct line with her post. She knew it was overhead, but stayed put - the beastly thing 'cut out' and blew her and the post to pieces.'[103] In 1944, the school was destroyed completely by a flying bomb.[104]

YWCA

Women working for the YMCA in the First World War had fulfilled essential voluntary roles. By the time of the Second World War, the Young Women's Christian Association (YWCA) was growing in prominence. Volunteers were based all over the world, in the service stations of Europe, North Africa, and Asia. The YWCA, in association with the Ministry of Labour and the Ministry of Supply, also provided many of the hostels where War and Munitions Workers lived. Besides this, YWCA members worked at rest rooms and hostels for the armed forces.

Other general services who provided relief after air raids and support for those made homeless included the Church Army, the Salvation Army, Toc H, Church of Scotland Huts, Methodist and United Board Churches, Catholic Women's League, and Women's Institutes.

Prisoners of War Camps

Some women worked at PoW camps in Britain, often in clerical roles. In at least three of these camps, male 'listeners', as they were termed, gained intelligence from the German prisoners via listening (or 'bugging') devices.

Girl Guides

Girl guides once again contributed to the war effort. Many former guides would join the WAAF, WRNS and FANY, using the quasi-military training they had received at meetings or on camps. The current Guides grew food on allotments, knitted, dug shelters, administered first aid, raised funds for the war effort, helped with the evacuation, fed bombed families and helped in children's homes. After working 96 hours in war-related roles, each Guide received a War Service Badge.

Brownies also contributed to the war effort, not least the 1st Chefoo Brownie Pack in the Far East concentration camp who helped maintain morale in very difficult circumstances. Their camp sports were overseen by the former Olympic athlete, Eric Liddell, whose story was told in the film, *Chariots of Fire* (1981). Liddell died a few months before the camp was liberated.

Outside of the services and camps, some women to contributed to the war effort by working as reporters or creating propaganda.

Conscientious Objectors

The Great War had been described as 'the war to end all wars'. Many women had fervently hoped this would prove true. Consequently, pacifism had increased during that war and over subsequent years, not least as the losses and injuries of that war continued to be apparent. Quakers and other pacifists were thus united in their desire for peace, and refusal to participate in another conflict, less than 20 years after the last had ended.

In 1941, conscription only affected a relatively small number of women. At this stage, therefore, there were around 1000 women who applied for recognition as conscientious objectors. Of these, around 500 were imprisoned. These tended to be women who were extremely committed to their protest and refused any option of informal exemption.

Notes on Researching Women in the Second World War

Changes of work and interruptions by marriage or birth of children were common among women in this war. This needs to be borne in mind when researching. Even though a woman may have finished working in one area, and even taken time to give birth, she may have volunteered to work in another service later. Mary Wesley (1912-2002), who went on to be a well-known novelist, began the war as an ambulance driver, but quickly left this to work for MI5 in London until her unit was moved to Bletchley Park. She later moved to Cornwall where gave birth to her third child, cared for evacuees, joined the WVS and worked on the land with the WLA.

Illegitimacy rose during the war. Some children were registered under their mother's husband's name rather than that of their biological father. There are useful websites that can help researchers find out more about soldier relatives from abroad, including **www.canadianrootsuk.org** and GI Trace **www.gitrace.org**

Records either do not survive or were not created for much of the work that women did in this war. Most service records are retained by the Ministry of Defence and can be accessed only by the veteran herself or by the proven next-of-kin. This leaves researchers reliant on published secondary sources or alternative primary records, such as letters, diaries, memoirs and personal accounts. Fortunately, local and family history societies, local and national museums, university departments, newspapers, television producers and others have been keen to record and retain personal histories from the Second World War. Oral histories and other personal accounts of women who worked or served in this war are widely available in museums, at sound collection websites, and in relevant archives. Many of these resources can be found in the Records Section at the back of this book. The best resource, of course, is the women themselves and those who remain are often happy to share their war experiences with a patient listener. Veterans' groups can help to put you in touch.

Medals
Women in civilian roles were eligible for non-combatant medals, including the civilian equivalent of the Victoria Cross - the George Medal. Details of non-combatant medal awards, for gallantry or otherwise, are held in TNA series WO 373/66-70. The following women's or mixed services were eligible for the Defence Medal: Local Authority Civil Defence Services, National Fire Service, Civil Nursing Reserve, nurses in government or voluntary hospitals and the WVS.

ARP
Few records survive for women who worked in ARP although some details could be found by searching local newspapers and some ARP records may be found at local

record offices. The West Yorkshire Archive Service holds a good collection of the West Riding of Yorkshire's ARP Service.

WVRS

The Women's Royal Voluntary Service archive has an online catalogue and offers a remote enquiry service. The Collection includes over 4,000 photographs, 263 posters and around 50,000 Narrative Reports from 1938-1945. The Archive is planning a new repository and free onsite access by 2018. The WVRS Archive and Heritage Collection's website is: **www.wrvs.org.uk/about-us/our-history/wrvs-archive-and-heritage-collection** Outside the Collection, records on the formation of the organisation are held at TNA; poster, uniforms and a full series of the Bulletin magazine are held at IWM; there is a small collection of material at the NAS; and a collection of oral histories can be found in The Women's Library @ LSE.

Evacuation

Few evacuation records survive of teachers, administrators or schools. School records that do remain may be held either at the local record office or with the school itself. One of the most useful type of record that may survive is the school log book of both the host and sending school. These can give details on the related schools, medical provision and so on. School admission registers often include the names of evacuees and sometimes the names and addresses of their hosts. Some were lost in later records as children from city schools were spread across many different rural areas and schools. For example, Ealing brought back 708 children from 60 places.

At LMA, reference LCC/EO/WAR (Education Officer's Department: Emergency Wartime Measures) is particularly useful. LMA's catalogue has more details **http://search.lma.gov.uk**, but as these records are subject to the Data Protection Act, it is worth contacting the archive concerned before visiting.

Parish magazines 1938-1945 may contain references to registration and evacuation. These would be particularly worth checking if the evacuee was sent to a small village. Local newspapers may also feature information. The Evacuees Reunion Association (ERA) is the largest organisation for British evacuees, with over 2,200 members worldwide. Its newsletter helps former evacuees to keep in touch and could answer enquiries regarding administrators and teachers of the evacuation.

Details of some of the women who rescued children from Europe via the Kindertransport and other schemes can be found in records at the Wiener Library for the Study of the Holocaust & Genocide, 29 Russell Square, London WC1B 5DP **www.wienerlibrary.co.uk**; the Hampstead Garden Suburb Care Committee for Refugee Children; the Movement for the Care of Children from Germany (or British

Inter-Aid Committee). Other useful organisations are Save the Children, the Central British Fund and the Society of Friends.

Women's Land Army

There are no surviving service records for the Women's Land Army 1939-50. The index cards are held at TNA, with originals at the Imperial War Museum.

Women's Land Army Employment figures are given by county in Vita Sackville-West's well-illustrated the Women's Land Army (MAF, London, 1997; original 1944). The book is very detailed on the work done by Land Girls. Chapter 9 gives a List of Chairmen and County Secretaries. The 'chairmen' were all women. Other chapters cover welfare, details of everyday life, training (and the documents generated by it), employment (which gives an insight into the work done), wages received. There is even the sheet music for the Land Army Song, *Back to the Land*. Documents that were created were application forms, medical certificates, forms of undertaking (rents], membership cards, badges and items of uniform. Transfers from one county to another were possible, but not encouraged. There are also records of county war agricultural executives committees (or similar), such as that in Cheshire.

A memorial statue to the Women's Timber Corps (WTC) stands in the Queen Elizabeth Forest Park near Aberfoyle in Scotland.

NAAFI

A NAAFI Collection exists at the Imperial War Museum. The National Army Museum (NAM) also has a good collection of related artefacts.

War Work

The National Register of Archives: **www.nationalarchives.gov.uk/nra/** holds information on the whereabouts of records on factories where women worked in the war. Pathe and other contemporary films (such as those on: **www.movietone.com**) regularly showed women working in factories. Some individual factories, like the Royal Ordnance Factory in Aycliffe, Durham, have dedicated websites on their workers' experiences of war: **www.aycliffeangels.co.uk**

Enfield Local Studies Centre & Archives holds a register of female workers at the Ediswan factory 1920s-1931. Some of these women continued to work in the factory during the war.

Records of civilian workers at the War Office were retained but few survive. Some information may be found in unindexed Home Office papers at TNA.

AFS/NFS
London Fire Brigade Museum has a useful guide for researching AFS and NFS members within the capital and beyond: **www.londonfire.gov.uk/Research.asp**. A comprehensive list of online resources can be found at **http://archiveshub.ac.uk/features/firefighters.shtml**

YWCA records
These are held at the University of Warwick, Modern Records Centre.

Girl Guides
Archive film footage shows the Guides at work. More detail on this can be found in Janie Hampton's How Girl Guides Won the War (see bibliography]. Some local troops have also produced their own histories. There are archives for the Girlguiding movement across the world, including that of Girlguiding UK at 17/19 Buckingham Palace Road, London SW1W 0PT. These include photographs, log books, and publications, such as *The Girl Guide Gazette*, *The Guide* and *Guiding*. For further details, see: **www.girlguiding.org.uk**. More information can be found at local Girl Guide Archives (often found at local record offices), in scrapbooks at the Imperial War Museum, local newspapers and further items deposited with local archives.

Conscientious Objectors
Material includes leaflets and pamphlets held at the Peace Pledge Union archives, periodicals and private papers at IWM, Manchester records at the Working Class Movement Library and Quaker records at the Friends House Library. Reports on tribunals were covered in local newspapers.

Casualties
Women lost their lives in this war while serving in a variety of roles, both at home and abroad. Their names can be found on the Debt of Honour database at: **www.cwgc.org**

Images
During the war, women were commissioned as Official War Artists. Among these was Evelyn Dunbar (1906-1960) who is celebrated for her paintings of the WLA. A website dedicated to Dunbar's works is **www.evelyndunbar.com**

Memorials
The Memorial to the Women of World War Two was unveiled by the Queen on 9 July 2005 in Whitehall, London. It stands next to the Cenotaph.

79th General Hospital at Bayeux (Normandy Campaign) 20 June 1944. Royal Army Medical Corps nurses and women of the Queen Alexandra's Imperial Military Nursing Service (QAIMNS) carry a wounded soldier. By Laing (Sgt), No. 5 Army Film & Photographic Unit. Public domain image.

CHAPTER NINE

Women Nurses, Doctors and Medical Services in the Second World War

'... the thanks of this House be accorded to the women of the Auxiliary and Nursing Services for the ready self-sacrifice and efficiency with which they performed their arduous duties of sustaining their brothers in action against the enemy.'

Prime Minister Clement Attlee, addressing the House of Commons, 30 October 1945.

By September 1939, the military nursing service in Britain and across the Empire was well established. The Queen Alexandra's Imperial Military Nursing Service (QAIMNS) now numbered 624[105] serving in military hospitals in Britain and overseas. Changes had taken place in medical care in Britain. Suggestions had been made for a national health service, and city councils had built new general hospitals. Domestic civilian nurses were working voluntary hospitals, a residue of Poor Law establishments and institutions belonging to local government. Other women in the Civil Defence Services helped to run the Wartime Nurseries. The numbers of women doctors remained low, with many struggling to obtain a place to study medicine. Of those that were practising doctors, many were welcomed by the War Office, particularly to help with the treatment of other women, such as those serving in the ATS. By the end of the war, 150 medical women had served as officers in the Royal Army Medical Corps[106].

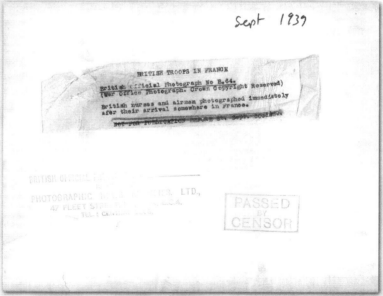

Sept 1939

BRITISH TROOPS IN FRANCE

British (Official Photograph No E.64.
(War Office Photograph. Crown Copyright Reserved)

British nurses and airmen photographed immediately
after their arrival somewhere in France.

NOT FOR PUBLICATION BEFORE 8th Sept. cooidat

BRITISH OFFICIAL P

PHOTOGRAPHIC   R. LTD.,
47 FLEET STR   U.S.A.
TEL: GE

PASSED
BY
CENSOR

32. This is an official press photo of British nurses and airmen photographed immediately after their arrival somewhere in France, and the caption on the back says: reads 'British Troops in France (1939)'. Below: reverse of the above.

In 1939, military hospitals across Britain were mobilised for increasing numbers of patients from the theatres of war. These establishments included many of the hospitals where military nurses had served in the First World War, including those at Aldershot, Haslar, Netley and Woolwich. Military nurses who served in these included members of the QAIMNS, QAIMNS Reserve (R) and the Territorial Army Nursing Service (TANS).

At the outset of war, military nurses were also stationed at regimental bases overseas. The nurses of the QAIMNS (or QAs, as they were known), QA Reserve and TANS continued to be sent to work overseas. The first nurses in France, including QAs and members of the Voluntary Aid Detachments (VADs), embarked in September 1939. Throughout the six years of war, military nurses were sent to British bases like Gibraltar, Hong Kong, Malta and Palestine, as well as France, Africa, Burma, Italy and Singapore. At the frontline, nurses worked from Regimental Aid Posts, Walking Wounded Clearing Posts, Mobile Field Hospitals or Advanced Dressing Stations.

Civilian nurses had been volunteering for the QAIMNS Reserves (R) from 1938. The TANS was ready for service. Other civilian nurses formed the new Emergency Military Nursing Service (EMNS). Hospitals in vulnerable parts of Britain were evacuated, leaving the wards free for Casualty Clearing stations. From 1940, well-trained and experienced nurses were needed across Britain to care for the casualties of air raids. Nurses were also required in the Civil Nursing Reserve. The essential role performed by civilian nurses in tending to domestic casualties has often been under appreciated.

QAIMNS

The Matron in Chief of QAIMNS in 1939 was Catherine Murray Roy, who had been one of the first British nurses sent to the Western front in 1914.

The QAs made a significant contribution to the evacuation of Dunkirk in May 1940, ensuring their patients were safely evacuated, driving ambulances and working with the Royal Engineers. Amidst gunfire and aerial bombing, over 1,000 nurses were evacuated along with members of the British Expeditionary Force and other servicewomen.

After the evacuation the service was run by Matron-in-Chief, Kathleen Henrietta Jones (1888-1967), a QA of the First World War, who had been Mentioned in Despatches for service in Palestine. In 1941, when the government made changes to women's services and their role in the war, the ranking system of the QAIMNS was restructured along Army lines. From then on nurses wore badges to show their rank.

From December 1941 to October 1942, the citizens and military personnel of Malta were subject to an intense period of aerial bombing. The QAs based on the island were called upon to tend to those hit as well as allied pilots, who had been injured while trying to defend the population of 270,000. This required nurses to be flexible, adapting to the needs of those injured or ill, giving first aid or assisting in the operating theatre as required. Conditions were difficult, not only with more than 3,000 air raids in less than a year, but with a siege preventing supplies from reaching the island. This affected not only food supplies, but the fuel, medicines and equipment that were essential for the treatment of the sick and wounded. In 1942, a typhoid epidemic led to further demands on the nurses.

After the bombing of the US military base of Pearl Harbor on 7 December 1941 by Japan, British Territories in the Far East also came under attack. QAs were based at Military Hospitals in Singapore, Hong Kong, and Shanghai. During the war, some QAs were taken prisoner by Japanese forces. Members of the Colonial Nursing Service were also taken prisoner. They and members of the Indian Army Nursing Service, based in India and Burma, are discussed in Chapter 14, as are the VAD nurses who were recruited in India.

At its peak, there were 12,000 nurses serving with QAIMNS. In 1944, the War Office appealed publicly for State Registered Nurses to enlist or immediate commission as an army Sister. Ex-nurses were also called upon for whatever service they could contribute. QAIMNS, along with members of the QAIMNSR and TANS, were sent into France in the later years of the war as the Allies surged into Europe following D-Day in June 1944. Over 1,000 nurses assisted the evacuation of injured men during the Normandy Landings and were present at the liberation of concentration camps.

Territorial Army Nursing Service (TANS)
The TA nurses served alongside QAs.

Audrey Hayward OBE (1916-2011) trained as a civilian nurse, qualifying in nursing, midwifery and as a health visitor. She signed up for TANS in the Second World War, and was sent to serve in West Africa, India and Europe, where she was sent to care for the wounded in the aftermath of Operation Overlord.[107] She remained a TA nurse for over 30 years, finally being promoted to Lieutenant Colonel.

Voluntary Aid Detachments (VADs) / Red Cross Nurses

The British Red Cross and the Order of St John formed the Joint War Organisation at the beginning of the war. At first, their main function was to provide auxiliary homes and hospitals. St Andrew's Ambulance Association provided first aid across Scotland after air raids, and also taught classes for ARP. After Dunkirk, the War Office urgently needed more beds for casualties, and requested help from the Joint War Organisation in finding beds in large private homes. Volunteer Red Cross Nurses served in similar roles performed by the organisations in the First World War, such as cooking, driving ambulances, running hospitals, caring for convalescents and supporting qualified nurses. While many served in civilian and military hospitals in Britain, others served as Naval VADs or were sent overseas.

Josephine Edwina 'Hattie' Jacques (1922-1980) who later became a well-known actress, volunteered as a Red Cross Nurse in the war.

The Queen Alexandra's Royal Naval Nursing Service (QARNNS)
This service was attached to the Royal Navy, caring for sick or injured naval personnel at home, on board ships and overseas. It numbers were supplemented in the war by the VADs, taking the size of the organisation from the pre war 78 to 1,341 nurses by the end of the war[108].

Princess Mary's RAF Nursing Service (PMRAFNS)
This had remained attached to the RAF after the First World War. Now known as the Princess Mary's Royal Air Force Nursing Service (PMRAFNS), the service was 1,126 strong in 1943. During the war, PMRAFNS worked alongside WAAF medical orderlies, dental attendants and female medical officers. The Service played a major role in caring for the sick and injured of the Normandy Landings, helping to evacuate 300,000 casualties.

Acts of bravery by women were common in war, and not all received recognition. However, some nurses were rewarded. PMRAFNS Sister Miss V K Stone was awarded the MBE for her quick action in April 1944 when an aircraft crashed into nearby WAAF huts. With no regard for herself or the fact that she had only recently completed 12 hours duty, Sister Stone rescued wounded women from the huts and administered first aid. Small fires burning close to the crashed aircraft added to the air of panic, but Stone remained calm. After everyone was rescued, she then spent the night working in the operating theatre. In the morning she reported for duty as usual[109].

Medical Women

The War Office was quick to recruit qualified women doctors to military roles, rewarding recruits with pay equal to that of their male counterparts. However, women did not receive commissions within the Royal Army Medical Corps (RAMC). Once four weeks of training was complete, women entered the Corps as officers, with the rank of Lieutenant. Many suffered discrimination as they were not fully welcomed by all their male colleagues. They wore the uniform of the ATS, but with the corps buttons of the RAMC.

Female doctors also worked as civilians with the Emergency Medical Service in Britain.

Casualties

According to official statistics, there were 207 QAIMNS casualties of the Second World War, 33 TANS, 30 VADs, 12 QARNNS and 7 PMRAFNS. All are remembered on the Register of Honour on the CWGC website.

In the confusion of war, the families of nurses sent overseas often received no notification that their relative had been killed. Notices from such families may be found in the personal columns of national and local newspapers. In October 1945, the family of Sister Beatrice Le Blanc Smith QAIMNS published a notice in *The Times* asking for information on her whereabouts. They had last heard from her aboard *SS Taniong Penang*. Unbeknownst to her family, Le Blanc Smith had died more than three years earlier on 18 February 1942, aged 31. Sister Beatrice Le Blanc Smith is remembered on Column 114 of the Singapore Memorial.

Notes on Researching of the Second World War

Service Records are retained by the Ministry of Defence and can be accessed only by the veteran or her next of kin. Further details on how to access these records are available at the Service Personnel and Veterans' Agency website: **www.veterans-uk.info/service_records/ service_records.html** or by writing to the Agency at Norcross, Blackpool FY5 3WP.

Service record cards and other documents relating to VADs and Red Cross nurses are held by the Red Cross. These can be accessed by writing, with full details of the VAD you are researching, to the British Red Cross, Museum and Archives department, 44 Moorfields, London EC2Y 9AL.

Some records of nurses in the Second World War can be found on Findmypast.

Medals
The Royal Red Cross registers at TNA in WO 145. Citations are held at TNA or can be found in the *London Gazette.* A transcription of the Register by Sue Light can be found on Findmypast.

Specialist Collections

The Army Medical Service (AMS) Museum holds private papers, letters and diaries of QAIMNS nurses from the Second World War. QARNNS documents and books are held at the Royal Naval Museum: **www.royalnavalmuseum.org/research.htm**

The RAF Museum Library and Archive holds Regulations for the PMRAFNS. Related items can be found in the collections of the IWM.

A list of QAIMNS and TANS officers 1939-1945 is online at: **www.unithistories. com/officers/QAIMNS_officers.html**

Useful history websites featuring memories and images of nurses who served in the Second World War are: **www.qaranc.co.uk**

Sue Light has transcribed numerous documents from TNA onto her website: **www.scarletfinders.co.uk**. These include Nominal Rolls of Nurses with the BEF 1939-1940 (WO 1777/14 Findmypast), nurses' accounts of service overseas in the Second World War (including Katharine Jones) and locations of the 122 British General Hospitals of the war (TNA ref. WO222/1568).

Some of the records mentioned in Chapter 5 can help in researching a Second World War nurse. For example, nurses' names (up to 1956) may be found in the archive of the British Journal of Nursing: **http://rcnarchive.rcn.org.uk/**

The names of female officers of the RAMC can be found in Peterkin & Johnston, *Commissioned Officers in the Medical Services of the British Army 1660-1960.*

Medical doctors possessed degrees. Records of their education, which include biographical information, addresses, and next of kin details, may be found in the relevant university archives. Lists of successful physicians and surgeons were printed in *The Times*. Women examinees were identified by their forenames printed in full. Males were identified by initials only.

'Join the ATS': poster issued by His Majesty's Stationery Office, 1941. Public domain image.

CHAPTER TEN
Auxiliary Territorial Service (ATS)

*'Women will, of course, be employed only on work for which they have a
special aptitude, but the House should know that such work included
duties at searchlight and gun stations.'*

Captain the Right Hon. HDR Margesson MC, MP, the Secretary of State for War,
addressing the House of Commons, 10 April 1941.

Established by Royal Warrant on 9 September 1938, the Women's
Auxiliary Territorial Service (ATS), was formed out of the Women's
Auxiliary Defence Service that had been established three months
earlier. At first, its role was defined as 'Non-combatant duties with military
units. Motor driving, clerical and other services calling for energy and
initiative.' The ATS was attached to the Territorial Army (TA) and its
Command Units were based on the structure of the TA with similar sub
divisions and groups.

Great War veteran, Helen Gwynne-Vaughan, served as Chief Controller
from July 1939 to July 1941. Katherine Jane Trefusis Forbes (known as Jane:
1889-1971) was appointed Chief Instructor at the ATS School of Instruction
in 1938, and in August, Winston Churchill's daughter, Mary Spencer-
Churchill (b. 1922), was appointed honorary Controller-Commandant.
Through these aristocratic leaders, the officers of the ATS tended to be drawn

from the upper classes, which caused some resentment. It also did not help the service's popularity among potential recruits, most of whom were from a working class background.

ATS recruits were aged between 18 and 43, with an extension to 50 for former servicewomen. For the first year and a half of the war, the ATS was a voluntary organisation. In April 1941, the War Office, desperate to recruit more women to the service, gave the ATS full military status. From then on its members were known as 'Auxiliaries'. All the auxiliary services would now be part of the armed forces, rather than the Civil Establishment. The higher status of the service made it more popular with potential recruits and the conscription enforced by National Service Act of 1941 led to a huge increase in numbers. From only 65,000 officers and auxiliaries in September 1941, the number had grown to 210,308 by June 1943.

Some members of the ATS were seconded as agents to SOE. These included Violette Reine Elizabeth Szabo, GC (nee Bushell: 1921-1945). Violette was born in Paris to an English father and a French mother, but grew up in Brixton, south London. She married the Franco-Hungarian officer, Etienne Szabo in 1940, and enlisted in the ATS in 1941. After Etienne's death in 1942, Violette volunteered as a special agent and was promoted to an Ensign of FANY. Her first mission in 1944 involved successful acts of sabotage by the Resistance, which Violette reported back via wireless to London. During her second mission she was captured. Following this she was imprisoned and tortured, finally being executed by firing squad in February 1945.

Training

ATS training took place at army bases, or Training Depots, across the UK. These included Wellesley Park Barracks in Halifax, Pontefract Barracks, Tonfanau Camp in Merionethshire, Cowdray Park in Hampshire, Talavera Camp at Northampton Racecourse, Chicheley Hall near Newport Pagnell, Ketteringham Hall in Norfolk and Droitwich in Worcestershire.

Training usually took four weeks and recruits undertook a number of examinations.

Previous qualifications were required to even take the examinations for some roles. ATS members of the Gunnery Experimental wing (of the Royal Artillery) needed a science degree to qualify as an officer, or a strong mathematical background for junior positions.

Roles

Drivers of the Women's Transport Service, First Aid Nursing Yeomanry (FANY), which had been renamed in 1933, were incorporated into the ATS as its transport section. Confusingly, FANY continued its other activities as a separate private service.

Duties were varied, and, by the end of 1943, women of the ATS were occupied in more than 80 trades. Your ATS ancestor may have worked in clerical roles, as cooks, anti-aircraft signallers, postal workers, radio mechanics, drivers, radar operators or ammunition inspectors. In the ATS, women also operated guns, particularly against enemy aircraft, and served as military police.

Although most women who were attached to the British Army served in the ATS, female medical, dental and veterinary officers and chaplains were members of the same corps as the men of their respective regiments.

Women were paid at two thirds of the rate of equivalent male ranks in the Territorial Army.

33. Kathleen 'Kit' Donnelly ATS (in boiler suit, in centre) worked as an Artillery Predictor Operator. Pictured, with friends Aldershot 1942.

Ranks

The ATS was reorganised on 9 May 1941. Prior to this its ranks were:

Chief Controller
Senior Controller
Controller
Chief Commandant
Senior Commandant
Company Commander
Deputy Company Commander
Company Assistant
Senior Leader
Section Leader
Sub-Leader
Chief Volunteer
Volunteer

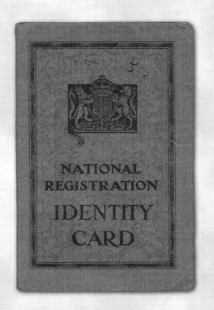

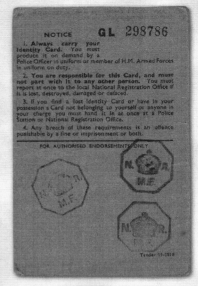

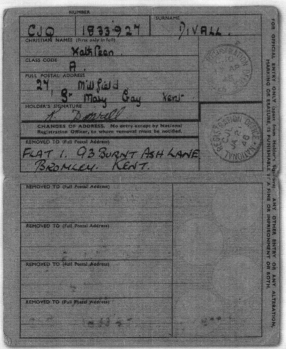

34. Kathleen Divall (nee Donnelly) ID card for the period 1945-1946.

After the restructure, the ranks were:

Chief Controller
Senior Controller
Controller
Chief Commander
Senior Commander
Junior Commander
Subaltern
Second Subaltern
Warrant Officer 1st Class/Warrant Officer 2nd Class/Staff Sergeant
Sergeant/ Lance Sergeant
Corporal/Bombardier
Lance Corporal/Lance-Bombardier
Private/ Gunner

Locations

ATS Command Units were based at barracks including Pontecraft Methley Hall, Queen Ethelburga's School in Thorpe Underwood in Yorkshire, Cavalry Barracks in York, Westbourne in Emsworth, Newburgh in Fife, Newbattle Abbey in Dalkeith, Balthayock in Perth, Linlithgow in West Lothian, Brigstock in Northamptonshire, Heathfield at Honiton in Devon, Garat's Hay near Woodhouse Eaves in Leicestershire, Fenham Barracks in Newcastle, Ramsey in Huntingdonshire, Arbury Park at Nuneaton, Bowerham Barracks in Lancaster and Wollaton Park in Nottinghamshire.

From the onset of war, the women of the ATS were sent to cook, drive, manage stores and perform other essential roles in overseas theatres of operation. 300 ATS members travelled to France in September 1939 and returned during the evacuation of Dunkirk in May 1940. ATS casualties during the war died or were killed while serving in Belgium, Egypt, Ireland, Palestine, Italy, the Netherlands and South Africa. In Ceylon, there were casualties from ATS (Ceylon).

A list of where the various batteries and sections of the ATS were based on 7 May 1945 can be searched at: **www.atsremembered.org.uk/WO331717pdf.pdf**

Life in the ATS

Women servicewomen in the Second World War did not live in comfort. Standards of accommodation were so bad for some members of the ATS that by the end of 1940, over a fifth of the membership resigned over their poor conditions.

ATS members wore a khaki uniform, designed by Gwynne-Vaughan (a more attractive version was introduced after her retirement) and a badge with a laurel leaf and ATS insignia. Along with the uniform, ATS members were given stockings, shirts, panties, khaki knickers, gloves, combs and toothbrushes. All of these were replaced free of charge when worn out or damaged.

Medals

All full time servicewomen who had served for 28 days between 3 September 1939 and 2 September 1945 were eligible for the British War Medal 1939-1945. Members of the ATS who served in the theatre of operation in North Africa, Abyssinia, Somaliland, Eritrea and Malta between 10 June 1940 and 12 May 1943 were also eligible for the Africa Star.

Violette Szabo was awarded the George Cross, the Croix de Guerre (1947) and the Medaille de la Resistance (1973). The George Cross was bestowed on her posthumously on 17 December 1946.

Casualties

There were 717 official casualties of the ATS in this war. A list of casualties of the Auxiliary Territorial Service can be read online at: **www.atsremembered. org.uk/ CWGCpdf.pdf**

Princess Elizabeth

In 1944, 18 year old Elizabeth, elder daughter of King George VI, joined the ATS. There was great publicity surrounding this as the Ministry of Information used the Princess's enlistment as a propaganda tool; Pathé newsreels of Elizabeth at work proved very popular. Becoming an ATS subaltern in February 1945, the Princess trained as a mechanic and truck driver. She was soon promoted to honorary Junior Commander and ended the war with the honorary commission of Brigadier.

35. The grave of Pearl Helen Emma Biffin, ATS.

First Aid Nursing Yeomanry (FANY)

In the Second World War, the Women's Transport Service/FANY formed the first ATS Motor Driver Companies.

FANY members were also attached to the Polish Army.

Some of the most well-known FANY of the war were agents for Special Operations Executive (SOE). These include Odette Marie Celine Sansom (nee Brailly; later Hallowes; 1912-1995) GC MBE L d'H. The women of SOE are discussed further in Chapter 13.

Notes on Researching ATS and FANY Ancestors of the Second World War

Service Records

Service records are currently retained by the Ministry of Defence. More details of how to obtain a copy of your relative's record can be found at: **www.veterans-uk. info/service_records/service_records.html**

Recommendations for awards are held in TNA reference WO 373.

Some details of your ancestor's work may be found in War Diaries held at The National Archives (TNA) which can be searched for using 'Auxiliary Territorial Service' via Discovery. In cases where the ATS members were attached to other units, the relevant units must be identified in order to locate their War Diaries.

ATS material, formerly held in the WRAC's museum, is now held by the National Army Museum: see: **www.national-army-museum.ac.uk**

A comprehensive website for ATS information is: **www.atsremembered.org.uk**

A veterans' organisation exists for former members of the ATS, the Women's Royal Army Corps Association. Its website is: **www.wracassociation.org.uk**

Numerous memoirs exist for former members of the ATS in archives and collection. Published memoirs of serving in the ATS include Sylvia Wild's *Women at the Front: Memoirs of an ATS Girl* (Amberley, 2012).

The National Memorial Arboretum in Staffordshire has a dedicated section for the ATS.

Other memorial statues and plaques exist in towns and cities.

A memorial statue to Violette Szabo stands on the Albert Embankment, London. *Carve Her Name with Pride*, a film marking her life starring Virgina McKenna, was released in 1956. A dedicated website created by her daughter, Tania, is: **www.violetteszabo.org**

IWM holds the medals of Odette Samson, as well as the jacket and lozenge tin she had with her in Ravensbrück Concentration Camp. Her wartime experiences were made into a film, *Odette* (1950).

CHAPTER ELEVEN

Women's Auxiliary Air Force (WAAF) and the Air Transport Auxiliary (ATA)

'Women's place is in the W.A.A.F., and Britain is calling on as many people as possible to take that place. If the W.A.A.F. cap fits you ... wear it. Join to-day and line up with the R.A.F.'

Recruitment advertisement for the WAAF, July 1941.

Women's Auxiliary Air Force (WAAF)

The Women's Royal Air Force was reformed as the Women's Auxiliary Air Force (WAAF) on the 28 June 1939. By the beginning of the war on 1 September 1939, 1,734 women, aged 18 to 43, had enlisted. Katherine Jane Trefusis-Forbes DBE LLD served as Commander, or Senior Controller[110] of the service and also became the first WAAF Director (1939-43). Forbes was relieved in 1943 by HRH Princess Alice, Duchess of Gloucester, the Commander of the WAAFs. Lady Mary Welsh, was then appointed Air Chief Commandant in 1943 and director in 1944.

After nearly two years of WAAF operations, on 25 April 1941, Defence (Women's Forces) Regulations were passed to make all personnel subject to RAF discipline and rules. In July 1943 numbers peaked at 182,000 - 16% of the entire RAF. In total around 250,000 women served in the WAAF during

the Second World War. Women enrolled for the WAAF from all parts of the Empire, including the West Indies, the Dominions and India. There were also 800 recruits from Palestine[111]. Separate to the WAAF were air forces created across the Empire, including the Royal Canadian Air Force (Women's Division), Women's Auxiliary Australian Air Force, New Zealand Women's Auxiliary Air Force, Women's Auxiliary Air Force (S.A.A.F.) and the Southern Rhodesia Women's Auxiliary Air Service. These are discussed further in Chapter 14.

The Ministry of Defence made a conscious decision that WAAFs would be auxiliary to the Royal Air Force (RAF). Women were not to be fighter pilots. This differed from other European countries where women were flying military aircraft. In the Soviet Union women pilots were armed. Soviet Lieutenant Tamara Pamyatnykh, for example, served in the 586th Fighter Regiment as a combat pilot. She and fellow Lieutenant Raisa Surnachevskaya are celebrated for protecting a railway junction from 42 enemy bombers on the night of 19 April 1943. The 588th Bomber Regiment were known as *Nachthexen* or Night Witches, by members of the German armed forces who complained the pilots stopped them from sleeping.

The celebrated female Spitfire pilots of the Second World War were not members of the WAAFs nor fighter pilots. Their role was one of transit under the remit of the Air Transport Auxiliary, or ATA (see below).

After the excellent service provided by the WAAFs during the Battle of Britain 1940, many transferred to the Royal Observer Corps of the RAF.

Training

Recruits - some still untrained - were sent to RAF stations. WAAF Training Depots through the war included West Drayton, Harrogate, Innsworth, Bridgnorth, Morecambe and Wilmslow.

Roles

On 22 December 1939, the first WAAF regulation was issued, relaying terms of service, ranks, discipline, uniform and leave.

WAAFs were employed in up to 15 types of duty, including mechanics, cooking, driving of staff cars, codes and ciphers, operating radios or balloons, waitressing, telephony and telegraphy, which enabled the fast communication of messages.

One of the most significant contributions of the WAAFs to the war effort was their work in Intelligence, Security and Operation Rooms. These operation rooms were where WAAFs plotted the raiding of enemy aircraft.

Roles undertaken at this time included cooking, clerical work, meteorologists, butchers, radio (wireless) operators, waitresses, flight mechanics, mess orderly, driving mechanical transport and working on fabric in the Balloon Centres. At the onset of war, teleprinter operators, plotters and radar operators were urgently required. However, only officers could be employed on code and cipher duty.

Others acted as barrage-balloon girls and drivers operated vehicles ranging from tractors (for bombing-up aircraft) to 3-ton lorries. Electricians undertook concentrated 3-year courses in 9 months.[112] Parachute packers provided an essential role, ensuring that airmen could parachute safely.

WAAF Ranks

In the Second World War, WAAF officers received commissions, for which they had to be interviewed. Both officers and other ranks were selected by interview.

OFFICERS	OTHER RANKS
Air Commandant (Air Cmdt)	Warrant Officer (WO)
Group Officer (Gp Off)	Flight Sergeant (Flt Sgt)
Wing Officer (Wg Off)	Sergeant (Sgt)
Squadron Officer (Sqn Off)	Corporal (Cpl)
Flight Officer (Flt Off)	Leading Aircraft Woman (LACW)
Section Officer (SO)	
Assistant Section Officer (ASO)	

Officer Branches (WAAF Officer branches 1946: AP3234)[113]

Accountant	Administrative and Special Duties
Catering	Code and Cypher
Equipment	Filter
Intelligence	Interception Controller
Medical and Psychological Assistant	Meteorological
Motor Transport	Movements Liaison
Operations 'B'	Operations 'C'
Orthoptist	Personnel Selection
Photographic Interpretation	Provost

Signals 'G'	Signals, Special Radar
Signals, Supervisory Radar	WAAF G (WAAF only)
Dentist (RAF branch)	Doctor (RAF branch)

In the Signals Branch, radar operators were known as Special Duties Clerks (clks sd) for secrecy. Perhaps their finest hour was for work done during the Battle of Britain in 1940. Most of the code and cypher officers, including at the War Cabinet cypher office of Churchill, were members of the WAAF. By July 1943 there were 7,395 Special Duties Clerks, many of whom had been employed for their language skills.

Locations

The WAAFs in 1939 were divided into 47 companies, located across the UK. Some of these were attached to Flying Squadrons.

Benjamin Disraeli's former home, Hughenden Manor in Buckinghamshire, was taken over by the Air Ministry for the war, and code-named 'Hillside'. WAAFs based here were involved in secret aerial reconnaissance and mapping work, plotting enemy movements, and were required to sign the Official Secrets Act. Many died before being able to reveal to family members that they had worked there.

WAAFs of the 41 Group at Dover were employed mainly as drivers of staff cars or in clerical positions.

Thousands of WAAFs were posted overseas. Among these were the code and cypher officers sent to the British High Commission in New York in 1940 and the RAF Delegation in Washington D.C.. Others were posted to the Bahamas, Bermuda, Newfoundland, Labrador, Malta and Gibraltar. 250 WAAFs were sent to Egypt in 1944 to perform clerical, equipment and signal duties. By 1945, there were nearly 3,500 airwomen in the Middle East[114], many having been sent to Palestine in 1941 and later to Syria and Iraq. 800 WAAFs served in Algeria and Tunis, and others were posted to India and Ceylon in 1944. In the same year Italy received 150 domestic and clerical airwomen, along with cyphers.

Life in the WAAFs

The Air Ministry was responsible for the welfare of the WAAFs. However, comfort was not high on the Air Ministry's list of priorities and life as a WAAF could be difficult, particularly for those unused to being away from home. Those boarded in huts shared a room with 11 others, and slept on mattresses filled with straw. Women were paid fortnightly at two thirds of the rate of RAF pay, but received free uniforms, accommodation, food, medical and dental care.

The WAAF had its own band, which marched in the Victory Parade held in 1946,

Secret Service

Several WAAFs worked for the Special Operations Executive and evidence of this should be found on their service records.

Holder of the George Cross and the French Croix de Guerre, Noor-un-Nisa Inayat Khan (1914-1944), joined the WAAF on 19 November 1940 as an Aircraft Woman 2nd Class. She initially trained as a wireless operator and was known to her fellow WAAFs as 'Nora', but later received a commission as an Assistant Section Officer. A great-great-great granddaughter of the warrior ruler Tipu Sultan, Noor was a pacifist, raised as a Sufi Muslim. Despite her upbringing, Noor was committed to defeating Nazism. Although her mother was American and her father Indian, Noor had been raised at first in London's Bloomsbury and then in France. The family fled to London in June 1940. Her fluency in English and French marked her out for the Special Operations Executive (SOE) and she was seconded to FANY. In June 1943, Noor was the first female wireless operator sent to work with the Resistance in France. After other wireless operators were captured, Noor was invited to return to Britain. Bravely she refused, and remained in Paris transmitting messages until she was captured in October. She was eventually sent to Dachau Concentration Camp where she was executed on 13 September 1944. Her George Cross award was announced in the *London Gazette* of 5 April 1949. The citation stated that, 'Assistant Section Officer INAYAT-KHAN displayed the most conspicuous courage, both moral and physical over a period of more than 12 months.'

A memorial stature to Noor Inayat Khan was unveiled in London on 8 November 2012.

Medals

WAAFs were entitled to the British War Medal on the same terms as men. WAAFs who served in the theatre of operation in North Africa, Abyssinia, Somaliland, Eritrea and Malta between 10 June 1940 and 12 May 1943 were also eligible for the Africa Star. WAAFs who received medals for gallantry included, in 1940, Flight Officer Elspeth Henderson, Sergeant Joan Mortimer and Sergeant Helen Turner, who were awarded the Military Medal for bravery during the Battle of Britain. Three other WAAFs received the MM for gallantry in the Second World War.

2,497 WAAFs were Mentioned In Despatches (MIDs), 97 were awarded MBEs, 93 received BEMs - 3 for special gallantry: Aircraftwoman Kathleen McKinlay, Corporal Alice Holden and Leading Aircraftwoman Lilian Ellis; and an ordinary BEM to Leading Aircraftwoman Ivy Cross.

For service in the WAAF as an ACW 1 (Aircraft Woman 1st class) Radio Operator in the Radar Chain Home system station at Rye in Sussex, Margaret Gosling (pictured) was awarded the British War Medal 1939/45, but only received it in 1967. A letter from the RAF Records Office states that she was not entitled to the Defence Medal also as she 'did not complete three years service prior to the cessation of hostilities on 8 May 1945'. Margaret married in 1941: her marriage to RAF Squadron Leader William ('Bill') Y. Craig was announced in *The Times* of 23 October.

36. Margaret Gosling in WAAF uniform with steel helmet as an ACW 1 Radio Operator in the Radar Chain Home system station at Rye in Sussex.

Casualties

Around 600 WAAFs are believed to have died while serving in the Second World War. There are 731 WAAFs recorded on the Roll of Honour at the CWGC website for those killed up to 1949. They can be located on the database by using the term 'Women's Auxiliary Air Force' in the Regiment box on the Advanced Search page.

Joan Marjorie Easton (1917-1943) served as a Section Officer with the WAAFs. Easton was killed 8 September 1943, aged 26 years, while trying to rescue civilians from a crashed Stirling bomber in Cambridgeshire. Her gravestone reads:

SHE GAVE HER LIFE 8TH SEPTEMBER 1943
GALLANTLY SAVING OTHERS AND WAS
POSTHUMOUSLY MENTIONED IN DISPATCHES:
'GREATER LOVE HATH NO MAN THAN THIS.'

37. The British War Medal 1939-1945 awarded to ACW 1 Margaret Craig (nee Gosling), Radio Operator WAAF.

Air Transport Auxiliary (ATA)

Separate from the WAAFs was a civilian organisation, the Air Transport Auxiliary (ATA). Male and female members of the ATA flew RAF aircraft from manufacturer to the Aircraft Storage Units (ASU), where they were up-armoured and flight tested, and then onwards to operational squadrons.

The ATA was controlled by Gerard d'Erlanger, a private pilot and a director of the British Overseas Airways Corporation (BOAC). Based in White Waltham, Berkshire, the civilian ATA began operating in February 1940. In 1941, the Ministry of Aircraft Production (MAP) took overall control, but retained d'Erlanger as the administrator.

The women's section was commanded by Pauline Gower (1910-1947), who had spent the 1930s running Air Trips, a Kent-based air taxi and joy ride company. She had hundreds of hours of experience flying and was well-connected with the political establishment. The first female pilots, of Ferry Pool No. 5, were based at Hatfield Aerodrome from where the first non-training flights of the women's section of the ATA took off on 19 June 1941. By 1944 congestion at the airfield led to the Ferry Pool moving away.

To be selected as an ATA pilot, women had to be 22-45 years old, the holder of an A or B licence and have at least 250 flying hours. ATA shortages allowed 30 WAAF to join out of 1,400 volunteers.[115] All ATA pilots had to pass a practical flying test and a medical examination. One of the unique features of the ATA for women serving in the war was that the pilots were all paid exactly the same as males of equal rank from 1943. Overall, there were 166 female pilots in the ATA, recruited from, Britain, the Empire, the USA, Netherlands, Poland and Argentina.

Over the course of the war, the ATA transported 308,000 aircraft of 147 types. The pilots are particularly celebrated for flying Spitfires, but other aircraft included Fairey Swordfish, Fairey Barracudas, Halifaxes, Hawker Hurricanes, Lancasters and Mustangs. Fifteen women pilots were killed before the end of the war. They were:

Second Officer Irene Arckless (d. 3 January 1943)
Flight Captain The Hon. Margaret Fairweather (d. 4 April 1944)
Second Officer Elsie Joy Davison (d. 8 July 1940)
Flight Engineer Janice Margaret Harrington (d. 2 March 1944)
Third Officer Bridget Grace Marian L. Hill (d. 16 March 1942)
Flight Officer Amy V. Johnson (d. 5 October 1941)
Second Officer Kathleen Mary Kershaw (d. 3 April 1944)
First Officer Dora Lang (d. 2 March 1944)

Third Officer Joan Esther Marshall (d. 20 June 1942)
Second Officer Mary Webb Nicholson (d. 22 May 1943)
First Officer Honor Isabel Salmon (d. 19 April 1943)
Cadet Betty Eileen Sayer (d. 15 March 1942)
Flight Captain Eleanor Isabella (Susan) Slade (d. 13 July 1944)
Second Officer Taniya Whittal (d. 8 April 1944)
Second Officer Jane Winstone (d. 10 February 1944)

On the disbandment of the ATA in November 1945, Lord Beaverbrook praised the pilots for their service in the Battle of Britain when they 'sustained and supported' RAF pilots through their efficient delivery of aircraft: 'They were soldiers fighting in the struggle just as completely as if they had been engaged on the battlefront.'

Amy Johnson (1903-1941)

One of the most famous members of the ATA was the experienced aviator, Amy Johnson, who drowned in January 1941 after bailing out of an Airspeed Oxford. Amy was a celebrated aviator before the war, and she was personally invited to join the new women's section at Hatfield in Hertfordshire by the Commanding Officer, Pauline Gower, who wrote:

'At the outbreak of war, British Airways [BOAC], in conjunction with the Air Ministry, initiated a National Services organisation known as the 'Air Transport Auxiliary'. Their organisation is now being enlarged to encompass a women's section and it is to the section that women pilots will be attached.

The ATA is a self-contained unit with its own executive and senior officers and I have been invited and have accepted the post of 'Officer in Charge of the women's section' ... Admission to the women's section of the ATA will be on a competitive basis in view of the fact that at this stage at any rate, the number of women pilots whom it is contemplated engaging will not be large, and upon admission pilots will be required to enter into a contract with British Airways, the terms of which have yet to be settled, but it will provide for a rate of pay, insurance, and under the contract pilots will be given the rank of Second Officer and a uniform.'

Amy Johnson was flying an aircraft from the ASU at Silloth, near Carlisle, to a squadron in Kent. RAF Flight Sergeant O D Jolly, whose role was to be officially aware of every aircraft, noted that it had not arrived. Later the plane was discovered in the Thames Estuary.

Case Study of Winifred Le Page
(nee West: 1924-2011)

Winifred West, known as Win, was evacuated from Guernsey to Blackpool in June 1940. Her first experience of war work was with Wellington bombers and then as an Engine Fitter. She yearned to join the WAAF, but had to wait until the end of 1941 when she was 17 and a half.

38. Winifred West - centre.

'In November 1941, I went to join up in Preston: me and Eunice and another friend Pam. We asked to do clerical work but they didn't need any, only had openings for mechanics. We said, 'Well we will have a go!', so volunteered to be flight mechanics. The second group of women ever to do so!

The day before the Medical [examination] I had fallen in the snow and hurt my elbow, in such pain, the WAAF doc said, 'If you can't lift your arm, I can't pass you fit to register.' She let me off. I actually joined the WAAF in 1942.

We had female drill sergeants at Hednesford. We trained to be flight mechanics for 6 months. We mixed with the men - they saw us a bit of a joke, six women amongst all these men. One girl was from Jersey (Irene) but we called her Jersey.

I got mumps then and went to Bridgnorth Isolation Hospital. When got back I had sick leave but I had missed some of my training so had to slip back to a group that had started after mine.

I took the exams and was posted to [RAF Station] Sealand, just near Chester. Good place: maintenance unit and small airport there. They trained Commonwealth pilots from New Zealand. Aircraft were trainee ones with in-line engines. I made good friends there, went to dances in Queensferry, but got sick of being in uniform as the Sealand base men didn't want to know us in our uniforms. So one night, we dressed up in our civvies and put our uniforms over the top, we walked right past the guards, we had a bag to put our shoes and stockings in to change later at the dance hall. Got there and changed in the ladies, glorious evening cos the lads never recognised us.

At Sealand a few months when I got pleurisy! Had terrible pain in my side and couldn't sleep went to see the doctor to report sick. She gave me 24 hours off duty (August 43). I lay on the grass all day and slept, then back to my hut. I was bad that night, went sick again and crawled to the medical centre. Same doctor. I was transferred to a hospital in Chester, there for 6 months, and had medical exam to determine what they were going to do with me. Sent me to an air station near Warrington - Padgate - to go before Medical board, who said, 'I'm afraid we are going to have to discharge you. Although you are better, your lung isn't 100% functional.' I had fluid on the lung. I was disappointed. I really enjoyed the life and my friends. Was home by Christmas in Blackpool. Got final discharge January 31st, 1944. Full pension until 1950s and reduced it gradually until 1960s when my lung was 100%.'

Unable to serve further in the WAAF, Win spent the last years of the war in a civil service job in the Treasury Finance Department. There, she was trusted with a position managing the accounts of ports in the south of England which were building up stocks as part of Operation Overlord: D-day. For this, Win was required to sign the Official Secrets Act.

Notes on Researching WAAF and ATA Ancestors

Service records are retained by the Ministry of Defence. Records can be released to former WAAFs or their next of kin via the Service Personnel and Veterans Agency or RAF Disclosures Section, Room 221b, Trenchard Hall, RAF Cranwell, Sleaford, LINCS. NG34 8HB. The WAAF Association of former WAAFs has a useful website at: **www.waafassociation.org.uk** with details of local branches.

The RAF Air Historical Branch: **www.raf.mod.uk/ahb/** provides details of RAF casualty enquiries and aircraft accidents.

The archive collection at the RAF Museum's Department of Research & Information Services contains private papers of a number of women involved in WAAF and aviation. Besides personal documents, such as diaries, letters, photographs and memoirs, the collection includes operational records and some service documents. Among the women represented in the collection is Amy Johnson. A small number of logbooks are held there for members of the ATA.

Several hundred personnel files for ATA members are held at the RAF Museum. They are only available to next of kin. There are usually no restrictions on the papers of Pauline Gower, Amy Johnson and Diana Barnato Walker.

An interview with former Spitfire pilot Margaret Frost can be read at:
www.bbc.co.uk/blogs/tv/2010/09/spitfire-women-margaret-frost.shtml

The Imperial War Museum has a good collection of private papers, memoirs, objects and images relating to the WAAF, including portraits of WAAF Servicewomen based at RAF Watnall.

The RAF Museum's online exhibition on the WAAF is at:
www.rafmuseum.org.uk/research/online-exhibitions/women-of-the-air-force.aspx

WAAF casualties are remembered on the WAAF memorial at the National Memorial Arboretum, Alrewas, Staffordshire. The Roll of Honour can be searched at: **www.veterans-uk.info/afm2/index.php** Airwomen are also remembered on The Air Forces Memorial at Cooper's Hill, Runnymede, Surrey.

ATA obituaries and details of work can be found in *Flight* magazine at its online archive **www.flightglobal.com**

A permanent exhibition to the ATA, 'Grandma Flew Spitfires', is held in Maidenhead Heritage Centre, along with the Air Transport Auxiliary Archive.

39. The grave of Joan Marjorie Easton, Section Officer, WAAF.

The Women's Royal Naval Service during the Second World War. Wrens at a naval exchange, Greenock, Scotland. By Coote, R G G (Lt), Royal Navy official photographer. Public domain image.

CHAPTER TWELVE

The Women's Royal Naval Service and Women of the Merchant Navy in the Second World War

'Never At Sea.'

The motto of the WRNS.

L
ike the WAAF, the Women's Royal Naval Service (WRNS) was re-established in 1939. First World War Wren veteran, Elvira Sibyl 'Vera' Laughton Mathews (1888-1959: later Dame), was appointed WRNS Director in April of that year. Again it was to act as an auxiliary to the Royal Navy, focusing on shore duties and freeing men for service at sea. It would not replace work being done by women in Admiralty Headquarters.

Advertisements for recruits were posted from July. The service proved popular with former Wrens and with younger girls, some of whom were attracted by the smart uniform. Unlike the ATS and the WAAF, the WRNS actually had a waiting list of recruits. This meant new recruits had to prove themselves worthy of enrolment, through qualifications or a specific reason for wanting to join, such as previous service or experience of boats. The organisation was regarded by contemporary observers as being middle class, but in practice recruits came from a variety of backgrounds.

At first, many rating recruits received no training, although officers were sent to Greenwich Royal Naval College. From 1940, training was introduced for ratings. Training took place at Royal Naval training bases, such as *HMS Raleigh* near Plymouth, New College in London's Finchley Road and Mill Hill, North London. After training, Wrens were assigned to Sections.

Initially, the only women serving on boats were the crews who delivered the post. However, as the war progressed, more women worked in boats. Others took on tasks such as mechanics, radar, electrician and maintaining torpedoes. These Wren Torpedomen helped to free further male Naval personnel for service at sea.

Although many women who served in the Second World War were land-based, thousands in the auxiliary services were sent overseas to the theatres of operation. The constant perils of the sea during this period led to the hundreds of women's deaths. Passenger and troop ships carrying servicemen and women were struck by U-boats, hit mines, were bombed from the air or were otherwise lost throughout the war. On 19 August 1941, 21 Wrens and 1 QAIMNS officer lost their lives when *SS Aguila* (the merchant ship that was carrying them to Gibraltar where the Wrens were reporting for cipher and wireless duties) was sunk by a U-boat in the Irish Sea. They are remembered by the *Aguila Wren*, a retired Liverpool lifeboat, presented to the RNLI in 1952 by Edward Benjamin, the father of Chief Wren Cecilly Monica Bruce Benjamin (1921-1941) who died in the disaster. There is a memorial to the victims of the *Aguila* in the National Memorial Arboretum in Staffordshire. There were 303 official WRNS casualties in this war; they are commemorated on the CWGC's Register of Honour. Some of those who have no known grave are remembered on the Portsmouth Naval Memorial in Southsea, Plymouth Naval Memorial in Devon and the Chatham Naval Memorial in Kent.

WRNS ratings and officers were engaged in clerical work, stewarding, cooking, driving and as radio mechanics. In 1939, Wrens were organised around three categories: office duties branch, motor transport branch and general duties branch. The number of categories and branches grew over the course of the war. At its peak, the service had 74,000 officers and ratings working in 90 categories and 50 branches.

As with the ATS, Wrens' wages included food and lodging. For Wrens, however, and in keeping with naval custom, sleeping quarters were known as cabins and their kitchens were 'galleys'.

Like the other auxiliary forces, the WRNS became a military service from April 1941.

Wrens who served more than 28 days in the war were eligible for the 1939-45 War Medal. Examples of Wrens who were rewarded for gallantry include the 1941 commendation for Wren Petty Officer M W Lunnon (TNA reference ADM 1/11483). Wren I Marriott, and Leading Wren Nina Marsh were awarded the OBE on 17 December 1940 (WO 373/66). Acting Chief Officer Felicite Potter, First Officer Letitia Ethel Medley, Second Officer Florence Priscilla Chase, Second Officer Barbara Mary Brownell Drabble, Second Officer Nesta Dorothy May and Third Officer Joan Margeurite Frances Soper were named Additional Members of the Military Division of the said Most Excellent Order 'for distinguished services in connection with the planning of operations which led to the invasion of Normandy.'[116]

Fleet Air Arm

The Fleet Air Arm (FAA) is the flying branch of the Royal Navy. In war, the FAA was responsible for maintaining, transporting and operating all the Navy's aircraft. Wrens who served in this branch fulfilled a variety of roles, but some 'Flying Wrens' did travel by air as part of their duties as wireless mechanics or aerial photographers.

Wrens also supported the work of the Royal Marines.

Merchant Navy

Few women served with the Merchant Navy. Those that did were employed in similar roles to those in the First World War, as stewardesses. Some had been working on ships before the war. Others worked as children's nurses, cooks or hairdressers. Victoria Drummond (1894-1978)[117] became the first woman engineer and her award of the Lloyds Medal for bravery at sea was mentioned in the *London Gazette*. Casualties of the Merchant Navy are commemorated at the Tower Hill Memorial in London. The Memorial Register is held by the Trinity House Corporation.

Gwendoline Page (née Acason)

Gwendoline Acason was 14 years old at the outbreak of war. At 16, she registered for service and at 17 she formally volunteered. Although her war service only began when she turned 18, volunteering a year in advance made it more likely that a girl would be given the service of her choice. Gwendoline chose the WRNS as her brother was volunteering to be apprenticed to the Merchant Navy. Soon after enlisting, Gwendoline was interviewed for what she discovered was to be war service in Bletchley Park, or Station X as it was known. Although she had been educated at a grammar school, Gwendoline had only basic German and French. However, she feels that the interview was a test of character and that the recruiting officers were looking for those good at keeping secrets.

40. Gwendoline Page.

Gwendoline was then posted to work at Station X (from December 1942 *HMS Pembroke V*[118]) at Bletchley Park, boarding first at its outstation at Wavendon House in Woburn Sands. There she slept in the garages and was glad when nearby Stockgrove Park was requisitioned as WRNS quarters in August 1944 and she could sleep there. Some of her fellow servicewomen were billeted at the cold and draughty Woburn Abbey.

Eventually, Gwendoline was sent to work in Block A with other Wrens. WRNS officers, cooks and stewards staffed the Wrens' own canteen, which no longer survives. The Wrens lived, worked and ate together, rarely meeting members of other services, nor the many civilians who also worked in the Park. If they did meet it might have been at local dances, where they were taught the new jive by American GIs.

Most of her fellow Wrens were, like her, young, with many officers only in their twenties. Between them they worked on vital roles, although Mrs Page observes that many were unaware of what their work meant. Most were not code-breakers; that was usually reserved for those from university, or with advanced language skills.

Gwendoline was assigned the role of indexing U-boat signals. Unlike some of her colleagues, Gwendoline was fully aware of what she was reading. The signals had all been decoded and translated before they reached her desk. One of the most frightening moments of her war was seeing the name of her brother's ship, *SS Beckenham*, shown as one of convoy that had been dive bombed by Stuka bombers. Duty came first, and Gwendoline continued her work, but she was relieved to discover that her brother's ship was safe.

Serving as a Wren at Bletchley was distinct from working elsewhere as there was no promotion. Those at Station X remained there throughout the European War to limit the risk of secrets being exposed. Gwendoline served there until after VE Day on 8 May 1945, when she was transferred to Japanese signals. Around a month later, she was posted to Ceylon, and was in Colombo when the atomic bombs were dropped on Japan on 6 and 9 August.

Veterans agree that one of the hardest aspects of serving at Bletchley was the secrecy. Gwendoline said that, at the time, they were used to not asking each other what they did. Those who worked there were compelled to sign the Official Secrets Act and were threatened with prison if they talked. No badges or insignia were worn, which marked out Bletchley staff from others in the Wrens who all wore some kind of badge. A 'W' insignia on the sleeve, for example, would indicate the Wren was a Writer. At the end of the war, Gwendoline could only say she had served in the WRNS near Leighton Buzzard. Occasionally she might say 'near Bletchley', but she could not discuss her role with anyone for 30 years. Only in the 1980s and 1990s were reunions allowed, supported by the Bletchley Trust.

Unlike non-Bletchley Wrens, Gwendoline had to wait 60 years for her badge. Many others who served at Bletchley Park did not receive a badge at all, having died in the meantime. This can make researching a Bletchley ancestor difficult. Gwendoline was given a copy of her service record, the only documents that she was able to keep from that time. No one was allowed to write a diary or take photographs. The pass that she used to enter Bletchley Park each day was taken off her at the end of the war.

Gwendoline recalls feeling 'a bit ignored' at the end of the war despite her own knowledge that her work had saved the lives of others. It was only after the 30 year ban was lifted that she was able to reveal to her own brother that she knew about his convoy being hit. The one small perk she received at the end of the German war for her years of service was to be allowed to go aboard a captured U-boat and see from where some of the signals she had worked on had been sent.

Gwendoline Page is the author of six books, all of which are detailed in the bibliography.

One of the women who scouted for women to work at Bletchley Park was WRNS Third Officer Marjorie Noble (1913-2012). She was later promoted to First Officer.

Notes on Researching the Women's Royal Naval Service and women of the Merchant Navy in the Second World War

Service records of all WRNS 1939-1955 can be obtained from the Ministry of Defence or by writing to the Director of Naval Personnel

Records of some of the WRNS documents and photographs that form the WRNS Historic Collection, held at the Royal Naval Museum, can be searched online via the Sea Your History website. Others can be accessed in person in the Library reading room of the Museum in Portsmouth. More details are available at: **www. royalnavalmuseum.org/collections_display.htm**

Information on Wrens who served with the Fleet Air Arm can be found at the Museum. Further details can be found online **www.fleetairarm.com/womens-royal-navy-service-wrens-tpyf.aspx** and in the online archive: **www.fleetairarmarchive.net/Index.html**.

WRNS Benevolent Trust was formed in November 1917 and has provided financial relief to former Wrens for over 70 years. Its website is: **www.wrnsbt.org.uk**.

Ship records are held at TNA.

41. The National Archives online guide to the records of the WRNS.

CHAPTER THIRTEEN
Spies and Intelligence Work

'... and now, set Europe ablaze!'

Winston Churchill's Instruction for the Special Operations Executive.

Thousands of women working at home and abroad were required to sign the Official Secrets Act during wartime. Some of these women were recruited by branches of the government explicitly for intelligence work, such as code breaking. Others were to operate overseas as special agents or spies. Most, however, worked in offices in Britain doing work that was highly confidential but which has not always been recognised for the vital contribution it made to winning the war. This includes the war work of WAAF Win West (see page 145), and the monotonous hole punching of 300 members of the ATS between 1939 and 1940 at the offices of MI5 that assisted in early codebreaking[119]. Girl Guides again played a useful role in this war, collecting items which would be used to help British Prisoners of War, and assisting with patriotic propaganda such as War Weapons Week in 1941[120].

Office Work and the Cabinet War Rooms

Government offices in and around Whitehall in London were filled with women doing all kinds of secret tasks. One of the main government command

centres of the war was that of the Cabinet War Rooms, situated below the Treasury building. Churchill and his cabinet met here around 100 times. Plans for the war were created here, particularly in the large map room. Female civil servants, typists, censors and switchboard operators worked in the offices from when the rooms opened on 27 August 1939 to the day the lights were switched off for the first time - 16 August 1945. Life for those who worked in War Rooms was unpleasant. Administrative staff worked, ate and sometimes slept, underground in dark, dusty, smoky and cramped conditions. Women in the typing pool worked 14 hour shifts, and the lack of natural light led to some staff being given weekly sun lamp treatment.

Air Intelligence

During the Second World War, air intelligence work was performed under the control of the Directorate of Intelligence. Air Intelligence involved reconnaissance flights, interrogation of PoWs, monitoring aircraft, analysing the effects of bombing raids and the assessment of aerial photographs.

Photographic reconnaissance and the interpretation of aerial photographs played a key role from 1943 in what became known as *Operation Crossbow*. This involved defending Britain from, and attacking, the launch sites of Germany's long-range weapons programme. One aspect of the operation was to identify missile sites though the aerial photographs and maps. In 1941 RAF Medenham, based at Danesfield House in Buckinghamshire, became the centre of photographic air interpretation. 1,715 people worked here over the war, including 1,270 RAF personnel and 130 WAAFs. Among the WAAFs working here were Elizabeth Hick, Sarah Churchill and Constance Babington-Smith (1912-2000) MBE, who, in 1943, was the first person in Britain to identify from a photograph the German V1 flying bomb. As a result of her observation, Allied bombers were sent to destroy V1 launch sites in France, saving many lives and homes in Britain. For her work in Britain and America, Babington-Smith was Mentioned in Despatches, appointed MBE and received the US Legion of Merit.

WAAFs at Medenham worked closely with their counterparts at Bletchley Park, probably the most renowned centre of military intelligence in the Second World War.

Bletchley Park: Station X

From 1939, the headquarters of the Government Code and Cypher School (GC&CS) were situated on a 55 acre site at Bletchley Park in Buckinghamshire, codenamed Station X. Most female operatives there belonged to one of the forces although some were civilians, employed by the Foreign Office (FO), the Air Ministry, and the General Post Office (GPO). Not all women there were employed as code-breakers - some were administrators, cooks, cleaners or drivers. Further intelligence work, involving more than 200 Bombe machines, was carried out at the GCCS outstations of Eastcote, Stanmore, Wavendon, Adstock, and Gayhurst. Later in the war, Wrens, including Gwendoline Acason (see page 151), were sent to GCCS outstations overseas, such as *HMS Anderson* and *HMS Lanka*, in Colombo, Ceylon (now Sri Lanka).

The GC&CS had been formed in 1919 and oversaw all Signals Intelligence work in the war. In recent years, the work done at Bletchley Park has become increasingly well-known. It was there that code-breakers, including women, worked on codes used by the Axis powers. The Enigma code is perhaps the best known of these. This was broken using the Bombe decryption machine, created by the mathematician Alan Turing and others. Women code-breakers produced the 'crib', the first part of the process of decoding. For the code-breakers, a crib was a section of German text believed to be the original text. This crib had been enciphered to produce the intercepted Enigma cipher text[121] sent from German U-boats. The 'crib' was often the wording at the beginning of a message, and would usually include a date. After this the Bombe was programmed with the crib and used to find the correct class of the code. In the early stages, this was based on code books from captured German U-boats. Members of WRNS operated the Bombe machines, with the mechanical help of RN and RAF former General Post Office engineers. In 1944, around 12,000 people were employed by GCCS. Many of the code-breakers had language, chess or crossword skills or had been recruited from universities.

Wrens serving here were categorised as *HMS Pembroke V* from December 1942. In total, 2,963 WRNS worked at Bletchley Park during the war. Once accepted for this posting, women could only be transferred on medical or compassionate grounds, or if they were deemed 'unsuitable'. Most *HMS Pembroke V* Wrens worked in Bombe Section at the various outstations.

Ratings at Wavendon (later WRNS quarters) were employed in teleprinting and operating the switchboard. There were 1,699 Wrens here by December 1944. Naval Section had 570 Officers and ratings by August 1945. Hut 6 had 161 by May 1945.

A partial lifting of secrecy restrictions occurred only in 1974.

42. Barbara Baker.

43. Barbara Baker and her husband.

Barbara Baker (1925-2011: pictured) enlisted in the WRNS and was selected to be sent to *HMS Pembroke V* (P5), the Royal Naval designation at Bletchley Park. After working under the mathematician, Max Newman, Barbara later retrained to operate Colossus Mk 1 - the world's first electronic computer. From February 1944, this computer enabled code-breakers to decipher encrypted enemy messages within hours of them being sent.

Before the Morse coded messages reached Station X, they had been intercepted by the women and men of the Y Service at listening stations in Britain and overseas. Members of the ATS and WAAF were recruited to work in wireless interception of the military intelligence, and were described by Churchill as his 'geese that laid the golden eggs that never cackled'. The intelligence gathered at Station Y was codenamed 'Ultra', but it was only long after the war that the agents of Station Y were able to understand the full significance of the work they had been doing. Together with that of Bletchley Park, the war work of the Y Service is believed to have shortened the war by at least two years and saved countless lives.

The Y stations were situated across Britain in stately homes, like Beaumanor Hall, and RAF bases, such as those at Canterbury, Kingsdown and Waddington.

Spies: Special Operations Executive (SOE)

SOE was formed in the summer of 1940 under the control of Hugh Dalton, the Minister of Economic Warfare. Its main role was to support Resistance groups on the Continent in disrupting enemy activity, but agents also operated in the Middle and Far East. In 1944 its agents played a key role in the planning of the Normandy Landings.

The work of SOE was of utmost secrecy and importance to national security. Women were recruited from a variety of backgrounds. Recruiting officers sought special skills, temperaments and knowledge. Fluency in languages such as French and German was highly prized. Some agents volunteered their services, but others were recruited from other organisations.

Training took place in around 60 specially created schools, usually in requisitioned country houses. Recruits were assessed and then given para-military training, parachute training and the finishing skills required for the locality to which they would be sent. Most women became couriers and were trained at communications schools and in industrial sabotage.

Within SOE were sub-groups: SO1 Propaganda, SO2 Active Operations and SO3 Planning.

Some SOE agents were well-connected, known to senior SOE staff through family members. These women tended to come from the upper classes. Hermione, Countess of Ranfurly, for example, worked in the Cairo office of SOE so that she could be with her husband, Dan, in Egypt.

Some of the most renowned women who served in the Second World War operated as secret agents in France for SOE. All had first enlisted into the women's services. As explored in previous chapters, Odette Sansom, for example, was in FANY, Noor Inayat Khan was in the WAAF and Violette Szabo served in the ATS. It was only after this that the three were recruited by SOE.

Not all women SOE received the kind of recognition experienced by Odette Sansom, who was portrayed by the glamorous film star Anna Neagle in a film about her war experiences. With the Official Secrets Act still applicable, most women were unable to reveal their bravery and frightening experiences to anyone for decades after the war was over. For some, this had long lasting psychological effects.

One former agent who experienced psychological problems after the war was Eileen Mary 'Didi' Nearne (1921-2010). A member of FANY in wartime, Nearne was diagnosed with 'exhaustion neurosis' in 1946. As with men who were described as 'shell-shocked' after the First World War, Nearne did not receive good medical support for her post-traumatic condition. However, she did receive care from her sister, Jacqueline, also an SOE veteran.

Like Noor Inayat Khan, Eileen Nearne had lived in France and trained as a wireless operator before being recruited into SOE. In March 1944, Nearne was parachuted into France where she worked with the Resistance, sending messages back to Britain. On 21 July 1944, she was captured by the Nazis and sent, like Violette Szabo whom she later met, to the Ravensbruck women's concentration camp. One of Eileen Nearne's greatest skills was her ability to maintain her cover as an ordinary French girl. Even under torture she was able to convince her captors that she was not a spy. It was this skill that saved her life - on more than one occasion.

As a result of her bravery in the war, Nearne received the MBE and the French *Croix de Guerre*. Her personnel file can be viewed at The National Archives.

Another notable SOE agent was Nancy Grace Augusta Wake (1912-2011), the most decorated woman of the Second World War. Born in New Zealand and raised in Australia, Wake married a French industrialist, Henri Fiocca (1898-1943) in 1939 and after war was declared the couple acted as key organisers of a Resistance network. Until 1943 when Henri was captured by the Nazis, the Fioccas helped refugees and servicemen escape over the Pyrenees. After the capture of her husband[122], Nancy had to make the same journey, into Spain and then on to Britain. As a significant figure in the French Resistance, she was quickly accepted by SOE when she volunteered in London in 1944. At the time she was one of only 39 women in the French section. She is celebrated perhaps most of all for leading 7,000 guerilla fighters in the northern Auvergne in June 1944 in the sabotage of Nazi operations in the lead up to D-day. The guerilla skills Nancy learned in training proved useful when she was required to kill a sentry with her bare hands. After the war, she was awarded the George Medal by the United Kingdom and the Resistance medal, Legion d'Honneur and Croix de Guerre with two bronze palms and a silver star by France, the Medal of Freedom by the USA, but nothing, at first, by Australia. When she was offered an award she refused, but eventually accepted the Companion of the Order of Australia in 2004. Nancy Wake spent her last years spent in London, but she requested that after death her ashes be scattered over the hills of Montlucan in the Auvergne.

Not all women who spied for Britain were British. Maria Krystyna Janina Skarbek was born in Poland, the daughter of a Jewish count. In 1938, Krystyna married Jerzy Gizycki, becoming Krystyna Gizycka, and went on to work as a secret agent for the Allies during the war. Well-educated, Gizycka was fluent in Polish, French, German and English. Motivated in part by the Gestapo's murder of her Jewish mother, Gizycka volunteered for service with SOE. Her British alias was Christina Granville, and in France she was known as Pauline Armand.

After the war, while living in Cairo, Gizycka was no longer welcome in the newly-Communist Poland and became a British citizen. She was awarded the George Medal and the OBE. France awarded her the Croix de Guerre.

Krystyna is believed to have been immortalised by her colleague Ian Fleming as the spy Vesper Lind in his novel, *Casino Royale*. Vera Atkins[123] (1908-2000), who recruited and deployed SOE's female agents for the F (French) section, described Krystyna as 'utterly loyal and dedicated to the Allies,' while being 'a law unto herself'. She struggled to find work after being let go by the Intelligence Services, and eventually took a job as a stewardess on merchant ships. She was murdered by an obsessed former steward on 15 June 1952 and is buried in St Mary's Catholic Cemetery, Kensal Rise in London under the name of Krystyna Skarbek-Granville.

Notes on Researching Spies and Intelligence Work

Most SOE operational files were destroyed. Those that do survive are in the HS series at TNA. Details of FANYs attached to SOE, and their wartime activities, may be found in the Index Cards at TNA (HS 19). While SOE files often give aliases, it is sensible to check indexes with all possible variation of name used by your ancestor, including any married names.

Agents of SOE and those who worked at Bletchley Park and in Y stations were also members of the auxiliary services. Their service records are retained by the Ministry of Defence.

The Personnel File of Eileen Mary Nearne aka Alice Wood aka Jacqueline Duterte is held at TNA reference HS 9/1089/2. Nearne's FANY war pension record is held in PIN 93/2. PIN 93 is the series of Second World War Pensions Award Files of Notable Individuals.

Nancy Wakes's memoir of her war years, *The White Mouse,* was published by Macmillan in 1986. Her personnel file at TNA includes photographs and is in reference HS 9/1545.

Kristina Gizycka's personnel file is held at TNA in HS 9/612 and her naturalisation certificate is in HO 334/167/20605.

The Imperial War Museum holds loose prints and papers relating to Vera Atkins' work as a member of the War Crimes Investigation Team. These include items of the French Resistance. Other private papers related to secret service work are those of Mrs C Wrench of SOE 'F' Section.

Hermione, Countess of Ranfurly (1913-2001) recalled her experiences of SOE in Cairo in her memoir, *To War With Whittaker.* Her aristocratic connections were perhaps less important in securing her role as her years of secretarial experience. She was appointed secretary to the head of SOE, George Pollock.

Bletchley Park Archives has so far catalogued over 14,000 documents, images, sound recordings, objects and software. The records do not contain detailed personal information. The archives are separated into separate collections, including Codes & Cryptology 1938-1946, ISOS and ISK Series Reports, Government Code & Cypher

School Card Indexes, Creed Telegraph Equipment, and BT Connected Earth Collection. A digitised Archives Online is in progress at: **www.bletchleypark.org.uk /content/hist/history/archivesonline.rhtm**

Official records of GC&CS are held at TNA in the HW record series.

The Bletchley Park Roll of Honour is an alphabetical list of those who served at the Park or its outstations in the Second World War. Details have been provided by veterans and their relatives or friends, and gleaned from surviving documents. New names and information are added regularly. The Roll of Honour is online at: **www.bletchleypark.org.uk/content/hist/history/RollofHonour.rhtm**. No full list of Bletchley staff survives, but there is a December 1940 list at TNA series HW 14/9. Other names can be found in the HW series.

A full list of Y stations can be found in Robin Denniston's *Churchill's Secret War Diplomatic Decrypts, the Foreign Office and Turkey, 1942-44* (The History Press, 2009). Oral history interviews with some of the women who served at Bletchley Park and in the Y Service are collated at the website *Churchill's Secret War Diplomatic Decrypts, the Foreign Office and Turkey, 1942-44* (The History Press, 2009). Details and images of Y stations are online at: **http://ystations.webs.com**

For a thorough review of the history of the secret services and those who worked for them, Phil Tomaselli's *Tracing Your Secret Service Ancestors* is recommended.

The Churchill War Rooms, as they are now known, have been open to the public since 1984 and are run by the Imperial War Museum.

The oral accounts of four staff members, including the custodian of the Cabinet War Rooms and a shorthand typist, are also available online at: **http://cwr.iwm.org.uk/server/show/ConWebDoc.6563**

Olive Margerison worked as a secretary in the war rooms, and accompanied Churchill to the Cairo Conference of 1943. She died in 2008, aged 93; her obituary from *The Times*, can be read online: **www.timesonline.co.uk/tol/comment/ obituaries/article5303488.ece**

Joan Bright Astley was also a secretary. She died in 2008, aged 98, and a website dedicated to her (including links to obituaries) can be found at: **www.joanbrightastley.co.uk/**

Some staff at the war rooms worked as censors: an article from *The Times* (22 November 2001) features an interview with one such veteran, Ruth Ives. A copy of this article is held at the Second World War Experience Centre in Leeds: **www.war-experience.org/** or can be read online: **www.fpp.co.uk/History /Churchill/WarRoom.html**

To find out more about the context of some of the work being done in the war rooms, search the Wartime Cabinet Papers by keyword at: **www.nationalarchives.gov.uk /cabinetpapers/**. To browse the Second World War papers by theme see: **www.nationalarchives.gov.uk/cabinetpapers/themes/total-war.htm?WT. ac=Total%20war**. Copies can be ordered online or originals can be viewed in person at The National Archives in Kew.

For official documents on work in the bunker, the Cabinet War Rooms Collection, including papers, maps and miscellanaea, are held at the Cabinet War Rooms in reference CAB 156. Daily Situation Reports are held in CAB 100. Full details on these records can be read at: **www.nationalarchives.gov.uk/records/research-guides/war-cabinet-1939-1945.htm**

Hundreds of records relating to photographic reconnaissance can be found at TNA in series AIR 2, AIR 20, AIR 29, AIR 40 and AIR 51.

West Indian ATS: Women working in one of Britain's ordnance depots with members of the WVS and the British Legion Women's Section, Bicester (1939-1945). Ministry of Information official photographer, Public domain image.

CHAPTER FOURTEEN
Women of the Empire and British Commonwealth

'Let me again emphasize that in expressing our gratitude to those who delivered us we thank not just only those who come from these islands but all the peoples of the Commonwealth and Empire.'

Prime Minister Clement Attlee, in a speech to the House of Commons, 30 October 1945.

From the day Britain declared war on Germany on 3 September 1939, one by one the dominions and her imperial colonies committed themselves to stand beside her as allies. More than 5 million fighting troops volunteered. Auxiliary to these were thousands of women, some of whom had previously made a major contribution to Britain's cause in the First World War.

Besides nursing services (see Chapter 9), women's colonial and British Commonwealth forces of the Second World War, include the following:

Australia
Australian Women's Army Service
Women's Auxiliary Australian Air Force
Women's Royal Australian Naval Service (WRANS)

Canada
Canadian Women's Army Corps
Royal Canadian Air Force (Women's Division)
Women's Royal Canadian Naval Service

East Africa
Women's Service Corps (of Kenya)
Women's Territorial Service (East Africa)

New Zealand
New Zealand Women's Army Auxiliary Corps
New Zealand Women's Auxiliary Air Force
Women's Royal New Zealand Naval Service

South Africa
South African Women's Auxiliary Services
South African Women's Auxiliary Naval Service
Women's Auxiliary Air Force (S.A.A.F.)
Women's Auxiliary Army Services, S.A. Forces
Women's Auxiliary Defence Services, S.A. Forces
Women's Auxiliary Military Police Corps, S.A. Forces

Southern Rhodesia
Southern Rhodesia Women's Auxiliary Air Service
Southern Rhodesia Women's Auxiliary Military Service

India and Burma
Women's Auxiliary Corps (India) (WAC(I))
Women's Auxiliary Air Force in India and Ceylon
Indian Army Nursing Service
Women's Auxiliary Service (Burma)
Women's Royal Indian Naval Service

Colonial Nursing Service

Women from across the world served in the Queen Alexandra's Imperial Nursing Service, its Reserve or the Territorial Army Nursing Service (see Chapter 9). Others enlisted in the Colonial Nursing Service. The Unified Colonial Nursing Service was formed in 1940, but the organisation had been created in 1896 when the Voluntary Society sent trained nurses to Mauritius to fulfil a need for skilled care of British officials and their families. All nurses were fully trained, and were state registered from its introduction. There were only a few hundred nurses in the Service in the war, of whom 52 were killed. Most of the Colonial Nursing service casualties died in Malaya. Barbara Mitchell-Heggs, a Nursing Sister with the Colonial Nursing Service, received a Commendation for her actions in the sinking of the *Anchises* off Malaya in 1940 and Norah Mary Brown was awarded the MBE for her actions after the Dutch steam merchant ship *Alphacca* was torpedoed by a German U-boat on 4 April 1942.

Prisoners of War

1,020 women were interned following the fall of Singapore on 15 February 1942. 330 children and thousands of servicemen and civilian men were also made prisoners of the Japanese. Many of the women were secretaries, wives and mothers, or nurses of the military and voluntary services. Most were interned in Changi, the notorious group of prison camps in Singapore.

One Far East Prisoner of War (FEPOW) was Phyllis Mary Erskin Briggs (later Thom: 1908-2008) who was working as a Colonial Nursing Service sister in Malaya when the Japanese invaded in December 1941. After being evacuated to Singapore, Phyllis nursed victims of the aerial bombardment. On Friday 13 February 1942, just two days before Singapore fell, Phyllis was among a number of women and children who were being evacuated on the *Mata Hari*, bound for Australia. Before the boat could leave Asian waters, she was captured by a Japanese warship and her passengers taken prisoner. Phyllis was taken to Sumatra, where she was imprisoned in cramped and insanitary conditions. Although most women and children were moved three months later, Phyllis and five other nurses stayed to care for the remaining male prisoners. After this, they were imprisoned for 20 months at the Women's Internment Camp, Palembang, where Phyllis nearly died from illness. She was saved by massage from her friend, Alice Rossie. Phyllis Briggs' war experiences are included in Lavinia Warner and John Sandilands' *Women Beyond the Wire* (1982), the television series *Tenko* (1981-1984) and the film, *Paradise Road* (1997). One of her fellow internees was the missionary and composer, Margaret Dryburgh (1890-1945).

Australia

On 13 August 1941, Australia set up its Australian Women's Army Service whose 24,026 members served through the war in similar roles to the British ATS. Women across the country signed up for war work, military nursing and in the auxiliary services. In July 1942, the Australian Women's Land Army was formed.

Major Margaret Joan Spencer (no TF424) of the AWAS was awarded the OBE on 6 March 1947 for service in the South West Pacific theatre of operations.

Captain Vivian Bullwinkel (1915-2000)[124] enlisted in the Australian Army Nursing Service in 1941. She was sent to Malaya in September of that year and was there when the Japanese invaded. After escaping to Singapore, Vivian, 65 other nurses and several civilians escaped aboard the *Vyner Brooke*. The ship was sunk in an air raid and some of its survivors swam to nearby Banka Island. After the group had agreed to surrender, everyone, except Bullwinkel, who had pretended to be dead and one private, who died a few weeks later, was massacred. Vivian and the private surrendered again after two days and were imprisoned. After the war, Major Vivian Bullwinkel was awarded the Florence Nightingale Medal, the MBE and the Member of the Order of Australia.

Canada

The Canadian Women's Army Corps (CWAC) was established on 13 August 1941 as the Canadian Women's Auxiliary Corps. The name was changed when the Corps was absorbed into the Canadian Army on 13 March 1942. Over the course of the war, 22,000 members, or CWACs, served in the USA, UK, Italy and North West Europe. The Canadian Women's Auxiliary Air Force was established in July 1941 but was restructured along the lines of the WAAFs in February 1942 when it became the Royal Canadian Air Force Women's Division. Its members were WDs. The Women's Royal Canadian Naval Service was formed in July 1942.

East Africa

The Women's Territorial Service (East Africa) was part of FANY (see Chapter 10).

New Zealand

The New Zealand Women's Army Auxiliary Corps was established in 1939. New Zealand's Prime Minister, Michael Joseph Savage, was eager for the country to join in the war, and committed to Britain's side on 5 September 1939. The Women's Auxiliary Air Force (NZWAAF) was set up in 1941 and the Women's Royal New Zealand Naval Service came into being in 1942.

South Africa

South African Women's Auxiliary Services comprised the Women's Auxiliary Air Force (S.A.A.F.), the Women's Auxiliary Army Services, S.A. Forces, which was formed in 1940, the Women's Auxiliary Defence Services, S.A. Forces, and the Women's Auxiliary Military Police Corps, S.A. Forces, set up in 1942.

Southern Rhodesia

The Southern Rhodesian Prime Minister, Geoffrey Huggins, was also firmly committed to supporting Britain's war effort. White Southern Rhodesians, in particular, agreed and enlisted in large numbers. The Southern Rhodesia Women's Auxiliary Air Service and the Southern Rhodesia Women's Auxiliary Volunteers (SRWAV) were established in 1 June 1941. They were supported by the Southern Rhodesia Women's Military and Air Force Police.

India & Burma

The Women's Auxiliary Service (Burma) functioned there until Burma was invaded by Japan in 1942. The Women's Auxiliary Corps (India) (WAC(I)) was formed in May 1942 to assist the Indian Army in a similar manner to that of the ATS in Britain. Membership of the WAC(I) peaked at 11,500, with the majority being Anglo-Indian. The Women's Auxiliary Air Force had bases in India and Ceylon, while the Women's Royal Indian Naval Service (WRINS) assisted with shore work at the Royal Indian Navy bases. In appreciation for the excellent service rendered, the Indian Nursing Service was incorporated into the Indian Army in 1943. Women working in factories also made an essential contribution, with 37,000 of the 50,000 textile articles needed by the Allies for the war coming from India.

The West Indies

Women from Barbados, Jamaica, Trinidad and across the Caribbean volunteered to work overseas. Initially, the British War Office had been hesitant to accept black women recruits into the ATS, but their arguments of West Indian women being unable to cope in a cold climate rang hollow and now appear to be racist. Despite this rejection, white and black West Indian women were keen to contribute. In 1943 politicians altered their stance, and welcomed 300 middle-class Caribbean women into the ATS, with some posted to Britain and others working in military bases and hospitals in the West Indies[125]. More women later sailed to Britain to join the ATS and around 80 women enlisted in the WAAF. ATS Emmie Greenhalgh from Barbados had previously worked as personal secretary to Brigadier Stoke-Roberts, the commanding officer to the south Caribbean.

Notes on Researching Women of the Empire and British Commonwealth

Where women received awards from Britain, details of these are held at The National Archives. Details of Major Margaret Joan Spencer's OBE award can be downloaded from DocumentsOnline in TNA reference WO 373/65/2475. War diaries and operations records books for some of the services are also held at TNA.

At the British Library (BL), reference IOR:L/AG/20/39/1 contains release leave accounts and records of the payment of gratuities to members of the Indian Army Nursing Service, and IOR:L/AG/21/13/97 includes service pensions paid to retired members of the Indian Army Nursing Service in the UK.

Records relating to VADs who served in India include BL reference IOR: L/MIL/14 Personal Files, but these are available to next of kin and to those requesting career details only. Also useful are IOR:L/AG/20/41/1-4 payment books on appointment and records of VADs released in the UK 1946-47 in reference IOR:L/AG/20/41/5-6.

Ranks of Nursing Sister and above of the Indian Army Nursing Service are recorded in the *Indian Army List*.

Service records of West Indian women who served in the ATS and WAAF are held in Britain and can be obtained via the Service Personnel and Veterans Agency.

The Imperial War Museum and the National Army Museum hold documents, images and sound recordings of West Indian women who served in Britain during the war.

Liverpool School of Tropical Medicine is undertaking research into the Far East PoW experience and has established a website at: **www.captivememories.org.uk** to reflect its findings, including interviews with former internees.

The National Archives has online catalogues of index cards for British FEPOWs in reference WO 345 and WO 367. Other TNA records include questionnaires of liberated PoWs, lists of names, enquiries into missing personnel, selected notifications of deaths and PoW camp reports.

Film footage of women from across the Empire can be seen at:
www.colonialfilm.org.uk

The names of female casualties from across the Commonwealth can be found in the CWGC's Register of Honour. Images of the headstones of some of these casualties are online at the website of the War Graves Photographic Project: **http://twgpp.org/index.php**

Relevant records held in collections outside Britain can be found via the following organisations:

Australia

National Archives of Australia: **www.naa.gov.au/**
Trove: **http://trove.nla.gov.au/**
Australian Women's Register: **www.womenaustralia.info/**
Australian Department of Defence: **www.defence.gov.au/footer/contacts**
World War Two nominal Roll: **www.ww2roll.gov.au**

Canada

Library and Archives Canada: **www.collectionscanada.gc.ca**
Second World War Service Files: Canadian Armed Forces War Dead:
www.collectionscanada.gc.ca/databases/war-dead/001056-100.01-e.php
CFB Esquimalt Naval & Military Museum
www.navalandmilitarymuseum.org/index.asp
Canada at War: **www.canadaatwar.ca/index.php**
Canadian War Museum: **www.warmuseum.ca/home**
Canadian Newspapers and the Second World War:
www.warmuseum.ca/cwm/exhibitions/newspapers/intro_e.shtmls

New Zealand

New Zealand Defence Force (NZDF) Archives:
www.nzdf.mil.nz/personnel%2Drecords/nzdf-archives/default.htm

South Africa

South African National Defence Forces
Documentation Service Directorate, (Personnel Division)
Private Bag X289, Pretoria, 0001, South Africa.
Fax: +27 12 323 5613
(Mail or fax inquiries only)

Zimbabwe (formerly Rhodesia)

The National Archives of Zimbabwe: **www.archives.gov.zw/**

V.E. Day Celebrations in London (Whitehall), England, UK, 8 May 1945. Public domain image.

CHAPTER FIFTEEN
End of War and Demobilisation

Sixty-eight long months of war ended in August 1945. Crowds of people across the UK and the world met to celebrate the end of the conflict. For service personnel, however, work was not over. The men and women of the armed forces, auxiliary services and nursing corps continued to serve until they were demobilised, or 'de-mobbed'.

Not everyone was celebrating. Over 400,000 British lives had been lost in the Second World War. This contrasted with over 1,000,000 in the First World War, but included far higher civilian casualties and higher numbers of women. In the theatres of operation, 624 women had been killed on active duty and 260,000 men. On the domestic front, thousands of men and women returned between 1945 and 1947 to find they were homeless. Although some members of the services received an allowance on discharge or demobilisation, this was small change (members of the ATS, WAAF and WRNS received £12/10s) in a country where austerity and rationing continued. Ironically, austerity was to be greater in the first five years after the war than it had been during. Perhaps as a reflection of this difficult time, the British electorate chose a socialist Labour government in 1945, rejecting the Conservative Party - including, to his surprise, the immensely popular wartime Prime Minister and Conservative leader, Winston Churchill. The Conservatives had been tainted by the appeasement of the 1930 and the sense of 'we are the masters now'[126] presaged the dawn of a new age.

In this new Britain, thousands of women would not speak in detail, if at all, of their role in the war for decades. Literally thousands of women were prevented from discussing their activities as a result of signing the Official Secrets Act. Others wished to focus on the present and the opportunities a post-war world presented rather than dwell on the horrors and hardships of war. Some migrated to distant parts of the British Commonwealth. Until 1974, when some confidentiality restrictions were lifted, the actions of most women in the Second World War, particularly in Britain, were barely considered. In recent years, that has begun to change.

Demobilisation

Although Britain was still at war, some services began to be demobilised as early as 18 June 1945. Married women in the ATS were the first to be demobbed. Besides marital status, length of service, current age and number of children or elderly dependents affected how soon a woman would be released from service. Some women were sent on courses to prepare them for civilian life, such as training for a peacetime career, but many were concerned that the various skills they had developed during the war would not be taken into consideration by future employers. There were further worries that women would not be accepted by trade unions.

Women from the WAAF reported to their designated Release or Demobilisation Centres, such as RAF Wythall in Worcestershire. WAAFs were given a letter and a number for their order in demobilisation. Dates of release were advertised in Air Ministry Orders (AMOs), starting on 18 June 1945. They received their discharge papers and their final wages. An ATS Ex-Service Employment Office worked with the War Office and the Ministry of Labour to help former ATS personnel into suitable jobs.

Women who had not worked in the services, such as those in the WLA, were not given a medal, a discharge payment, nor extra clothing coupons for civilian clothes. They were given a Release Certificate rather than discharge papers and received fewer ration coupons. WLA members were shocked to be asked to return their uniforms. A group of WLA protested for equal pay with male land workers in Westminster in 1946.

However, civilian services did march alongside the armed forces at the Victory Day parade held in London on 8 June 1946.

What Happened to the Women's Services and Organisations?

The Women's Voluntary Service (WVS) continues to exist, becoming the Women's Royal Voluntary Service in 1966. It is now known simply as WRVS. No longer needed for its initial purposes of assisting civilians with air raids, after the war the WRVS provided social care and support. Today, the focus is on providing practical help for older people. The organisation currently has over 40,000 volunteers.

Air Raid Precautions (ARP) services were disbanded in 1946. However, a Civil Defence Corps was established in 1949 and continued to exist until 1968. This was similar to the ARP except that the defence precautions were taken in respect of a nuclear attack rather than an air raid.

The YWCA of Great Britain continues today, providing opportunities for young women to develop skills in 'working together for a better world'. This involves working to promote women's sexual health and helping to prevent violence against women. The YWCA of GB contains a network of YWCAs and is affiliated to the World YWCA. There are further independent YWCAs across Britain and their hostels have provided accommodation for young men also since the 1960s.

The Navy, Army and Air Force Institutes (NAAFI) continues as the official trading organisation of Her Majesty's Forces.

The Women's Timber Corps was disbanded in August 1946. The Women's Land Army continued to recruit after the war, but after a few years the need for female agricultural workers reduced and the WLA disbanded for the second time in its history in 1950.

The National Fire Service was disbanded in 1948, with control of the fire services reverting to local authorities.

The Army and Air Force (Women's Service) Act of 1948 altered the status of the services, determining that from then on women in the ATS and WAAF would be serving officially as members of the armed forces.

The Women's Royal Naval Service became a permanent service in February 1949, later formalised as part of the Royal Navy under the Naval Disciplines Act of 1977.

On 1 February 1949, Queen Alexandra's Imperial Military Nursing Service (QAIMNS) became the Queen Alexandra's Royal Army Nursing Corps (QARANC). From the 1950s, nurses undertook State Registered Nurse training within the Corps. QARANC nurses continued to serve across the world. From 1992, male nurses were admitted into QARANC, and female nurses could serve with the RAMC and RADC. In recent years, QARANC nurses have served in Iraq, Bosnia and Afghanistan.

The QAIMNS Reserve and Territorial Army Nursing Service (TANS) continued to support the QAIMNS/QARANC.

Nurses who had served in the reserves returned to civilian nursing. Others who had served in a civilian role continued nursing. The introduction of the National Health Service in 1948 dominated the lives of female and male health professionals after the war. Most were not given the respect or acknowledgement they deserved for their role in the war.

After the creation of the NHS, the Red Cross continued to run auxiliary hospitals as part of a five year plan to support the new service. British Red Cross volunteers worked with the International Red Cross to help refugees displaced by the war and its aftermath. The Red Cross continues to provide aid to victims of wars, as well as natural disasters. In Britain, Red Cross volunteers help those who need care at home after a stay in hospital, operate transport services and provide therapeutic massage.

St Andrew's Ambulance Service continues to administer first aid and to run courses across Scotland. The organisation is now publicly known as St Andrew's First Aid.

Queen Alexandra's Royal Naval Nursing Service (QARNNS) continued, but in 1949 a separate nursing branch of the WRNS was set up. The QARNNS reserve had been formed from many VADs and other volunteers. In 1960, the two organisations combined and in 1983 this single service admitted men for the first time. In 2000, QARNNS officially became part of the Royal Navy.

RAF nurses (PMRAFNS) continued to care for Royal Air Force personnel, their families and foreign nationals around the world after the war, broadening their role to include in-flight nursing.

The ATS became the Women's Royal Army Corps (WRAC) in 1949 and its members served as full members of the armed forces until 1992 when women were incorporated into the Army.

In 2012, the First Aid Nursing Yeomanry (FANY) celebrated its 105th anniversary. After the war, the Corps focused on military and civil communications, aiding civil and military authorities in the UK during a major event or planning to prevent such an event from taking place. In 1999, the corps was renamed as FANY (The Princess Royal Volunteer Corps.).

On 1 February 1949, the Women's Auxiliary Air Force was renamed Women's Royal Air Force (WRAF), becoming a permanent service within the RAF. Three years later, Jean Lennox Bird of the WRAFVR became the first woman to be awarded a RAF pilot's badge. In 1994, the WRAF merged fully with the RAF and the name WRAF disappeared.

The Air Transport Auxiliary was disbanded in November 1945.

After the war, some women teachers worked with the British Families Education Service (BFES), which was created in 1947. There is more information on them at the TACA website.

The various structural changes to the services have resulted in women serving alongside their male counterparts in the British armed forces since 1991.

Notes on Researching Women after the Second World War

Service records for all women from this period are retained by the Ministry of Defence and can be accessed via Veterans UK.

The contents of the WRAC Museum are held in the main at the National Army Museum, but some are at the Adjutant General's Corps Museum in Hampshire. The WRAC Association's website is: **www.wracassociation.org.uk**

Women who served as officers in WAAF, WRAF and RAF may found in the annual *Air Force List*.

Officers of the WRNS and QARNNS are recorded in the *Navy List*.

IWM has a good collection of papers, photographs and other material relating to demobilisation of women's services, including examples of WLA Release Certificates.

Films of the Allied Victory Parade can be found on youtube.com, Pathe and itnsource.com. Other material is held by the Museum of London and can be seen at their website: **www.20thcenturylondon.org.uk**

Recommendations for awards up to 1990 can be found at TNA in reference WO 373.

The WRVS website is: **www.wrvs.org.uk**
St Andrew's Ambulance Association/First Aid: **www.firstaid.org.uk**

For further reading, Alan Allport's *Demobbed: Coming Home After the Second World War* is recommended.

ENDNOTES

1. Hacker, 1981.
2. *The Hamilton Papers. Letters and papers illustrating the political relations of England and Scotland in the XVIth century* (1890), li. 466.
3. *The Hamilton Papers*, li. 469-470.
4. www.clanborthwick.com/history2.htm
5. A proclamation of 13 July 1643.
6. Fraser, p.199.
7. www.earlymodernweb.org.uk/warlives/wlbiographies.htm.
8. *The Grand Quarrel*, p.92 Alice Thornton.
9. Sir Simmond D'Ewes, quoted in Weigall, David, *Women Militants in the English Civil War*, History Today, 22:6 (1972: June) p.434.
10. 'Historical Collections: July-December 1643', *Historical Collections of Private Passages of State*: Volume 5: 1642-45 (1721), pp. 341-387. URL: www.british-history.ac.uk/report.aspx?compid=80739 Date accessed: 30 November 2012.
11. Samuel Butler, *Hudibras*: In three parts, written in the time of the late wars, Volume 1.
12. Collections of private passages of state, weighty ..., Volume 5, p.302.
13. Clarendon in Alison Plowden, *Women All on Fire: The Women Of The English Civil War* (Stroud: 1998), p.127.
14. *The History of England*, p.610.
15. Lynn, p.13.
16. Lynn, *Women, Armies, and Warfare in Early Modern Europe* (CUP, 2008), p.1.
17. Mrs Eaton, *Waterloo Days*, quoted in M. De Lancey, *A Week at Waterloo* in June 1815, ed. B. R. Ward, London 1906, p.107.
18. Andrew Uffindell.
19. Andrew Uffindell.
20. in 1813.
21. Philip Haythornthwaite, *The Armies of Wellington* (Arms and Armour Press, 1996), pp.130-131.
22. *The Times*, 2 August 1803.
23. *London Chronicle,* 10 December 1795.
24. Howard R. Clarke www.achart.ca/articles/army_education/armymistress.htm
25. *The Standard* (London, England), Wednesday, September 23, 1874; p.4; Issue 15649.
26. Marian Petrie, *Strength, composition, and organization of the army of Great Britain,* p.152.
27. Marian Petrie, *Strength, composition, and organization of the army of Great Britain,* p.152.
28. Margaret Breay, Editorial, 'The nursing of the sick under Queen Victoria', *British Medical Journal,* 1897, I: 1644-8, p.1645.

29. Sept. 1855, reproduced in Sue M. Goldie, ed., *I Have Done My Duty*: Florence Nightingale in the Crimean War, 1854±56 (Iowa City: University of Iowa Press, 1987), pp.151-6 (quote at p.154).

30. www.countryjoe.com/nightingale/38.htm .

31. R G Huntsman, Mary Bruin & Deborah Holttum, *Twixt candle and lamp: the contribution of Elizabeth Fry and the Institution of Nursing Sisters to Nursing Reform.* (Med Hist. 2002 July; 46(3): p.356.

32. www.historytoday.com/lynn-mcdonald/florence-nightingale-and-mary-seacole-nursings-bitter-rivalry.

33. www.qaranc.co.uk/netleyhospital.php.

34. *The Graphic* (London, England), Saturday, August 9, 1879; Issue 506.

35. Deeble was appointed to the post in 1870 and remained there until 1889.

36. Anne Summers.

37. Princess Christian was the third daughter of Queen Victoria.

38. Summers, p.163.

39. *Times* (London, England) 5 Oct. 1931: p.19.

40. Helen G. Wilkie, *The Work of the Women's Emergency Canteens in France: 1915-1919*, compiled by Josephine Davies (Women's Printing Society, 1919).

41. 1911 Census Reference: RG14PN2277 RG78PN77 RD26 SD4 ED27 SN142.

42. MI5 report KV/49 (or KV 1/49 held at TNA) quoted in Hampton, *How Girl Guides Won The War* (Harper Press, 2010), p.26.

43. Hampton, p.26.

44. Hampton quoting MI5 report, p.26.

45. Woollacott, p.19.

46. The Norah Bristow papers are held in the Liddle Collection at Leeds University.

47. Marwick, p.74.

48. Marwick, p.72.

49. MS Allen, *The Pioneers Policewoman* (Chatto & Windus, 1925), p.19.

50. Grayzel, *Experiences of War* p.87.

51. Grayzel, *Experiences of War* p.66.

52. Marwick, p.115.

53. *Daily Express*, 19 August 1918, quoted in Woollacott, p.193.

54. Ministry of Reconstruction, *Report of the Women's Employment Committee* quoted in Woollacott, p. 17

55. Our Military Correspondent. 'Need For Shells.' *Times* [London, England] 14 May 1915: p.8. *The Times* Digital Archive.

56. Marwick, p.55.

57. Woollacott, *ibid.*

58. Woollacott, *ibid.*

59. Mrs Hodgkinson's Dissertation, General Section, Liddle Collection. Munitions topic box, Domestic Front Section in the Liddle Collection, Brotherton Library, University of Leeds.

60. Marwick, p.56.

61. Marwick p.60.

62. Ursula Birsting, *Autobiography*, item 12, Liddle Collection.

63. Marwick, p.176.

64. Woollacott, p.167.

65. I. F. W. Beckett, *The First World War* (PRO Publications, 2002).
66. Housego, p.61.
67. Dr Anne-Marie Claire Hughes.
68. www.newhamstory.com/node/2446.
69. Marwick, pp.68-69.
70. http://warmemscot.s4.bizhat.com/warmemscot-post-49675.html .
71. *Lancaster Guardian* Wednesday 26 September 2007.
72. *Flight,* 9 January 1919.
73. www.women.qmul.ac.uk/virtual/themes/1914-1945/page1.htm .
74. Marwick, p.84.
75. Bowser pp.71-2.
76. A full discussion of this tragedy can be read at the Great War Forum http://1914-1918.invisionzone.com/forums/index.php?showtopic=147631.
77. Housego, p.9.
78. Military Collection No 262a file 188.
79. Marwick, p.42.
80. www.roll-of-honour.com/Ships/HMHSLetitia.html.
81. ADM 1/8615/1971921.
82. Women's Collection at IWM.
83. Marwick, *ibid,* p.101.
84. Marwick, *ibid*, p.89.
85. listed in Marwick, p.89.
86. Housego, p.55.
87. Escott, p.3.
88. ww.telegraph.co.uk/news/uknews/9066371/Last-surviving-veteran-of-First-World-War-dies-aged-110.html.
89. Report of the Director, 1957.
90. Angela Jackson, *British Women and the Spanish Civil War* (Routledge, 2002).
91. Lucy Noakes, *Women in the British Army: War and the Gentle Sex 1907-1948*, p.96.
92. Beryl Escott, *The WAAF* (Shire, 2003).
93. *Manchester Guardian,* 10 March 1941 quoted: www.spartacus.schoolnet.co.uk/TUbevin.htm
94. quoted in *Wartime Camden*, p.123.
95. www.guardian.co.uk/world/2006/jun/19/secondworldwar.gender .
96. *Land Girl: A Manual for Volunteers in the Women's Land Army 1941* by WE Shewell-Cooper (Amberley, 2011).
97. Vita Sackville-West, *The Women's Land Army* (MAF, London, 1997; original 1944).
98. *Hansard* 12 October 1943, vol 392, cc730-1W http://hansard.millbanksystems.com/written_ answers/1943/oct/12/womens-land-army.
99. Margaret Harriman, *Bring Me My Bow* (London: Victor Gollancz, 1967).
100. Harriman, *ibid*, p.92.
101. *The Star & Garter Magazine*, Vol. XXVIII, October 1948, no.4.
102. www.paullewis.co.uk/archive/saga/2000_and_before/871001_asbestos.h.
103. *Wartime Camden*, p.31.
104. www.locallocalhistory.co.uk/ctown/p100/pages112-120.htm.
105. Ada Harrison (ed.), *Grey & Scarlet* (Hodder & Stoughton, 1944).

106. Martin Brayley, *World War II Allied Nursing Services* (Osprey, 2002).
107. Obituary of Audrey Hayward in *Nursing Standard* (16 February, 2011).
108. McBryde, *ibid.*
109. *The Times* (London, England), Wednesday, Aug 23, 1944; p.6; Issue 49942.
110. Later Air Commandant and after 1942 Air Chief Commandant (Dame 1944).
111. Sqn Ldr Beryl Escott, *The WAAF* (Shire, 2003), p.32.
112. Escott, p.17.
113. Escott p.19.
114. Escott, p.32.
115. Escott, p.18
116. 5454 Supplement to the *London Gazette* 28 November 1944.
117. www.militarian.com/threads/women-at-sea-during-wwii.1672/.
118. Details of this decision can be found in TNA reference HW 14/57.
119. Patrick Marnham, *Wild Mary* (Chatto & Windus, 2006).
120. Hampton, p.205.
121. G. Page, We Kept the Secret (p.105).
122. Nancy did not discover what had happened to her husband for more than a year after his capture. He was executed after being tortured extensively. He died refusing to reveal his wife's whereabouts. For her ability to slip through their fingers, Nancy Wake had been nicknamed 'The White Mouse' by the Gestapo, and became their most-wanted member of the Resistance.
123. Originally, Vera Maria Rosenberg.
124. www.awm.gov.au/people/1906.asp.
125. Ben Bousqet and Colin Douglas, *West Indian Women at War: British Racism in World War II* (Lawrence & Wishart Ltd, 1990).
126. This statement is attributed to Hartley Shawcross (later Baron Shawcross) when he was Attorney-General, although the exact words he used were, 'We are the masters at the moment, and not only at the moment, but for a very long time to come' (Commons Sitting of Tuesday, 2 April, 1946; *Hansard* Fifth Series, Volume 421). He was referencing Humpty Dumpty in *Alice in Wonderland*.

USEFUL RECORDS FOR ALL WOMEN AT WAR ANCESTORS

This section presents the records required to trace the war service or career of female ancestors. It is not intended as a detailed guide about these records, or how to use them.

General Records

Newspapers and Journals

Newspapers are an important source of historical material. When researching women at war, they are particularly useful for locating newspaper announcements and obituaries that mention your ancestor or her colleagues. Copies of paper newspapers can be found in several of the specialist archives listed below and in local archives. Others can be sourced through commercial companies such as Historic Newspapers: www.historic-newspapers.co.uk. Many newspaper collections have been uploaded to online databases.

Useful online historical newspaper databases include:

Australian newspapers via Trove: http://trove.nla.gov.au/ndp/del/home
British Medical Journal: www.bmj.com/archive
British Newspaper Archive: www.britishnewspaperarchive.co.uk/ includes national and local newspapers dating back to 1800. The database is continually adding titles from the British Library's newspaper collections, which are among the finest in the world containing most of the runs of newspapers published in the UK since 1800.
British Newspapers 1800-1900: http://newspapers11.bl.uk/blcs/
Google News: http://news.google.com/newspapers
(Manchester) *Guardian* and *Observer* Digital Archive: http://archive.guardian.co.uk/D
London Gazette: www.london-gazette.co.uk/ includes the names, ranks and some service numbers of women mentioned in Despatches and those who were awarded the Military Medal. All were listed in 9 May 1919.
National Library of Scotland's Digital Collection includes a number of online newspapers and journals: https://auth.nls.uk/ldc/
New Zealand Papers Past: http://paperspast.natlib.govt.nz
Newspaper Archive: http://newspaperarchive.com/
The Times (London): Digital Archive 1785-2006: http://gale.cengage.co.uk/times.aspx/

Historical journals relevant to women's military history that can be accessed in archives are:

Blackwood's
Common Cause
Emigration Gazette (an occasional paper), the official organ of the Salvation Army Emigration
    Department
English Review
Flight [see websites]
Girls' Friend
Girls Own Stories
Labour Women
Landswoman
Modern Woman
Newsletter (YWCA)
Old Comrade's Association Gazette (later the *QMAAC and ATS Comrades Association*
    Gazette)
Our Girls
Our Own Gazette (YWCA)
Pioneer and Labour Journal (Woolwich)
Police Chronicle
Police Review
The Cocoa Works Times (York's Rowntree Factory)
The Engineering
The Journal of the Women Police Service
The Limit (White & Poppe factory, Coventry)
The Suffragette
The Thistle - Scottish Women's Hospitals for Foreign Service (SCOTLAND) 1916
    The Thistle: souvenir book in aid of Scottish Women's Hospitals for Foreign Service.
    (With illustrations.]
The War-Worker
The Whistle (London, England : 1919)
The Woman Worker
Woman At Home
Woman's Dreadnought (later *Workers' Dreadnought*)
Woman Engineering
Women's Industrial News
Woman's Life

Essential Genealogy Records

Records of State Registration - Women's marriages are particularly important records. You may find your ancestor's service details under her maiden or married name. Do be aware that she may have had more than one marriage, or been unmarried but adopted the name of a common law husband.

Records of British subjects born overseas - Family Search; Find My Past GRO Army, Overseas and at Sea; FIBIS database.

UK Census Records for 1841, 1851, 1861, 1871, 1881, 1891, 1901 and 1911 can be searched online in full or in part at:

Ancestry www.ancestry.co.uk
Family Search www.FamilySearch.org
Findmypast: www.findmypast.co.uk/
FreeCEN: www.freecen.org.uk/
GenesReunited: www.genesreunited.co.uk/
National Archives Census of Ireland: www.census.nationalarchives.ie/
Origins: www.origins.net
RootsUK: www.rootsuk.com/
ScotlandsPeople: www.scotlandspeople.gov.uk
The Genealogist: www.thegenealogist.co.uk/
UK Census Online: http://ukcensusonline.com/
1911census.co.uk: www.1911census.co.uk/default.aspx
1901censusonline.com: www.1901censusonline.com

Parish Records - baptism, marriage and burial records; some can be found online at Family Search, Ancestry or Findmypast.

Passenger lists - some online at Ancestry and Findmypast

Divorce records - some indexed material on Findmypast and Discovery

Locate Records

Many archives have online portals or catalogues to enable access to specific areas of their collections. Some have links to online documents, but most help locate a document for copying or consulting within an archive. Search the portals by name, keyword or document reference.

Among the most useful for British family history research are:

A2A Access to Archives: www.nationalarchives.gov.uk/a2a/
Archives Wales: www.archivesnetworkwales.info/
COPAC: http://copac.ac.uk/search. Search over 70 UK and Irish academic national & specialist library catalogues
Discovery: http://discovery.nationalarchives.gov.uk/SearchUI/Home. Discover the collections of The National Archives (TNA)
Explore: http://explore.bl.uk/ Search, view and order items from the British Library's main catalogue of nearly 57 million records or search the contents of the Library's website.
Genuki: www.genuki.org.uk/ A virtual reference library of genealogical information of particular relevance to the UK and Ireland. Can be searched by keyword, acronym or phrase, such as 'ARP'.

London Metropolitan Archives: http://search.lma.gov.uk/ search by ancestor's name or keyword/phrase such as 'army nurse'.

National Library of Scotland (NLS) Digital Gallery: http://digital.nls.uk/

National Register of Archives: www.nationalarchives.gov.uk/nra/default.asp

Public Record Office of Northern Ireland (PRONI): www.proni.gov.uk/index/search_ the_archives.htm

Society of Genealogists catalogue (SoGCAT) http://62.32.98.6/S10312UK/OPAC/Index.aspx includes details of everything in the library except the Document Collections.

Other online catalogues for libraries and archives - usually available via the homepage of the relevant organisation. These can be found via the websites of archives in the list below.

Online book catalogues include:

Europeana: www.europeana.eu

Gallica: http://gallica.bnf.fr

Hathi Trust: www.hathitrust.org

Google Books: http://books.google.com/

Internet Archive: http://archive.org

Kirtas: http://kirtasbooks.com

Project Gutenberg: www.gutenberg.org

Cemetery and crematoria records

Commonwealth War Graves Commission: www.cwgc.org

Geoff's Search Engine: www.hut-six.co.uk/GreatWar/

Ancestry parish burials and Commonwealth War Graves, 1914-1921/1939-1947: www.ancestry.co.uk

Deceased Online: www.deceasedonline.com/

Find A Grave: www.findagrave.com

Local projects

Monumental inscriptions can be found in published sources or in some online databases

The National Memorial Arboretum in Staffordshire is the UK's Centre of Remembrance. Its website is: www.thenma.org.uk

The location of names of those remembered in the Arboretum can be identified on the Veterans UK Roll of Honour, which can be searched online at: www.veterans-uk.info/afm2/index.php

From 1989, the UK National Inventory of War Memorials has been recording non-Commonwealth War Graves Commission memorials to all conflicts. Further details can be found at their website: www.ukniwm.org.uk

The Ministry of Defence is responsible for recording members of the Armed Forces who died in service from 1948. They can be contacted at:

MoD - Non-War Graves
SO3 Memorials and Graves, Armed Forces Personnel Administration Agency, Joint Casualty and Compassionate Centre, Building 182, Innsworth Station, Gloucester GL3 1HW.
Email: JPAC@afpaa.mod.uk
Tel: 01452 712612 ext 6304 or 6063

Further Commonwealth Casualties may be found at:

Australia: www.awm.gov.au/ http://www.ww2roll.gov.au/ World War Two Nominal Roll
Canada: www.vac-acc.gc.ca/remembers/sub.cfm?source=collections/virtualmem
New Zealand: www.aucklandmuseum.com/130/cenotaph-database
Private papers (letters, diaries etc) - some are found in archives, others are in private collections, include family documents.

Probate records - see ScotlandsPeople, Ancestry, Findmypast, Discovery, The Genealogist, FamilyRelatives, the National Wills Index www.nationalwillsindex.com, Origins and Irish Origins, National Library of Wales, LDS Family History Centres, PRONI and via local projects (some online).

Military Records

Service Records - ledgers; papers; many do not survive; for women born less than 100 years ago, records are usually retained by the Ministry of Defence.

Pension Records - not all women were entitled to these. They were usually awarded after a set period of service. Women may have received pensions after serving in the auxiliary services as well in roles of essential war work, like the Women's Land Army.

Musters and Pay Lists; Regimental Rolls - not all survive.

Medals; Army Recommendations for Honours & Awards - see TNA guide at: www.nationalarchives.gov.uk/documentsonline/browse-refine.asp?CatID=22&search Type=browserefine&pagenumber=1&query=*&queryType=1 , William Spencer's *Medal's The Researcher's Guide* and books on specific medals (see Bibliography).

Military announcements in local and national newspapers - some can be found by searching online newspaper databases

Shipping announcements in newspapers

Medal awards can be found in the *London Gazette*: www.london-gazette.co.uk/. These and other military announcements may includes names, ranks and service numbers

Casualty lists, military obituaries, rolls of honour, memorials - Commonwealth War Grave Commission www.cwgc.org casualty records and Register of Honour, York Minster Women's Screens (see Appendices) and local memorials. In From The Cold www.infromthecold.org was formed to research and identify all service women (and men) who are missing from the official Commonwealth War Graces Commission (CWGC) list of casualties from the First and Second World Wars.

Archives

Adjutant General's Corps Museum Collection (AGC)
The Guardroom, Peninsula Barracks, Romsey Road, Winchester, Hampshire SO23 8TS.
Email: curator@agcmuseum.co.uk

Air Historical Branch (RAF)
RAF Northolt, West End Road, Ruislip, Middlesex HA4 6NG.

Archives New Zealand
National Office, Wellington
10 Mulgrave Street, Thorndon, Wellington 6011, New Zealand.
PO Box 12-050, Wellington, New Zealand.
Tel: (64-4) 499 5595
http://archives.govt.nz/

Army Medical Services Museum (AMS)
Keogh Barracks, Ash Vale, Aldershot, Hampshire GU12 5RQ.
www.ams-museum.org.uk

Army Museums Ogilby Trust
Brigadier CS Sibun, 58 The Close, Salisbury, Wiltshire SP1 2EX.
www.armymuseums.org.uk

Association of Jewish Ex-Servicemen and Women (AJEX)
Shield House, Harmony Way off Victoria Road, London NW4 2BZ.
Tel. 020 8202 2323
www.ajex.org.uk

Bletchley Park Archives
Archives Department, Bletchley Park Trust, The Mansion, Bletchley Park, Milton Keynes, Bucks MK3 6EB.
Tel. 01908 272650
www.bletchleypark.org.uk/edu/archives

Bodleian Library
Department of Special Collections and Western Manuscripts, Broad Street, Oxford OX1 3BG.
Tel. 01865 277158
www.bodley.ox.ac.uk

British Library (BL)
96 Euston Road, London NW1 2DB.
Tel. 020 7412 7676
www.bl.uk

British Nurses' & Hospital Badge Society (BNHBS)
Email: bnhbsarchive@hotmail.com
Tel. 020 8543 9514

British Red Cross Museum and Archives
44 Moorfields, London EC2Y 9AL.
Email: enquiry@redcross.org.uk
Tel. 020 7877 7058

Camden Local Studies and Archives (Camden LS)
Holborn Library, 32-38 Theobalds Road, London WC1X 8PA.
www.camden.gov.uk/localstudies

Churchill College, Cambridge
Director of Archives, Churchill Archives Centre, Cambridge CB3 0DS.
Tel. 01223 336087
www.chu.cam.ac.uk/archives

Commonwealth War Graves Commission
2 Marlow Road, Maidenhead, Berkshire SL6 7DX.
Tel. 01628 634221
www.cwgc.org

Enfield Local Studies Library & Archive
First Floor, Thomas Hardy House, 39 London Road. EN2 6DS.
Tel. 020 8379 2724
www.enfield.gov.uk/info/1062/libraries-local_collections/1011/enfield_local_studies_
library_and_archive

Florence Nightingale Museum
2 Gassiot House, Lambeth Palace Road, London SE1 7EW.
Email: info@florence-nightingale.co.uk
Tel. 020 7620 0374

Great War Archive
University of Oxford
www.oucs.ox.ac.uk/ww1lit/gwa

House of Lords Record Office
Clerk of the Records, House of Lord, London SW1A 0PW.
Tel. 020 7219 3074
www.parliament.uk

Imperial War Museum (IWM)
Explore/ research centre, London SE1 6HZ.
Tel. 020 7416 5221/2/3
www.iwm.org.uk

International Red Cross and Red Crescent Museum
17, Avenue de la Paix
1202 Geneva, Switzerland
Email: mus@micr.org

International Institute for Social History
Cruquiusweg 31, 1019 AT Amsterdam, The Netherlands.
http://socialhistory.org/

Irish War Memorials Project
www.irishwarmemorials.ie/

Library and Archives Canada
395 Wellington Street, Ottawa, ON K1A 0N4, Canada.
Tel. 613-996-5115 or 1-866-578-7777
www.collectionscanada.gc.ca/

Liddle Collection
Leeds University Library, Brotherton Library, University of Leeds LS2 9JT.
www.leeds.ac.uk/library/spcoll/liddle
Liddle Collection Database Catalogue: http://brs.leeds.ac.uk/~lib6osp/liddle.html
Tel. 0113 343 5513

London Metropolitan Archives (LMA)
40 Northampton Road, Clerkenwell, London EC1R 0HB.
Email: ask.lma@cityoflondon.gov.uk
www.cityoflondon.gov.uk/lma

London Transport Museum Library
Covent Garden Piazza
London, WC2E 7BB
www.ltmuseum.co.uk/collections/research/library

Marx Memorial Library
37a Clerkenwell Green
London EC1R 0DU
Tel: 020 7253 1485
www.marx-memorial-library.org

Museum of London
Tel: 020 7001 9844
email: info@museumoflondon.org.uk

National Archives And Records Service Of South Africa
The National Archivist, Private Bag X236, Pretoria 0001, South Africa.
www.national.archives.gov.za/
Tel: 012 441 3200

National Archives of Australia
Head Office, Canberra, Australia.
Tel. + 61 2 6212 3600
www.naa.gov.au/

National Army Museum (NAM)
Royal Hospital Road, Chelsea, London SW3 4HT.
Tel. 020 7730 0717
www.national-army-museum.ac.uk

Templar Study Centre
www.nam.ac.uk/research/templer-study-centre

National Library of Scotland (NLS)
George IV Bridge, Edinburgh EH1 1EW.
www.nls.uk

National Maritime Museum (NMM)
Greenwich, London SE10 9NF.
Tel. 020 8312 6632
www.rmg.co.uk

Order of St John Library and Museum
St John's Gate, Clerkenwell, London EC1M 4DA.
Email: museum@nhq.sja.org.uk
Tel. 020 7324 4070
www.sja.org.uk

Parliamentary Archives
Parliamentary Archives, Houses of Parliament, London, SW1A 0PW.
Tel. 020 7219 3074
www.parliament.uk/archives

Peace Pledge Union
Peace Pledge Union, 1 Peace Passage, London N7 0BT.
Tel. 020 7424 9444
www.ppu.org.uk/coproject/research.html

People's History Museum
Left Bank, Spinningfields, Manchester M3 3ER.
Tel. 0161 838 9190
www.phm.org.uk/

Police Federation of England and Wales
Federation House, Highbury Drive, Leatherhead, Surrey KT22 7UY.
Tel. 01372 352000
www.polfed.org

Public Record Office of Northern Ireland (PRONI)
2 Titanic Boulevard, Titanic Quarter, Belfast BT3 9HQ.
Tel. 02890 534800
www.proni.gov.uk

Queen Alexandra's Royal Army Nursing Corps Museum (QARANC Archive)
Regimental Headquarters QARANC, Keogh Barracks, Ash Vale, Aldershot GU12 5RQ.
Tel. 01252 340212
www.ams-museum.org.uk/museum/

QARNNS Archive
Institute of Naval Medicine, Crescent Road, Alverstoke, Gosport, Hampshire PO12 2DL.
www.qarnns.co.uk

Royal Air Force (RAF) Museum
Department of Research & Information Services, Grahame Park Way, London NW9 5LL
Tel. 020 8358 4873
www.rafmuseum.org.uk/research

Royal British Nurses Association
The Princess Royal House, The Territorial Army Centre, London Road, Stonecot Hill, Sutton, Surrey SM3 9HG.
Email: enquiries@rbna.org.uk
Tel. 020 8335 3691

Royal Naval Museum (RNM)
HM Naval Base, Portsmouth, Hampshire PO1 3NH.
Tel. 02392 727562
www.royalnavalmuseum.org

The National Archives (TNA)
Ruskin Avenue, Kew, Surrey TW9 4DU.
Email: enquiry@nationalarchive.gov.uk
Tel. 020 8876 3444

The Wellcome Library (WLL)
183 Euston Road, London NW1 2BE.
Tel. 020 7611 8722
http://library.welcome.ac.uk

Transport for London (TfL) Corporate Archives
8th Floor, Windsor House
42-50 Victoria Street
London SW1H 0TL
Tel: 020 7918 4535
Email: corporatearchives@tfl.gov.uk

The Women's Library @ LSE
Archives Services Group Library, London School of Economics and Political Science,
10 Portugal Street, London WC2A 2HD.
Email: Document@lse.ac.uk
www.lse.ac.uk/library/archive/Home.aspx

UK Centre for the History of Nursing
Royal College of Nursing Archives, 42 South Oswald Road, Edinburgh EH9 2HH.
Email: archives@rcn.org.uk
Tel. 0131 622 1010

Wiener Library for the Study of the Holocaust & Genocide
29 Russell Square, London WC1B 5DP.
www.wienerlibrary.co.uk

Working Class Movement Library
51 The Crescent, Salford, U.K. M5 4WX.
Tel. 0161 736 3601
www.wcml.org.uk/

Women's Transport Service (FANY)
TA Centre, 95 Horseferry Road, London SW1P 2DX.
Tel. 020 7976 5459
www.fany.org.uk

Yorkshire Museum of Farming
Murton Park, Yorkshire
Tel. 01904 489966
www.murtonpark.co.uk/

Archive Collections

Women's Work Collection

This collection can be searched in the Imperial War Museum's Explore History Centre in Kennington, South London. The Imperial War Museum (IWM) was created in 1917 as the National War Museum. Lady Norman became 'Chairman' of the Museum's Women's War Work Sub-Committee, with Miss Agnes Conway as Secretary. The Collection was formed when the two women gathered together documents and photographs on women's war work by contacting every person and organisation they could think of which had anything to do with work. It includes reminiscences, letters and diaries, and can be searched by name.

To access the collection in the Explore History Centre, click on online resources, then the 'Women's Work' tab. This takes you into a Gale databases site which includes historic news pages as well as 'Women, War and Society, 1914-1918', which can be searched by text. The collection includes images of press-cuttings, minutes, reports, correspondence, photographs and recent essays, which can be printed or emailed. This database is taken from the *Women at Work Collection*.

The Imperial War Museum's Collections include thousands of papers, oral recordings, films, photographs, paintings and other objects relating to women at war. The Museum holds examples of uniforms, including badges, ties, caps, buttons and belts.

Liddle Collection

The Liddle Collection is held at the University of Leeds and is one of the major resources for researching women at war. Although the Collection is usually associated with the First World War, it also has major holdings on the Second World War. Included in the archive are the personal papers of well over 4,000 people who lived through the First World War, and approximately 500 who experienced the Second World War.

Searches can be made of two separate catalogues, the 1914-1918 Catalogue, which is online at: http://brs.leeds.ac.uk/cgi-bin/brs_engine?*DB=LIDL&*ID=0 and the 1939-1945 Catalogue http://brs.leeds.ac.uk/cgi-bin/brs_engine?*DB=LIDX&*ID=0

The Women's Library @ LSE

The Library is now based at LSE and holds over 500 archives of women's history. These are arranged within 11 sections: Female Emigration Societies, Women's Suffrage Societies, Societies for the Abolition of State Regulation of Prostitution, Societies for the Suppression of Traffic of Persons, Campaigning Organisations, Personal Papers, Records of Oral History and Research Projects, Autograph Letter Collection, Fawcett Library Scrapbooks and Records of the Women's Library predecessor and associated bodies.

Young Women's Christian Association (1855-1995) Collection

The YWCA records (Ref. MSS.243) are held at the University of Warwick, Modern Records Centre. They contain constitutional papers, a large series of minutes 1884-1957, administrative records, correspondence and subject files 1855-1979, reports 1862-1993, almanacs, directories, journals, etc. 1879-1970, and leaflets 1877-1980; branch records 1861-1977; historical notes, press cuttings 1870s-1979. Includes records for women who served in First World War, between the wars and in the Second World War.

Websites

Achart - military history: www.achart.ca
Ancestry: www.ancestry.co.uk
Air Transport Auxiliary exhibition and archive: www.atamuseum.org
Anglo Boer War website: www.angloboerwar.com
ATS Remembered: www.atsremembered.org.uk
Australian Women in Wartime: http://australia.gov.au/about-australia
    australian-story/women-in-wartime
Auxiliary War Hospitals of Kent: www.juroch.demon.co.uk/kentvad.htm
BBC People's War: compiled between 2003-2006; search by name or by category, such as
    Land Army, Fire Duty etc: www.bbc.co.uk/ww2peopleswar
BBC WWI: ww.bbc.co.uk/topics/world_war_1
Bletchley Park Roll of Honour: http://rollofhonour.bletchleypark.org.uk
Bradford WWI: www.bradfordww1.co.uk/content/research
Brenzett Aeronautical Museum Trust: www.brenzettaero.co.uk
British Army WWI Medal Rolls Index Cards 1914-1920:
    http://search.ancestry.co.uk/search/db.aspx?dbid=1262
British Civil Wars: www.british-civil-wars.co.uk
British Library Sound & Moving Image Collection:
    http://cadensa.bl.uk/uhtbin/cgisirsi/x/x/0/49/%20;%20charset=UTF-8
British Movietone Digital Archive: www.movietone.com
British Pathe: historic news clips: www.britishpathe.com
British Resistance Archive: www.coleshillhouse.com
Channel 4 WWI website: www.channel4.com/history/microsites/L/lostgeneration/ww1
Children on the Move: a lasting record of evacuation in Staffordshire:
    www.childrenonthemove.org.uk
Churchill War Rooms: www.iwm.org.uk/visits/churchill-war-rooms
Commonwealth War Graves Commission: www.cwgc.org
Connected Histories: www.connectedhistories.org
Crimean War Research Society: http://cwrs.russianwar.co.uk/cwrsentry.html
Diaries: www.firstworldwar.com/diaries/august1914.htm
District Nursing 150: www.districtnursing150
Edith Appleton: www.edithappleton.org.uk
English Civil War: www.englishcivilwar.org
Europeana: www.europeana1914-1918.eu/en/library
Evacuees Reunion Association: www.evacuees.org.uk
Families In British India Society: www.new.fibis.org
FANY (PRVC) Princess Royal's Volunteer Corps: www.fany.org.uk
Far East PoW experience (Liverpool School of Tropical Medicine):
    www.captivememories.org.uk
Far East Prisoners of War Community (FEPOW): www.fepow-community.org.uk

Find My Past: www.findmypast.com

First World War: www.firstworldwar.com

First World War Poetry Digital Archive:
www.oucs.ox.ac.uk/ww1lit/collections/item/1285?CISOBOX=1&REC=7

First World War Sources for History at The National Archives:
www.nationalarchives.gov.uk/pathways/firstworldwar/index.htm

Flightglobal Archive: Flight Magazine 1909-2005: www.flightglobal.com/pdfarchive

For the Fallen: www.forthefallen.co.uk

Forces Reunited: www.forcesreunited.org.uk

Gainsborough and District Heritage Association: www.gainsboroughheritage.com

George Cross database: www.marionhebblethwaiteart.com/gcindex.htm

Gertrude Bell Archive: www.gerty.ncl.ac.uk

Girlguiding UK www.girlguiding.org.uk

Girlguiding Norfolk's Historical Jigsaw: www.girlguidingnorfolkheritage.org.uk

Great War Forum: Women in The Great War: http://1914-
1918.invisionzone.com/forums/index.php?act=idx

Hilda Clark 1881-1955 (Society of Friends blog):
http://librarysocietyfriendsblog.wordpress.com/2012/07/03/world-war-i-and-its-aftermath-
cataloguing-the-papers-of-hilda-clark-1881-1955/

Historic Scotland - Gretna: A Munitions Town: www.historic-scotland.gov.uk/gretna

History to Herstory: Yorkshire women's lives online. 1100 to the present
www.historytoherstory.org.uk

Home Sweet Home Front (WWII): www.homesweethomefront.co.uk

HMS Belfast: www.iwm.org.uk/visits/hms-belfast

Hospital Records Database (Hosprec): www.nationalarchives.gov.uk/hospitalrecords/

Imperial War Museum: www.iwm.org.uk

International Committee of the Red Cross Archives: www.icrc.org/eng/resources/icrc-
archives/index.jsp

Irish Defence Forces Military Archives: www.military.ie/dfhq/archives/arch.htm

ITN Source: archive footage www.itnsource.com

IWM Catalogue, Photographic and Sound Archive: search by keyword for access to oral and
video collections, photographs, dairies, memoirs and items of uniform and medals. Some
can be accessed from home; others will require you to book an appointment at IWM.
Some women are mentioned by name. Others may be found within documents that include
lists of names: www.iwm.org.uk/collections/search

IWM Duxford: www.iwm.org.uk/visits/iwm-duxford

IWM First World War Centenary Website: www.1914.org

IWM North: www.iwm.org.uk/visits/iwm-north

Kent Voluntary Aid Detachments: www.kentvad.org

London Museums of Health and Medicine: www.medicalmuseums.org/Florence-Nightingale-
Museum/

London's Voices (Museum of London oral history archive):
www.museumoflondon.org.uk/archive/londonsvoices/default.asp

Lost Hospitals of London: www.ezitis.myzen.co.uk

Maidenhead Heritage Centre's Air Transport Auxiliary Exhibition and Archive:
www.atamuseum.org

Mary Seacole website: www.maryseacole.com

Mary Seacole's autobiography
http://digital.library.upenn.edu/women/seacole/adventures/adventures.html SoG (book)
Mass Observation Archive www.massobs.org.uk
Medical Women's Federation: www.medicalwomensfederation.org.uk
Medieval Soldiers Database: www.icmacentre.ac.uk/soldier/database/index.php
METWPA: History of Met Women Police Officers: www.metpwa.org.uk
Military History Encyclopedia on the Web: www.historyofwar.org
National Army Museum: www.nam.ac.uk
National Maritime Museum: www.nmm.ac.uk
National Register of Archives: www.nationalarchives.gov.uk/nra/default.asp
National War Museum, Edinburgh: www.nms.ac.uk/our_museums/war_museum.aspx
Our Secret War: oral history films of Britain's covert activities during the Second World War:
    www.our-secret-war.org/Introduction.html
Peace Pledge Union (includes details of researching conscientious objectors):
    www.ppu.org.uk/coproject/guide.html
PMRAFNS: www.raf.mod.uk/PMRAFNS/history/princessmary.cfm
Prisoners of War: www.btinternet.com/~prosearch/tomspage19.html
QARANC: http://qaranc.co.uk
Queen's Nursing Institute: www.qni.org.uk
Reading University's Research Centre for Evacuee and War Child Studies:
    www.reading.ac.uk/merl/collections/merl-archives.aspx
Reporting the English Civil War: www.reportingtheenglishcivilwar.wordpress.com
Roll of Auxiliary Home Hospitals in England and Wales 1914-1919:
    www.juroch.demon.co.uk/UKhospitals.htm
Roll of Honour: www.roll-of-honour.com/Databases
Royal Air Force Museum: www.rafmuseum.org.uk
Royal Armouries: www.royalarmouries.org
Royal College of Nursing Archive: http://rcnarchive.rcn.org.uk
Royal Naval Museum, Portsmouth: www.royalnavalmuseum.org
Royal Signals Museum and Archives: useful for Special Operations Executive:
    http://royalsignalsmuseum.co.uk
St Andrew's First Aid: www.firstaid.org.uk
Scarletfinders: www.scarletfinders.co.uk
Scottish Medical Service Emergency Committee - Index of Doctors in Scotland During The
    First World War: http://smsec.rcpe.ac.uk/
Scottish National War Memorial: www.snwm.org
Screenonline: guide to Britain's film and TV history: www.screenonline.org.uk
Sea Your History: twentieth century Royal Navy history: www.seayourhistory.org.uk
Second World War Experience Centre: www.war-experience.org
Service Personnel & Veterans Agency: www.veterans-
    uk.info/service_records/service_records.html
Society of Friends Library: www.quaker.org.uk/library
Society of Genealogists: www.sog.org.uk
Soldiers Letters (includes letters of nurses and other women):
    http://soldierletters.blogspot.co.uk/
The Army Children Archive: www.archhistory.co.uk/taca/home.html
The Genealogist: www.thegenealogist.co.uk

The Home Guard: www.home-guard.org.uk

The Long, Long Trail: The British Army in the Great War: www.1914-1918.net

The National Archives (UK): www.nationalarchives.gov.uk

The National Archives research guide on the Home Front 1939-1945, includes a Women at War section: www.nationalarchives.gov.uk/records/research-guides/home-front-1939-1945.htm

The Welsh Experience of World War One: http://cymruww1.llgc.org.uk/

Uboat.net - Ships hits by U-boats in WWII (includes passenger names): http://uboat.net/allies/merchants/

Victorian Wars Forum: www.victorianwars.com

WAACs online exhibition from the National Army Museum: www.nam.ac.uk/exhibitions/online-exhibitions/waacs-war

Wartime Memories Project: Women: www.wartimememoriesproject.co.uk/women

Wellcome Library electronic resources: http://library.wellcome.ac.uk/eresources.html

Wartime West Sussex 1939-1945: www.westsussex.gov.uk/learning/learning_resources/wartime_west_sussex_1939-45.aspx

Western Front Association: www.westernfrontassociation.com

Women at War website: http://caber.open.ac.uk/schools/stanway/index.html

Women's Land Army Leavenheath Hostel 1942-1950: www.bures.me.uk/wla/wla.htm

Women of the Air Force Online Exhibition: www.rafmuseum.org.uk/research/online-exhibitions/women-of-the-air-force.aspx

Women's Royal Army Corps Association: www.wracassociation.org.uk

Women's Timber Corps: www.forestry.gov.uk/womenstimbercorps

Women's War Services (Podcast 30) - First World War Centenary: www.1914.org/podcasts/podcast-30-womens-war-services/

World War One document Archive: www.lib.byu.edu/index.php/Main_Page

World War Two Survivors: The Women's Land Army and Timber Corps: http://landarmy.org.uk/home.html

Association of WRENS: www.wrens.org.uk

WW1 Centenary: Great War Centenary 2014-2018 website by Paul Reed: http://ww1centenary.net/

WWI Women's Organisations (The Long, Long Trail): www.1914-1918.net/women_orgs.htm

SoG indicates that there is a copy in the Society of Genealogists Library.

General

Ruth Adam, *A Woman's Place 1910-1975* (1975).

Kate Adie, *From Corsets to Camouflage: Women and War* (Hodder and Stoughton, 2003).

Mary Elizabeth Ailes, 'Camp Followers, Sutlers, and Soldiers' Wives'.

Margaret Barrow, *Women, 1870-1928: A Select Guide to Printed and Archival Sources in the United Kingdom* (Mansell, 1981).

Deirdre Beddoe, *Back to Home and Duty: Women Between the Wars 1919-1939* (River Oram Press, 1989).

Shleford Bidwell, *The Women's Royal Army Corps: Famous Regiments series* (Leo Cooper, 1977). SoG

Joanna Dean, *Women's archives guide: manuscript sources for the history of women* (National Archives or Canada, 1991). SoG

Eva Figes (ed.), *Women's letters in wartime 1450-1945* (Harper Collins, 1993). SoG

Nigel Fountain (ed.), *Women at War* (Michael O'Mara, 2002).

Clare Gibson, *Army Childhood: British Army Children's Lives and Times* (Shire Books, 2012).

Colonel Eric Gruber von Arni and Major Gary Searle, *Sub Cruce Candida 1902-2002: A celebration of one hundred years of Army Nursing* (The Queen Alexandra's Royal Army Nursing Corps Association, 2002).

H. Gwynne-Vaughan, *Service with the Army* (Hutchinson, 1942).

Janie Hampton, *How the girl guides won the war* (Harper Press, 2010).

Mary Ingham, *Tracing Your Service Women Ancestors: A Guide for Family Historians* (Pen and Sword, 2012).

Rose Kerr, *Story of the Girl Guides 1908-1938* (Girl Guides Association, 1976).

Mary Ann Lind, *The Compassionate Memsahibs: Welfare Activities of British Women in India, 1900-1947* (Greenwood Press, 1988).

Gillian McIntosh and Diana Urquhart, *Irish Women at War* (Irish Academic Press, 2010).

David Mitchell, *Women on the Warpath* (Jonathan Cape, 1966).

Lucy Noakes, *Women in the British Army: War and the Gentle Sex, 1907-1948* (Routledge, 2006).

William Spencer, *Family History in the Wars: Find how your ancestors served their country* (The National Archives, 2007). SoG

William Spencer, *Medals: The Researcher's Guide* (PRO, 2006). SoG

James Sutherland, 'The Distinguished Service Order 1924-2008' (2009). SoG

Roy Terry, *Women in Khaki: the Story of the British Woman Soldier* (Columbus 1988). SoG

D. Collett Wadge, *Women in Uniform* (1946, IWM reprint 2003).

Julie Wheelwright, *Amazons and Military Maids* (Pandora, 1999).

Women with the British Army (London: War Office, 1956). SoG

British women in conflict up to the mid nineteenth century

John Adair, By the sword divided: eyewitness accounts of the English civil war (Sutton Publishing Ltd, 1998). SoG

G E Aylmer, The civil war & interregnum: sources for local historians (National Council of Social Service, 1979). SoG

Maureen Bell, *Martha Simmonds* (Oxford DNB, 2004) F C Blackburne (ed.), *The manuscripts of the Marquess of Abergavenny, Lord Braye, G F Luttrell Esq. &c.* (includes the manuscripts of P Pleydell Bouverie, W Bromley Davenport & B R T Balfour) (HMSO, 1887). SoG

Stephen Bull, *The civil war in Lancashire* (Lancashire County Books, 1991). SoG

Kay Collins (ed.), A Georgian country parson: the Rev. John Mastin of Naseby (Northamptonshire Record Society, 2004). SoG

F H Blackburne Daniell et al., *The manuscripts of the Earl of Buckingham, the Earl of Lindsey, the Earl of Onslow, Lord Emly, Theodore J Hare Esq., & James Round Esq., MP* (HMSO, 1895). SoG

Daniel Defoe, *The Life and Adventures of Mrs Christian Davies, Commonly Called Mother Ross* (London: 1740) Google Books This account is exaggerated, but historians broadly agree that Davies did exist.

Jacqueline Eales, *Puritans and Roundheads* (Hardinge Simpole Publishing, 2001).

Wilfrid Emberton, *The English civil war day by day* (Sutton Publishing Ltd, 1995). SoG

Alan Everitt, *Suffolk & the great rebellion 1640-60 : Suffolk Records Society, vol. 3* (Suffolk Records Society, 1960). SoG

Antonia Fraser, *The Weaker Vessel* (Weidenfeld & Nicolson, 1984).

Peter Gaunt, *The Cromwellian gazetteer: an illustrated guide to Britain in the civil war & commonwealth* (The Cromwell Association ; Sutton Publishing Ltd, 1987). SoG

Tim Goodwin, *Dorset in the Civil War 1625-65* (Dorset Books, 1996). SoG

Elspeth Graham, *Her Own Life* (Routledge, 1989).

Malcolm Gratton, *Liverpool under parliament: the anatomy of a civil war garrison, May 1643 to June 1644: Transactions of the Historic Society of Lancashire & Cheshire, vol. 156* (The Historic Society of Lancashire & Cheshire, 2008). SoG

Jill Groves, *The impact of civil war on a community : Northenden & Etchells in Cheshire 1642-60* (Northern Writers Advisory Services, 1992). SoG

Barton C. Hacker, 'Women and Military Institutions in Early Modern Europe: A Reconnaissance', Signs, Vol. 6 (1981): 643-71.

Letters of the Lady Brilliana Harley (1854; Volume: 58, Printed for the Camden Society Year)

Healy and Sawday (ed.), *Literature and the English Civil War* (Cambridge University Press,

P M Higgins, *Women in the English Civil War* (Unpublished thesis, Manchester University, 1965).

Roger Hudson, *The Grand Quarrel: Women's Memoirs of the English Civil War* (Sutton Publishing Ltd, 2000).

Lucy Hutchinson, *Memoirs of the Life of Colonel Hutchinson*.

Thomas Taylor Lewis (ed.), *Letters of Brilliana Harley, wife of Sir Robert Harley of Brampton Bryan, Knight of Bath (1625-43)*, (Camden Society, vol. 58, 1854). SoG

John A Lynn II, *Women, Armies, and Warfare in Early Modern Europe* (Cambridge University Press, 2008).

Rosemary Anne Moore, *The Light in Their Consciences: Early Quakers in Britain* (Penn State Press, 2000).

Alison Plowden, *Women All On Fire: The Women of the English Civil War* (The History Press, 2004).

Matthew Stephens, *Hannah Snell: The Secret Life of a Female Marine, 1723-1792* (Matthew Stephens, 1997). SoG

Adrian Tinniswood, *The Verneys: Love, War and Madness in Seventeenth-Century England* (Vintage, 2008). SoG

David Weigall, 'Women Militants In The English Civil War' in *History Today*, 22:6 (1972, June, p.434).

Contemporary European History, Vol. 10, Issue 3: 'From Camp Follower to Lady in Uniform: Women, Social Class and Military Institutions before 1920'.

Letters on camp followers in *Family Tree* Magazine, Issue 2, volume 20, page 68 and Issue 5, volume 12, page 46. SoG

The Victorian Era

Monica E Baly, *A History of the Queen's Nursing Institute 100 years 1887-1987* (Croom Helm, 1987).

Brian Best and Kate Slossel, *Sister Janet: Nurse and Heroine of the Anglo-Zulu War 1879* (Pen & Sword, 2006).

Mark Bostridge, *Florence Nightingale: the woman and her legend* (Penguin, 2009).

Margaret Breay, Editorial, 'The nursing of the sick under Queen Victoria', *British Medical Journal*, 1897.

Kellow Chesney, *Crimean War Reader* (1960).

R M Coopland, *A Lady's Escape from Gwalior and Life in the Fort of Agra During the Mutinies of 1857* (Elder Smith, 1859). Google Books

Elizabeth Davis, *The autobiography of Elizabeth Davis, a Balaclava nurse, daughter of Dafydd Cadwaladyr*, ed. Jane Wiliams (Hurst and Blackett, 1857).

Byron Farwell, *Queen Victoria's Little Wars* (1973).

Sheila Gray, *The South African War 1899-1902: service records of British and colonial women: a record of the service in South Africa of military and civilian nurses* (Shelia M Gray, 1993). SoG

Elizabeth S Haldane, *The British Nurse in Peace and War* (Murray, 1913).

John Hannay, *The Crimea Goes To War - Photographs from the Crimean War* (Edinburgh, 1974).

Kathleen Harland, *Queen Alexandra's Royal Naval Nursing Service* (G. Shepherd Ltd). SoG

Ian Hay, *One hundred years of Army nursing the story of the British Army Nursing Services from the time of Florence Nightingale to the present day* (1953).

Michelle Higgs, *Tracing Your Medical Ancestors* (Pen & Sword, 2011). SoG

R G Huntsman, Mary Bruin & Deborah Holttum, 'Twixt candle and lamp: the contribution of Elizabeth Fry and the Institution of Nursing Sisters to Nursing Reform'. (*Med Hist*ory 2002 July; 46(3): 351-380.).

Lawrence James, *Crimea 1854-56. The war with Russia from Contemporary Photographs* (1981).

Catharine Grace Loch, *A Memoir, by Catharine Grace Loch, Royal Red Cross, Senior Lady Superintendent Queen Alexandra's Military Nursing Service for India* (1905). Archive.org

Lynn McDonald, 'Florence Nightingale and Mary Seacole: Nursing's Bitter Rivalry' (*History Today*, Volume 62, Issue 9, 2012).

Florence Nightingale, *Notes on Matters Affecting the Health, Efficiency and Hospital Administration of the British Army* (1858).

Florence Nightingale, *Collected Works of Florence Nightingale*.

Florence Nightingale, *Letters from Egypt* (Barrie & Jenkins, 1987). SoG

Thomas Packenham, *The Boer War* (1979).

QARANC, *Sub Cruce Candida: A celebration of one hundred years of Army Nursing 1902-2002* (QARANC Association, 2002).

Alan Ramsay Shelley, *The Victorian Army at Home* (London, 1977).

Edward M Spiers, *The Late Victorian Army* (Manchester University Press, 1992). SoG

Anne Summers, *Angels and Citizens: British Women as Military Nurses 1854-1914* (1987).

Myna Trustram, *Women of the Regiment; marriage and the Victorian Army.* Google Books

A N Wilson, *The Victorians* (Arrow, 2003).

WWI

Commandant Mary S Allen, *The Pioneer Policewoman* (Chatto & Windus, 1925).

Mary S Allen, *Lady in Blue* (Stanley Paul & Co. Ltd, 1936). SoG

Ian Beckett, *Home Front 1914-1918: How Britain Survived the Great War* (The National Archives, 2006).

Ian F W Beckett, *The First World War* (PRO, 2002).

Reginald H Brazier & Ernest Sandford, *Birmingham and the Great War 1914-1919 Birmingham in World War 1 (1914-1919)* (Solihull: Historical Data, 2003; original 1921) CD-ROM. SoG

Brian Bond, ed.. *The First World War and British Military History* (Oxford, 1991).

Thekla Bowser, *Britain's Civilian Volunteers: Authorized Story of British Voluntary Aid Detachment Work In The Great War* (1925; IWM reprint 2003).

Chris Brader, 'Policing the Gretna Girls: the Women's Police Service in World War I' (MA dissertation, University of Warwick, 1997).

Gail Braybon, *Women Workers in the First World War* (London, 1981).

Gail Braybon and Penny Summerfield, *Out of the Cage: Women's Experiences in Two World Wars* (London, 1987).

Paul Calahan, *Belgian Refugee Relief in England during the Great War* (New York, 1982).

Molly Coleclough, *Women's Legion 1916-1920* (Spearman, 1940).

Diana Condell & Jean Liddiard, *Working for Victory? Images of Women in the First World War* (Routledge Kegan & Paul, 1987).

Stephen Constantine, Maurice Kirby & Mary Rose (ed.), *The First World War Experienced* (London, 1996).

R M Douglas, *Feminist Freikorps: the British voluntary women police, 1914-1940* (Praeger, 1999).

V Douglas-Pennant, *Under the Searchlight* (Allen & Unwin, 1922).

Deborah Dwork, *War is Good for Babies and Other Young Children* (London, 1987).

Millicent Garrett Fawcett, *The Women's Victory - and After: Personal Reminiscences, 1911-1918*, (Sidgwick and Jackson, 1920).

H Gwynne-Vaughan, *The Junior Leader* (Hutchinson & Co., 1943).

Simon Fowler, *Tracing Your First World War Ancestors* (Countryside Books, 2008). SoG

Helen Fraser, *Women and War Work* (Arnold Shaw, 1918).

Susan R Grayzel, *Women and the First World War* (Longman, 2002).

Gerrard De Groot, *Blighty: British Society in the Era of the Great War* (London, 1996).

Andrew and Nicola Hallam, *Lady Under Fire on the Western Front: The Great War Letters of Lady Dorothie Feilding MM* (Pen & Sword, 2010).

Geoffrey Handley-Taylor, (comp.) ed., *Winifred Holtby (1898-1935): a concise & selected bibliography together with some letters* (A Brown & Sons Ltd, 1955). SoG

Marjory Harper, Stephen Constantine, *Migration and Empire. The Oxford History of the British Empire Companion Series* (Oxford: Oxford University Press, 2010).

Ada Harrison (ed), *Grey and Scarlet: Letters from the war areas by Army sisters on active service* (Hodder and Stoughton, 1944).

Nona Hermon-Hodge (The Hon. Mrs. Hermon-Worsley), *Call of the Land* (G. Allen & Unwin Ltd, 1936).

Gaynor Kavanagh, *Museums and the First World War: A Social History* (Leicester, 1994).

Monica Krippner, *The Quality of Mercy: Women at War. Serbia 1915-18* (David and Charles, Newton Abbot, 1980).

Dorothy Lawrence, *Sapper Dorothy Lawrence: The Only English Woman Soldier, Late Royal Engineers, Fifty-First Division 179th Tunnelling Company* (J Lane, 1919).

J H Leslie, *An Historical Roll (with Portraits) of Those Women of the British Empire to Whom the Military Medal Has Been Awarded During the Great War, 1914-1918, for 'Bravery and Devotion Under Fire.'* (Sir W C Leng, 1919).

Peter Liddle, ed., *Home Fires and Foreign Fields: British Social and Military Experiences in the First World War* (London, 1985).

Catriona Macdonald and E W McFarland, eds., *Scotland and the Great War* (East Linton, 1999).

Joyce Marlow (ed.), *The Virago Book of Women and the Great War* (Virago, 1999).

Arthur Marwick, *Women at War 1914-1918* (Fontana, 1977).

Arthur Marwick, *The Deluge: British Society and the First World War* (1965).

David John B. Mitchell, *Women on the warpath: the story of the women of the First World War* (1924; Cape, 1966).

Sharon Ouditt, *Women Writers of the First World War* (Routledge, 2000).

E Sylvia Pankhurst, *The Home Front* (Hutchinson & Co. Ltd, 1932).

Mrs C S Peel, *How We Lived Then, 1914-1918: a Sketch of Social and Domestic Life in England during the War* (Bodley Head, 1929).

Juliet Piggott, *Queen Alexandra's Royal Army Nursing Corps* (Leo Cooper, 1975 and 1990). SoG

Tammy M Procter, *Female Intelligence: Women and Espionage in the First World War.* (New York University Press, 2003).

Martin Pugh, *Women's Suffrage in Britain, 1867-1928* (London, 1980).

Martin Pugh, *Women and the Women's Movement in Britain, 1914-59* (London, 1992).

Peter Rees, *The Other ANZACS: Nurses at War, 1914-1918* (Allen & Unwin, 2008).

Flora Sandes, *The Autobiography of a Woman Soldier: A Brief Record of Adventure with the Serbian Army 1916-1919* (Hodder & Stoughton, 1927).

Elizabeth Shipton, *Female Tommies: The Frontline Women of the First World War* (The History Press, 1914).

Angela K Smith, *The Second Battlefield: Women, Modernism and the First World War* (MUP, 2000).

Angela Smith, *Women's Writing of the First World War* (MUP, 2000) - unpublished letters.

Neil B Storey & Molly Housego, *Women in the First World War* (Shire Library, 2010).

Kate Summerscale, *The Queen of Whale Cay: The Extraordinary Story of 'Joe' Carstairs, the Fastest Woman on Water* (Bloomsbury, 2012).

Deborah Thom, *Nice Girls and Rude Girls: Women Workers in World War I* (IB Tauris, 2000).

Helen G Wilkie, *The work of the Women's Emergency Canteens in France: 1915-1919*, compiled by Josephine Davies (Women's Printing Society, 1919).

Jay Winter and Richard Wall, eds, *The Upheaval of War: Family, Work and Welfare in Europe, 1914-1918* (Cambridge, 1988).

Women's (later Queen Mary's) Army Auxiliary Corps: WO 398 service record 1917-1920 (microfilm) (TNA). SoG

WRAF, *Women of the Royal Air Force on the Rhine* (Bachem, Cologne, 1919).

WRAF, *Handbook for WRAF* (Gale & Polden, 1919).

Louise Miller, *A Fine Brother: The Life of Captain Flora Sandes* (Alma Books Ltd, 2012).

Munitions and other factory work

Lottie Barker, 'My Life as I Remember It, 1899-1920', Brunel University Library (TS).

Ursula Birsting, *Autobiography, item 12, Liddle Collection.*

Sir Hall Caine, *Our Girls: their work for the war* (Hutchinson & Co., 1916).

Monica Cousens, *Lloyd George's Munition Girls* (London, 1916).

A K Foxwell, *Munition lasses six months as Principal Overlooker in Danger Buildings* (Hodder & Stoughton, 1917).

Elizabeth Gore *The Better Fight: the story of Dame Lilian Barker* by (Geoffrey Bles, 1965).

Peggy Hamilton, *Three years or the duration: the memoirs of a munitions worker, 1914-1918* (Peter Owen).

Marion Kozak, 'Women Munition Workers During the First World War with Special Reference to Engineering.' D. Phil. Thesis, University of Hull, 1976. (online at BL)

Annie Lord, 'My Life' (Brunel University Library, MS).

Barbara Ludlow, *She can sew a flannel cartridge: a brief social history of the Royal Arsenal* (1995).

Charlotte Meadowcroft, 'Bygones' (Brunel University Library, MS).

Ministry of Munitions, *Official History of the Scottish Filling Factory no. 4 (National), Georgetown, Renfrewshire.* (Glasgow, 1919) BL, IWM, NLS, NMM University of Glasgow.

Grace N. Pond, *The Forgotten Workforce: Women Gas Workers of the First World War* (Greater London Industrial Archaeology Society).

Elena Savvides, *An investigation into the pay, conditions and domestic lives of women munitions workers at the Woolwich Arsenal in the period 1914-1918* (Unpublished, 1987).

D Thom, *Women Munition Workers at Woolwich Arsenal in the 1914-1918 War* (MA Dissertation, University of Warwick, 1975).

Angela Woollacott, *On Her Their Lives Depend: Munitions Workers in the Great War* (University of California Press, 1994).

Miss Joan Williams, *A Munition Worker's Career at Messrs Gwynnes, Ltd., Chiswick, 1915-1919.* (documentary record). IWM

'T.N.T. Poisoning at Woolwich Arsenal', *The Pioneer,* 23 June 1916.

Between the Wars

Angela Jackson, *For Us It Was Heaven: The Passion, Grief & Fortitude of Patience Darton* (Sussex Academic Press, 2012).

Angela Jackson, *British Women and the Spanish Civil War* (Routledge, 2002).

Paul Preston, *Doves of War: Four Women of the Spanish Civil War* (Harper Collins, 2010).

WWII

Lincolnshire women at war: the vital role they played during World War II. A compilation of entries from the 1997 Women at War competition organised by Heritage Lincolnshire. (Heckington Heritage, 1997). SoG

Patsy Adam-Smith, *Australian Women At War* (Penguin Books, 1996).

Patsy Adam-Smith, *Prisoners Of War From Gallipoli to Korea* (Viking, 1992).

Alan Allport, *Demobbed: Coming Home After the Second World War* (Yale University Press, 2009).

Barbara Angell, *Wilma, a Woman's War, the exceptional life of Wilma Oram Young AM* (New Holland Publishers, 2003).

Pat Ayers, *Women at war: Liverpool women 1939-45* (Liver Press, 1988). SoG

Jill Banks, *Secrets and Soldiers, Kedleston Hall 1939-45* (National Trust booklet).

J Bassett, (ed.) *As We Wave You Goodbye: Australian Women and War* (Oxford University Press 1998).

Eileen Bigland, *The Britain's Other Army: the story of the A.T.S.* (Nicholson and Watson, 1946).

Angela Bolton, *The Maturing Sun: an army nurse in India 1942-45* (Imperial War Museum, 1986).

Ben Bousquet and Colin Douglas, *West Indian Women at War: British Racism in World War II* (Lawrence & Wishart Ltd, 1990).

Angus Calder, *The People's War* (Pimlico, 1969).

P G Cambray and G G B Briggs, *Red Cross and St John War History 1939-1947* (London: Red Cross, 1949). IWM

Anthony Cotterell, *She Walks in Battledress: the day's work in the A.T.S.* (Christophers, 1942).

Amy de la Haye, *Land Girls: Cinderellas of the Soil* (Royal Pavilion Libraries & Museums, 2009).

Anne de Courcy, *Debs at War: 1939-1945* (W&N, 2005).

The Pageant of the Lamp (Edison Swan Electric Co., c1949).

Theodora Fitzgibbon, *With Love* (1982) and *Love Lies a Loss* (1985).

Helen Fry, *The M-Room* (CreateSpace Independent Publishing Platform, 2012).

Peter Fryer, *Staying Power: The history of black people in Britain* (Pluto Press, 1984).

Midge Gillies, *The Barbed-Wire University: The Real Lives of Prisoners of War in the Second World War* (Aurum, 2012).

Clare Hardy, *SS Ceramic: The Untold Story* (Central Publishing, 2006).

Jacky Hyams, *Bomb Girls: Britain's Secret Army: the Munitions Women of World War II* (John Blake Publishing Ltd, 2013).

S Hardisty (ed.), *Thanks Girls and Goodbye: The Story of the Australian Women's Land Army 1942-1945* (Viking O'Neil, 1990).

S. Isaacs (ed), *The Cambridge Evacuation Survey* (Methuen, 1941).

Betty Jeffrey, *White Coolies* (Panther, 1963).

C Kenny, *Captives: Australian Army Nurses in Japanese Prison Camps* (University of Queensland Press, 1986).

Dorothy Brewer Kerr, *The girls behind the guns: with the A.T.S. in World War II* (Hale, 1990). SoG

Romie Lambkin, *My Time in the War: an Irishwoman's Diary* (Wolfhound Press, 1992).

Nella Last, *Nella Last's War: The Second World War Diaries of 'Housewife, 49'* (Profile Books, 2006). SoG

K D Luke, *Luke's Log* (Janus Publishing, 2005).

Ivor Matanle, *World War II* (Colour Library Books, Godalming, Surrey, 1989).

Brenda McBryde, *A Nurse's War* (Chatto and Windus, 1979).

Brenda McBryde, *Quiet Heroines* (Chatto and Windus, 1985).

Dr Stephen M Cullen, *The Home Guard and the Defence of the United Kingdom 1940-1944* (Pen & Sword, 2011).

E Brian Munt, *A Short History of Ediswan* (1989).

R M Neill-Fraser, *We Serve* (Hodder and Stoughton, 1942).

Mavis Nicholson, *What did you do in the War, Mummy?* (London: Chatto & Windus, 1995).

Virginia Nicholson, *Millions Like Us: Women's Lives in the Second World War* (Penguin, 2012).

J B Priestley, *British Women Go to War* (Collins, 1943).

Stuart A Raymond, *The Home Front 1939-1945: A Guide for Family Historian* (The Family History Partnership, 2012). SoG

Gwladys M. Rees Aikens, *Nurses in Battledress* (Nimbus Publishing, Halifax, N.S., Canada, 1998).

Vee Robinson, *On Target* (Verity Press, 1991).

Charles G Roland, *Long Night's Journey into Day* (Wilfrid Laurier University Press, Canada, 2001).

R Samways, *We think you ought to go.* (Greater London Record Office, 1995).

W E Shewell-Cooper, *Land Girl: A Manual for Volunteers in the Women's Land Army* (originally published 1941; present edition Amberley Publishing, 2011).

Jessie Elizabeth Simons, *In Japanese Hands* (Heinemann, 1985).

Daniel Smith, *The Spade is Mightier than the Sword: The Story of World War Two's Dig for Victory Campaign* (Aurum Press, 2011).

Neil R Storey and Molly Housego, *Women in the Second World War* (Shire Library, 2011).

Penny Summerfield and Corinna Peniston-Bird, *Contesting Home Defence* (Manchester University Press, 2007).

Obituary of Phyllis Thom (*The Times*, Thursday September 18, 2008).

Phil Tomaselli, *Tracing Your Second World War Ancestors* (Pen & Sword, 2011). SoG

Carol Twinch, *Women on the land: their story during two world wars* (Cambridge: Lutterworth Press, 1990). SoG

Nicola Tyler, *They Fought in The Fields: the story of a forgotten victory* (Arrow, 1999).

Stephen Wade, *Air Raid Shelters of the Second World War* (Pen & Sword, 2011). SoG

Sylvia Wild, *Women at the Front: Memoirs of an ATS Girl* (Amberley, 2012).

Mary Ziegler, *We Serve That Men May Fly - The Story of the Women's Division of the Royal Canadian Air Force* (RCAF (WD) Association, 1973).

ATA

Air Transport Auxiliary, *Air Transport Auxiliary* (Handbook) (White Waltham, 1945).

E C Cheeseman, *Brief Glot: The Story of the A.T.A.* (Harborough Pub. Co., 1946). Lettice Curtis. *The Forgotten Pilots: A Story of the Air Transport Auxiliary, 1939-45* (Nelson & Saunders, 1985).

Michael Fahie, *A Harvest of Memories: The Life of Pauline Gower M.B.E.* (GMS Enterprises, 1995).

Jacky Hyams, *The Female Few: Spitfire Heroines of the Air Transport Auxiliary* (The History Press, 2012).

Betty Lussier, *Intrepid Woman, Betty Lussier's Secret War, 1942-1945* (2010).

Helena Schrader, *Sisters in Arms.* (Pen & Sword Aviation, 2006).

Diana Barnato Walker, *Spreading My Wings* (Patrick Stephens. 1994).

Giles Whittell, *Spitfire Women of World War Two* (HarperPress, 2007).

WAAF

Air Ministry, *The Second World War, 1939-45: The Women's Auxiliary Air Force* (1953)

Bette Anderson, *We just got on with it: British women in World War II* (Picton Publishing, 1994). SoG

C Babington-Smith, *Evidence in Camera* (David & Charles, 1957).

E R Baker, *WAAF Adventure* (Lonsdale, 1946).

K B Beauman, *Partners in Blue* (Hutchinson, 1971).

K B Beauman, *Wings on her Shoulders* (Hutchinson, 1943).

Pip Beck, *A WAAF in Bomber Command* (Goodall Publications, 1989).

D Came, *The Eyes of the Few* (PR Macmillan, 1960).

Sqn Ldr Beryl Escott, *The WAAF* (Shire, 2003). SoG

Beryl E Escott, *Women in Air Force Blue: the story of women in the Royal Air Force from 1918 to the present day* (Stephens, 1989). SoG

Beryl E Escott, *The WAAF in Bomber Command in The Means of Victory* (Bomber Command Association, 1992).

Forbes & Portal, *Book of the WAAF* (Amalgamated Press Ltd, 1942).

John Frayn Turner, *WAAF At War* (Pen & Sword Aviation, 2011). SoG

D G Luke, *My Road to Bletchley Park: The Memoirs of WAAF LACW 2068978 Doreen Gertrude Spencer 1941-1946* (1999). SoG

Genevieve Moulard, *Les Femmes de la Royal Air Force: Engagees vers la victoire 1918-1945* (Marines Edition, 2012).

Clare Mulley, *The Spy Who Loved: The secrets and lives of Christine Granville* (Macmillan, 2012).

S Pickering, *Tales of a Bomber Command WAAF (and her horse)* (Woodfield, 2002).

Sylvia Skimmin, *Sand in my Shoes* (Oliver and Boyd, 1948).

A N Small, *Spit, Polish and Tears: Stories of WAAFs in World War II* (1995).

The WAAF in Action (Adam & Charles Black, 1942).

T Stone, *The integration of Women into Military Service: WAAF in WWII* (CUP, 1998).

Spies and Intelligence Work

Joan Bright Astley, *The Inner Circle* (Memoir Club, 2007).

L Atherton, *Top Secret: An Interim Guide to Recent Releases of Intelligence Records at the Public Record Office* (London, 1993).

Kathryn Atwood, *Women Heroes of WWII: 26 Stories of Espionage, Sabotage, Resistance* (Chicago Review Press, 2011).

Roderick Bailey, *Forgotten Voices of the Secret War* (Ebury Press in association with the Imperial War Museum, 2008).

Shrabani Basu, *Spy Princess: The Life of Noor Inayat Khan* (Sutton Publishing, 2006).

Marcus Binney, *The Women Who Lived For Danger: The Women Agents of SOE in the Second Word War* (Coronet Books, 2003).

Josephine Butler, *Churchill's Secret Agent* (Blaketon-Hall, 1984).

Robin Denniston, *Churchill's Secret War Diplomatic Decrypts, the Foreign Office and Turkey, 1942-44* (The History Press, 2009).

B E Escott, *Mission Improbable* (Patrick Stephens, 1991).

M R D Foot, *SOE in France* (Frank Cass Publishers, 2004).

Sarah Helm *A Life in Secrets: The Story of Vera Atkins and the Lost Agents of SOE* (Brown, 2005).

Sir Harry Hinsley (ed.), *British Intelligence in the Second World War* (HMSO, 4 volumes, 1979-1993).

Richard Holmes, *Churchill's Bunker: The Secret Headquarters at the Heart of Britain's Victory* (Profile Books, 2009).

Sophie Jackson, *Churchill's Unexpected Guests: Prisoners of War in Britain in World War II* (The History Press, 2010).

Liane Jones, *A Quiet Courage: Heart-stopping accounts of those brave women agents who risked their lives in Nazi-occupied France* by (Corgi Books, 1991).

R V Jones, *Most Secret War* (Penguin, 2009).

R Kramer, *Flames in the Field* (Michael Joseph, 1995).

Leo Marks, *Between Silk & Cyanide: A Codemaker's War, 1941 - 1945* (The Free Press, 1999)

Sinclair McKay, *The Secret Life of Bletchley Park: The History of the Wartime Codebreaking Centre by the Men and Women Who Were There* (Aurum Press, 2011).

Janet Morgan, *Secrets of Rue St Roch: Intelligence Operations Behind Enemy Lines in the First World War* (Allen Lane, 2004).

J Overton-Fuller, *Noor-un-nisa Inayat Khan* (Gollancz, 1952).

U Powys-Lybbe, *The Eye of Intelligence* (Kimber, 1983).

Hugh Skillen, *Spies of the Airwaves: History of the Army Y Sections in the Second World War* (Hugh Skillen, 1989).

Michael Smith, *Six: History of Britain's Secret Intelligence Service, Part 1: Murder and Mayhem, 1909-1939* (Biteback, 2010).

Tania Szabo, *Young, Brave and Beautiful: the Missions of Special Operations Executive Agent, Lieutenant Violette Szabo, George Cross, Croix de Guerre avec Etoile de bronze* (St Helier, 2007).

Phil Tomaselli, *Tracing Your Secret Service Ancestors* (Pen & Sword, 2009).

Nancy Wake, *The White Mouse: the Autobiography of the Woman the Gestapo called The White Mouse* (Macmillan, 1986).

A M Walters, *Moondrop to Gascony* (Macmillan, 1946).

WRNS

Stephanie Batstone, *Wren's Eye View: Adventures of a Visual Signaller* (Parapress, 2001).

John D Drummond, *Blue for a Girl, the story of the WRNS* (1960).

Christian Lamb, *I Only Joined for the Hat: Redoubtable Wrens at War Their Trials Tribulations and Triumphs* (Bene Factum, 2007).

Vera Laughton Mathews, *Blue Tapestry* (Hollis & Carter, 1948).

Ursula Stuart Mason, *Britannia's daughters: the story of the WRNS* (Leo Cooper, 1992). SoG

Captain C M Taylor (ed.), *Nursing in the Senior Service 1902-2002: Personal Histories of Queen Alexandra's Royal Naval Nursing Service* (2001).

Bletchley Park (Station X)

Judith Brearley, Obituary of Marjorie Noble: www.guardian.co.uk/theguardian/2012/apr/11/marjorie-noble-obituary.

Stephen Harper, *Capturing Enigma* (The History Press, 2008).

F. H. Hinsley and Alan Stripp (ed.), *Codebreakers: The Inside Story of Bletchley Park* (2001).

Sir Harry Hinsley and Ted Enever, *Britain's Best Kept Secret: Ultra's Base at Bletchley Park*

Sinclair McKay, *The Secret Life of Bletchley Park: The History of the Wartime Codebreaking Centre by the Men and Women Who Were There* (Aurum, 2011).

Gwendoline Page (ed), *We Kept the Secret: Enigma Memories* (George R Reeve, 2004).

Page, Gwendoline, *Coconuts and Coral* (George R. Reeve Ltd., 1994).

- *Growing Pains: A Teenager's War* (Book Guild Ltd., 1994).

- *They Listened in Secret* (George R. Reeve, 2003).

- *The Chocolate Elephant* (George R Reeve, 2007).

- *A Tropical Adventure in the 1950s* (George R Reeve, 2010).

Michael Smith, *The Secrets of Station X: How the Bletchley Park codebreakers helped to win the war* (2011).

Christopher White, 'Bletchley Park codebreakers' in *Your Family Tree* (Spring, 2012).

Nursing and Medical Services

Sister Edith Appleton, *War Diaries: A Nurse at the Front* (Simon & Schuster, 2012).

Joan Ash, *Catch Me a Nightingale* (1991). BL

Dr Diane Atkinson, *Elsie & Mairi Go To War* (Arrow, 2010).

Lynette Beardwood, *F.A.N.Y. at the Western Front 1914-1919* (FANY, 1997).

Pat Beauchamp, *Fanny went to war* (Routledge, 1940).

Bendall & Raybould. *A History of the General Nursing Council for England and Wales 1919-1969* (Lewis, 1969).

A Bolton, *The Maturing Sun: an Army Nurse in India 1942-1945* (IWM, 1986).

Martin Brayley, *World War II Allied Nursing Services* (Osprey Publishing, 2002).

B Cowell and D Wainwright, *Behind the Blue Door: The History of the Royal College of Midwives 1881-1981* (Balliere Tindall, 1981).

Dame Katharine Furse GBE RRC, *Hearts and Pomegranates: the story of forty-five years 1875-1920* (Peter Davies, 1940).

Janet Lee, *War Girls: The First Air Nursing Yeomanry in the Great War* (MUP, 2005).

Lyn MacDonald, *The Roses of No Man's Land* (London: Michael Joseph, 1980).

Susan Mann (ed.), *The War Diary of Clare Gass 1915-1918* (McGill-Queen's University Press, 2004).

Brenda McBryde, *A Nurse's War* (Chatto & Windus, 1979).

Brenda McBryde, *Quiet Heroines* (Chatto & Windus, 1985).

McGann, Crowther, & Dougall, *A Voice for Nurses: a history of the Royal College of Nursing 1916-1990* (MUP, 2009).

Dame Beryl Oliver GBE, RRC, The British Red Cross in action (London, Faber & Faber, 1966).

Hugh Popham, *F.A.N.Y.; the story of the Women's Transport Services 1907-1984* (2003).

A M Rafferty and D Solano, 'The rise and demise of the Colonial Nursing Service', *Nursing History Review* (2007, 15, 147-54).

M Robertson, *Sister Sahibs; the VAD's with the 14th Army, 1944-46* (1987).

The Red Cross: *Official Journal of the British Red Cross Society* 1914-19.

Diana Shaw, 'The forgotten army of women: the overseas service of Queen Mary's Army Auxiliary Corps with the British Forces, 1917-1921' in Hugh Cecil & Peter Liddle (ed.s), Facing Armageddon: The First World War Experienced (Pen & Sword, 1996).

Diane Sloggett, *Angels of Burma* (The Pentland Press Ltd, Bishop Auckland Co., Durham, 2000).

Sir John Smythe, *The Will to Live: The Story of Dame Margot Turner DBE RRC* (Cassell, 1970).

Sir John Smythe, *In This Sign Conquer: The story of Army Chaplains* (A.R. Mowbray, 1968).

Penny Starns, *Nurses at War: Women on the Frontline 1939-45* (Sutton Publishing, 2000).

Eric Taylor, *Front Line Nurse* (Robert Hale, 1997).

Eric Taylor, *Combat Nurse* (Robert Hale, 1999).

Susan Travers, *Tomorrow to be Brave* (Corgi, 2000).

Nicola Tyrer, *Sisters in Arms: British Army Nurses Tell Their Story* (Phoenix, 2009).

Reports by the Joint War Committee and the Joint War Finance Committee of the British Red Cross Society and the Order of St John of Jerusalem in England on the voluntary aid rendered to the sick and wounded at home and abroad and to British Prisoners of war 1914-1919 (London: HMSO, 1921).

RECORDS

British Women in Conflict up to the Mid Nineteenth Century

Anglo Saxon Chronicle. A contemporary history of the period c890 to c1154. Useful for details of The Anarchy. The original is written in Anglo Saxon, but translations are available. An edited version can be found online at: www.britannia.com/history/docs/asintro2.html

Legal and court martial records. Women's names occasionally appear in these. Submitted reports to the Judge Advocate General on individual courts martial 1715-1790 are at TNA in WO 71/34-64.

Parish records where they exist and survive; check parish registers for 'civil marriages' that were officiated by a Justice of the Peace but often blessed later and entered into the church books.

Heraldic visitations (1630s and 1660s) useful for research into middle and upper class families.

Sequestration and royalist composition papers

Tax lists. Protestation Returns are held either at the Parliamentary Archives or in the relevant local archive, and some have been transcribed by local family history societies. Hearth Tax records are held at TNA. Surviving records of ship money, including names of individuals, are held in reference E 179 at TNA.

Dissenters' records. Oaths of Allegiance and Supremacy which were recorded in the Association Oath Rolls - TNA; State Papers - Quakers; Recusant Roles at TNA.

Quarter Session Records. Locate your female ancestor through her husband or boyfriend participation in the Civil Wars? Pensions of ordinary soldiers can be found in Quarter Session records (many have been indexed on Discovery).

State Papers Domestic at TNA.

Chancery Records. Where royalists' estates were confiscated 1642-1660, they were required to pay a fine to the Committee for Compounding. Their records, in the main, do not survive. However, sales of these lands can be found in the close rolls in C54 (index in IND 1/17354) TNA.

Newspaper records - the seventeenth & eighteenth Century Burney Collection Newspapers is available from Gale databases and can be searched online at many libraries, including the British Library and academic institutions. The Collection includes hundreds of titles (pamphlets, newsbooks and newspapers). Civil war tracts and contemporary newspapers can be found in the Thomason Collection at the British Library.

Court Records. Women, especially those accused of prostitution, may be found in the court records for this period including: www.oldbaileyonline.org 1674-1913 records of the Central Criminal Court. Eighteenth century equity courts - include marriage contracts, family disputes, estate and inheritance issues, and contested wills.

The Victorian Period

The Florence Nightingale Museum holds over 100 letters written by Florence Nightingale. These are being digitised. A further 700 letters have been deposited with London Metropolitan Archive (LMA). The Florence Nightingale Museum Trust holds the parts of the Nightingale Collection that are not held at LMA.

LMA

H54. Records of the Florence Nightingale Hospital for Gentlewomen, Lisson Grove (1892-1953).

A/NFC. Records of the Nightingale Fund Council, includes papers relating to the registration of nurses and nursing in general (1832-1977).

HO1. Records of the Saint Thomas's Hospital Group, including the Nightingale Training School and documents which form part of the Nightingale Collection in reference H1/ST/NC. An example record is ref. HO1/ST/NC/08/002 (microfilm X042/015) Agreement between Florence Nightingale and Emma Fagg, for the Employment as a Nurse for the Sick and Wounded of the British Army in Turkey (21 Oct 1854). Army nurses can be found by name in ref. HO1/ST/NCPH/D/I Staff: Individual Nurses.

CLA/069. Administrative records of St. Thomas's Hospital, 1580-1894, includes staffing information.

TNA

Online guide on researching British Army nurses: www.nationalarchives.gov.uk/records/looking-for-person/britisharmynurse.htm

WO 25/264 c.1851-c.1856. Letters of recommendation for nurses applying to go to the Crimea, arranged alphabetically in bundles.

WO 43/963 1853-1857. Nurses in the Crimea. Correspondence and memoranda.

WO 43/991 1855-1858. Lists of ladies, nurses and orderlies embarked for England from the Crimea.

PMG 34. Army Establishment: Schoolmistresses and Nurses Pensions (1909-1928). Records of pensions of schoolmistresses and nurses, but including some rewards to warrant officers given for distinguished or meritorious services from 1917 to 1921 otherwise found in PMG 36.

WO 32/6964. War Office and successors: Registered Files (General Series). Education: General (Code 33(A)): Revised scheme of pay, allowances and pension for army schoolmistresses to aid recruitment. (1891-1893)

WO 329/2134. Army Schoolmistresses other ranks: medal rolls ED/103A. Pages 1A-6A. British War Medal and Victory Medal.

WO 339. War Office: Officers' Services, First World War, Long Number Papers (numerical). Officers Services (including Civilian Dependants and Military Staff Appointments): Long Service Papers.

WO 372/23. War Office: Service Medal and Award Rolls Index, First World War.

WO 374. War Office: Officers' Services, First World War, personal files (alphabetical).

WO 361/2154. War Office: Department of the Permanent Under Secretary of State: Casualties (L) Branch: Enquiries into Missing Personnel, 1939-45 War. Prisoners of War, Far East: Army Education Corps (AEC) and Queen's Army Schoolmistresses; nominal roll.

WO 145 War Office: Registers of Recipients of the Royal Red Cross 1883-1994. Transcriptions on Findmypast.

WO100. Medal Rolls - includes nurses who served in Egypt, the Nile and Boer Wars DocumentsOnline.

WO25/3955. National Aid Society Nursing Sisters records 1869-1891. Transcriptions on Findmypast.

Imperial War Museum (IWM)
E.J. 1147. *The Link That Binds* (newsletter of the Queen's Army Schoolmistresses Association).

Sound recordings of army schoolmistresses

British Library (BL)
IOR: L/MIL/7. India Office Records Military Collection files, some include names of army schoolmistresses.

Military Collection 262A
Indian Nursing Service Papers of Sisters appointed to Service Files 81-99 (5).

IOR: L/MIL/7/11803 - Papers of Nurses appointed to INS.

Sound recordings

St. John Ambulance Association
AR.514. Annual report of Central Committee, etc. Holdings note: 1878-1963.

Online

Findmypast
Army Nursing Service: a small but significant set of 238 nurses of often quite genteel origin, born in the nineteenth century, includes TNA series WO25/3955 & 3956.

Royal Hospital Chelsea Nurses: records of 165 largely untrained nurses, born between 1839 and 1876, who served at the hospital for pensioned soldiers between 1856 and 1910.

Women in the First World War

TNA
PIN 15/418. Women's Corps: grant of pensions. Ministry of Pensions and successors: War Pensions, Registered Files (GEN Series) and other records 01 January 1919 - 31 December 1920.

WO 145. Roll of those awarded the Red Cross medal.

WO 372. WWI Army service medals.

MUN 7/34. Agreement between Women's Police Service and the Ministry (of Munitions) on provision of women police for ministry factories (14 November 1916-19 August 1919).

HO 45/309485. Further details on the women's police and women's patrols 1914-18.

MEPO 2/1708 and 1720. Their role in controlling prostitution in parks and open spaces .

MEPO 13/56-6. Two photographs of women police in 1918 .

MEPO 2/1710 and 1748. Details on the London Women's Patrol Committee.

NATS 1/1292. File on volunteer motor drivers (Volunteer Motor Mobilisation Corps].

WO 32/5531. War Office and successors: Registered Files (General Series). Civil Staffs (Outstations): General (Code 47(A)): Rates of pay and uniform for women forage guards.

LAB 5/1 includes reports on the block system at the London Omnibus Company.

MT 6 holds files on women who worked on the Glasgow and South Western Railway, 1915-17 (MT 6/2454/12) and tramway drivers 1915-18 (MT 6/250/1).

KV 1/50. A report by H Branch (Organisation and Administration) of MI5 prepared in 1921, includes a supplement on women's work for the bureau.

MAF 42/8. Women's Land Army - need for more effective control.

MAF 42. Papers on the Women's Land Army, Women's Legion Agricultural Section and Women's War Agricultural Committee (MAF 42/8), work co-ordinated by the Women's Branch of the Food Production Department established in January 1917.

MAF 59/1-3. Records of the Women's Land Army, including details of Women's County Committees, a handbook, and miscellaneous articles and photographs.

NATS 1/1279. Women's Agricultural Volunteers in Wales.

NATS 1/560-64 and 1203. Women agricultural workers, including the Scottish Women's Land Army Scheme in 1918.

NATS 1/549-50. Transfer of women from munitions work to agricultural work.

Women's Police Service.

MUN 7/34. Agreement between Women's Police Service and the Ministry (of Munitions) on provision of women police for ministry factories (14 November 1916-19 August 1919).

HO 45/309485. Further details on the women's police and women's patrols 1914-18.

MEPO 2/1708 and 1720. Women's role in controlling prostitution in parks and open spaces.

MEPO 13/56-6. Two photographs of women police in 1918.

MEPO 2/1710 and 1748. Details on the London Women's Patrol Committee.

MT 23/652. War bonuses paid to temporary women clerks in the Admiralty's Transport Department, 1916.

MH 57/183. Government Committee on the Prevention and Relief of Distress: Women's Emergency Corps, Local Registered Files and Papers, Prevention and Relief of Distress (1914).

BT 71/1-4. Labour of women is mentioned in the records of Board of Trade: Timber Disposal Department and predecessors.

BT 71/3. Women's work on timber production in the papers of the Timber Supply Department 1917-19.

National Roll of Honour/ National Roll of the Great War 1914-1918. Published in the early 1920s, this Roll was intended to record all military and civilian personnel who had contributed to victory. However, only 14 volumes were produced. SoG holds all of the volumes. Online, Ancestry has I London, III London, IV Southampton, VI Birmingham, VII London, VIII

Leeds, X Portsmouth, XI Manchester, XIV Salford, Birmingham Roll of Honour 1914-18. Copies can also be accessed at IWM.

The Police Federation of England and Wales
National Council of Women Collection.

PRONI

D/3099 Edith, Lady Londonderry's papers. The 7th Marquess of Londonderry Papers, consisting of the bulk of the papers of the 7th Marquess (1878-1949), and his wife, Edith Helen, the rest of which are in Durham; together with the papers of Lady Londonderry's father, Henry, 1st Viscount Chaplin.

London Transport Museum Library
The full catalogue of the Museum's unique collection of over 12,000 books, journals and special collections is not available online, but full details on access can be read at: www.ltmuseum.co.uk/collections/research/library

Personnel records of London's bus and tram workers are managed by the Transport for London Archives: www.tfl.gov.uk/corporate/historicalarchives/17333.aspx

The Women's Library @ LSE
8ODH/02/01/15. Oral recording of Mrs Annie Fry (c.1988): Topics discussed: work during First World War as conductress - interview for the job, working conditions and hours, uniforms, working day; demonstration for equal pay; losing her job after First World War; attempts to become a conductress during Second World War and husband's opposition. (AltRefNo: T073; Research notes available at 8ODH/01/01. Tape reference: W12, W15).
3AMS/4/10/3 'Bristol Training School for Women Patrols and Police', Annual Report for 1918.
Suffragist organisation records. The Women's Library @ LSE holds the Records of the Fawcett Society and its Predecessors (1871-1967) in reference 2LSW (includes that of the National Union of Women's Suffrage Societies (NUWSS)).

Museum of London
Suffragette papers (**WSPU archive**): an internationally important holding of suffragette material, based on the archive of the Women's Social and Political Union.

International Institute for Social History in Amsterdam
Sylvia Pankhurst papers at the: www.ampltd.co.uk/digital_guides/women_suffrage_and _politics_sylvia_pankhurst/introduction-to-sylvia-pankhurst.aspx

National Library of Scotland
Collection of suffragette material is detailed at: http://suffragettes.nls.uk/
Digital collections, including Army Lists, can be accessed at: https://auth.nls.uk/ldc/
Women in the Great War resource: www.nls.uk/learning-zone/history/themes-in-focus/women-in-the-great-war

Imperial War Museum
The **Women, War and Society, 1914-1918** database (by GALE) can be searched in the Explore History Centre. The database contains masses of records on women in the First World War, including records of the early voluntary organisations, images, letters, cards, memoirs, and interviews. Further details on this can be found at: http://gdc.gale.com/assets/files/wws/GML40407_WomensMilitary.pdf

ARMY 1. Papers related to the Women's Legion.

London Metropolitan Archives (LMA)
MCC/CL/L/CON/05-5. The records of the Metropolitan Electric Tramways Limited (MET).

ACC/1297. London Transport Papers of predecessor companies of London Transport.

Women Munitions Workers of the First World War

Official History of the Ministry of Munitions (HMSO, 12 volumes: Volume I - Industrial Mobilisations 1914-1915, Volume II - General Organization for Munitions Supply, Volume III - Finance and Contracts, Volume IV - The Supply and Control of Labour 1915-16, Volume V - Wages and Warfare, Volume VI - Manpower and Dilution, Volume VII - The Control of Materials, Volume VIII - Control of Industrial Capacity and Equipment, Volume IX - Review of Munitions Supply, Volume X - The Supply of Munitions, Volume XI - The Supply of Munitions, Volume XII - The Supply of Munitions).

TUC Library Archives
National Federation of Women Workers records include some munitions workers.

TNA
MUN 5/146/1122/1. Lists of National Filling, Shell and Projectile Factories - 1915.
SUPP5/1051. Papers of the Committee on the Health of Munition Workers 1915-16.
MEPO 3/2434. Correspondence and papers on prohibition of women suffering from venereal disease from intercourse with member of the armed forces.
HO 45/10892/357517. Fraudulent claims by munitions workers for subsistence allowances.
HO 185/238. Fears women were picking up men's bad habits; reports on drinking by women and young people.
HO 45. Covers explosions at munitions factories including Morecambe (HO 45/10887/350619) and Chilwell (HO 45/10887/364648).
HO 45/10887/350619 Honours: List of awards in connexion with fire and explosion at Morecambe Shell Factory.
HO 45/10790/300791. Appointment of women factory inspectors 1915-18.
LAB 2 series. Records of named factories may be found here. For example, LAB 2/73/IC4366/1916 a dispute in the Humber Brass and Copper Works, Hull on the employment of women of work usually done by men and boys. Wage orders and regulations for women in controlled and uncontrolled firms producing munitions, 1917-18, can be found in LAB 2/243/LR142/9/1917/PtIII.

AIR 2/11. Air Ministry and Ministry of Defence: Registered Files. Committees, Commissions, etc. General (Code A, 18/1): Joint Committee between Representatives of Ministry of Munitions & Air Board on Training of Women for RFC.

FD 4/16. Labour wastage among women munitions workers.

FD 4/13. Medical Research Committee and Medical Research Council: Reports of Special Research Projects. Inquiry into the composition of dietaries: with special reference to the dietaries of munition workers 1918.

FD 4/11. Medical Research Committee and Medical Research Council: Reports of Special Research Projects. The causation and prevention of tri-nitro-toluene (TNT) poisoning.

MUN 4. Records of the Central Registry of the Ministry of Munitions.

MUN 5 Ministry of Munitions Historical Branch.

SUPP 5/861. Includes photographs of war workers at the Royal Gunpowder Factory, Waltham Abbey as well as records of the Royal Arsenal, Woolwich and the Royal Ordnance factory at Poole.

NATS 1. Includes the files of the Women's Work Department.

NATS 1/432-441. Financial and administrative records, including regional committees dealing with the discharge of people from Munitions Works.

LAB 15/94. Holds a report of a conference of employers, operatives and inspectors on the substitution of female for male labour in the bleaching, dyeing and printing works of Messrs. J. Jackson in 1916.

MUN 3. Ministry of Munitions: Specimens of Documents Destroyed. This series, formerly entitled Rochdale National Shell Factory Account Books, consisted originally of the records preserved in accordance with the Disposal and Liquidation Commission (late Ministry of Munitions) Third Schedule. Examples include 'Messrs Smith and Coventry Ltd of Manchester, machine tool makers, from March 1917 to June 1919 (MUN 3/273); Messrs Mellor, Bronley & Co., engineers from Leicester, May 1917 (MUN 3/275); and Messrs G. Beaton & Co., engineers from West London, also dating from May 1917 (MUN 3/276).

WO 142/263. Ministry of Munitions, Trench Warfare and Chemical Warfare Departments, and War Office, Chemical Warfare Research Department and Chemical Defence Experimental Stations (later Establishments), Porton: Reports and Papers. Chemical Defence Establishment, Porton Down: Historical (H) Collection. Anti-Gas Production and Work. Includes women workers.

Series CAB. Cabinet records.

Information on workers at the Royal Arsenal, Woolwich can be found at: http://yourarchives.nationalarchives.gov.uk/index.php?title=Royal_Arsenal_Woolwich_employees.

Ministry of Defence

Records of a few munitions workers may be held within the civilian personnel records of The Ministry of Defence. Contact: People Services, Access to Personal Information Service (APIS), Personnel, Pay and Pensions Agency, Ministry of Defence, J Block, Foxhill, Bath, BA1 5AB. For further details, see: www.mod.uk/DefenceInternet/FreedomOfInformation/FOIContact/RequestsForAccessToPersonalDataHeldByTheMinistryOfDefence.htm

IWM

Women's War Work during the First World War:

www.iwm.org.uk/history/womens-war-work-during-the-first-world-war

www.1914.org/podcasts/podcast-16-munitions

EMP 80/1. Employment Ministry of Labour 4 Jan 1919 - 24 May 1919 Department of Civil Demobilisation and Settlement. Weekly Report.

L R 122/3. Local Records/ Dumfriesshire/ List of areas in which work parties were organised

MUN 1/2-22. Munitions General Information Concerning Munitions Exhibition of the Womens Section, Catalogues etc..

MUN 10/2-6. Munitions - Anti-gas Work in France July 1915-Feb 1919.

MUN 11/2-5. Munitions: Report on the Work of Women in Connection with the Anti-Gas Dept.

MUN 12/2-7. Munitions: Cardonald National Projectile Factory, near Glasgow.

MUN 13/2. Munitions: HM Factory at Gretna 28 Aug 1917.

MUN 13/3-17. Munitions: Scottish Filling Factory, Georgetown 1919.

MUN 14/2-11. Munitions: HM Factory at Gretna 1917, 1919.

MUN 15 2/2-8. Munitions: Kingsnorth Airship Station.

MUN 15 3. Munitions; Work of Women Mathematicians in the New Designs Branch, Technical Dept. Aircraft Production.

MUN 18.2. Munitions: Ministry of Munitions Womens Service Committee 24 Nov 1916.

MUN VII. Munitions: Pamphlets, Magazines, and Leaflets 11 January 1918.

SUPP 31/201-222. Supplementary Material: Press Cuttings: Women in Munitions Work 1918-1919.

Women Nurses, Doctors and Medical Services in World War One

TNA

Online guide to researching British Army nurses' service records 1914-18: www. nationalarchives.gov.uk/records/army-nurses-service-records.htm

HO 372. Medals of FANY.

WO 145. Royal Red Cross medal.

WO 329/2308. Military Massage Corps: medal rolls MMC/101B. Pages 1-3; 1A-3A. British War Medal and Victory Medal.

WO 329/2324. First Aid Nursing Yeomanry: medal rolls.

PMG 42/1-12. Pensions of Officers (Army) and nurses, arranged alphabetically.

PIN 26/19985-20826. Ministry of Pensions and successors: Selected First World War Pensions Award Files - Nurses.

WO 32/9342-4. War Office's committee reports on the Supply of Nurses 1916-17.

MH 106. First World War Representative Medical Records of Servicemen - includes selected Medical Sheets of servicemen and women, including members of the VADs, the Scottish Women's hospital, the Women's League, WRNS, QMAC and as Nursing Sisters (MH/106/2207-11).

PIN 38. Disablement Services Branch Records (Ministry of Pensions) - useful if your ancestor worked at a hospital where artificial limbs were fitted.

PMG 42/1-12. A few pensions survive in PIN 26/19985-20826 and are indexed.

WO 145/1. You can consult the registers of the recipients of the Royal Red Cross to find a person who received this award.

PIN 26/19985-20286. The Disability Pension Files, held in the document series , contain records relating to nurses.

PIN 15/478. Nurses and medical auxiliaries employed with units of the Allied Armies. Ministry of Pensions and successors: War Pensions, Registered Files (GEN Series) and other records (1920).

WO 338/23 and in WO 339. Records of female doctors with temporary commissions as officers in the RAMC no longer survive, those who received permanent commissions can be found in these references.

WO 32/11226. File on the Duchess of Westminster's hospital in France in 1914.

WO 222. War Office: Medical Historians' Papers: First and Second World Wars .

D 1. papers of the Central Midwives Board. The Midwives Act 1902 (England and Wales) enabled the state enrolment of midwives and established the Central Midwives Board (CMB) for England and Wales.

DV 7. CMB England and Wales Roll of Midwives 1902-1983.

DV 12. CMB Rolls of Midwives for Scotland, Ireland and Overseas Reciprocal Boards.

NATS 1/1283. Voluntary Aid Detachment Department: hospital work, early correspondence.

WO 162/36. Employment of the General Service Section of the VAD in France: Conference.

WO 95/4386. War Diary of the Matron, Australian Nursing Service June 1916 - April 1918.

WO 95/4941. War Diary of the Australian Army Nursing Service.

HO 322/451. Women's Transport Service: First Aid Nursing Yeomanry Corps (FANY); oldest voluntary organisation of women in Great Britain; facing possible extinction due to cutbacks; detailed history.

WO399. Correspondence files of the Directorate of Army Medical Services and Territorial Force containing service records of women who served in Queen Alexandra's Imperial Military Nursing Service and Territorial Force Nursing Service and other associated bodies during the First World War. (c1902 - c1922).

The records in *WO399/1-15792* cover military nurses including members of the TFNS and the QAIMNS, which was supported by the QAIMNS Reserve (R). Documents Online.

Background to Lily Harris

http://professionaldescendant.blogspot.com/2010/11/remembrance-day-diary-of-ww1-nurse.html

Detailed information on nurses at sea: www.english-heritage.org.uk/discover/people-and-places/womens-history/maritime-women/shipboard-nurses/

ONLINE: DocumentsOnline

It is possible to find nursing personnel in the collection of First World War Medal Index Cards (WO 372). These too can be searched for and downloaded on DocumentsOnline.

You may wish to view First World War Unit War Diaries. A selection of First World War Unit War Diaries can be downloaded from DocumentsOnline. More are being digitised.

ONLINE: Hospital Records Database HOSPREC

www.nationalarchives.gov.uk/hospitalrecords

ONLINE: Findmypast

www.findmypast.co.uk/search/military/indexes/military-nurses/

Queen Alexandra's Imperial Military Nursing Service: records of 783 nurses, born between 1859 and 1904.

Queen Alexandra's Royal Naval Nursing Service (from 1902; from 1884 was the Royal Naval Nursing Service).

Scottish Women's Hospital: records of 1,575 women (and men) who were stationed in continental Europe during WWI.

ONLINE: ScarletFinders: www.scarletfinders.co.uk

One of the most comprehensive websites for military nursing information.

The Women's Library @ LSE

2SWH. Records of the London Committee of the Scottish Women's Hospitals (SWH) re their work during the First World War: authorisations, correspondence, staff files, circular letters, telegrams, postcards, photographs, statements of accounts, balance sheets, cheques and counterfoils, reports, lecture notes, lists of donors.

TWL also holds the Papers of Elsie Bowerman (7ELB); the Papers of Vera (Jack) Holme (7VJH); a Scrapbook (relating to the Scottish Women's Hospital) (10/22). The Women's Library Museum Collection holds postcards and photographs related to the Scottish Women's Hospital and of several of the women who served. Similarly the Printed Collections holds additional material such as 'The Scottish Women's Hospital at the French Abbey of Royaumont' by Antonio de Navarro (1917); 'The Little Grey Partridge : First World War diary of Isobel Ross who served with the Scottish Women's Hospital Unit in Serbia' introduced by Jess Dixon (1988) as well as biographies of individuals such as 'Dr Elsie Inglis' by Lady Frances Balfour (1918).

IWM

IWM BRCS 25/5.6/2 VADs who died in service.

DEC 8/175. An envelope of photographs of those who died.

FANY Gazette can be viewed on the WWS 1914-1918 database.

Liddle Collection

Recollections of serving as a VAD, including the Ada Clarke papers

FANY Archive

ONLINE Photographic Archive: www.fanyarchive.org.uk/

Email: hq@fany.org.uk

QARANC archives at Army Medical Services Museum

British Red Cross Museum and Archives

Original card index detailing service with the VADs 1914-19.

Trained/nurses index which names those who served with the Joint War Committee.

Sub-index of VADs who worked in military hospitals at home and overseas auxiliary hospitals.

The records of those who served in the First Aid Nursing Yeomanry (FANY).

ONLINE: FIBIS

www.new.fibis.org/

The 'British Military Nurses' section on the website contains useful resources for the Queen Alexandra's Military Nursing Service for India (as known from 1903; from 1926 was amalgamated with Queen Alexandra's Imperial Military Nursing Service).

Memorials

York Screens (see Appendices)
Scottish National War Memorial: www.snwm.org
Irish War Memorials: www.irishwarmemorials.ie

ONLINE: CWGC. www.cwgc.org. The official Register of honour for First World War casualties from the Commonwealth War Graves Commission does not include all nurses who died during this war.

Russian Red Cross Society

Holds the records of the few British women served with the Russian Army.

Local Archives

Perth and Kinross Archives holds an album of photographs showing nurses and homes that were turned into military hospitals in the First World War. For Perth and Kinross Archives visit www.pkc.gov.uk/archives, and for the Local Studies department at the A K Bell Library visit http://tinyurl.com/PerthLocalStudies

The Mitchell Library

Letters and reports of Elsie Inglis 1914-28: correspondence, financial records, subscriptions, personnel files, various committee minutes, reports from overseas units etc of the Scottish Women's Hospitals for Home and Foreign Service Reports from overseas units.

Imperial War Museum

Material about the Scottish Women's Hospitals in the Women's Work Collection.
Photographs of the SWH.
Femina patriae defensor: woman in the service of her country: Belgium, France, Great Britain ... (Paris: Charles-Lavauzelle, 1934) *lists all (allegedly) women who died for Britain.*

National Library of Scotland

Journals of SWH member, Mary Lee Milne.

Leeds Russian Archive

Memoirs of SWH member, Katherine North (nee Hodges).

Edinburgh Central Library

Papers of SWH members, Lilas Grant and Ethel Moir.

Lothian Health Archives

Letters of Yvonne Fitzroy.

Royal College of Physicians and Surgeons of Glasgow

RCPSG 74. Photograph album relating to the Scottish Women's Hospital in Salonika, 1907-1918.

Schleisinger Library, Harvard University

Papers of Ruth Holden of the SWH.

PRONI

D1982. Papers of the Scottish Women's Hospitals in Serbia.

LMA

H01/ST/C/06/001-003. Voluntary Aid Detachment. On cover 'Army Book 127'. With names of staff, dates of active service etc 1915-1919.

H01/ST/NCPH/E/014/001. Album compiled by Mrs Rita McLaren, a Canadian V.A.D., who nursed at St Thomas' Hospital 1918-1919, contains photographs, postcards and papers.

H01/ST/NTS/Y/40/001-002. Medals of the Territorial Nursing Force Service.

H01/ST/NCPH/C/V/A. Territorial Nursing Force Service.

The Wellcome Library

SA/CSP/F.1. Almeric Paget Massage Corps December 1915 - January 1916.

British Library

IOR: L/MIL/9/430-432. Indian Nursing Service: List of Candidates.

IOR: L/MIL/7/11617-11803. 1887-1917 Personal files of nursing sisters appointed to India.

IOR: L/MIL/7/11316-11616 1886-1940 Collection 262 Indian Nursing Service.

IOR: L/AG/20/39/1. Pay Accounts 1946 include names, when left India, when arrived in UK of the IMNS, address (occasionally care of a bank, sometimes personal, sometimes a hospital, some in Canada).

Military Collection 262A.

Indian Nursing Service Papers of Sisters appointed to Service Files 1-20 (volume 1).

Women's Auxiliary Services of the First World War

WAAC/QMAAC
IWM

ARMY 3/4-7/12-15 Records on QMAAC.

Holdings of the QMAAC journal, *Old Comrade's Association Gazette* (later the *QMAAC and ATS Comrades Association Gazette*).

TNA

NATS 1/1268, 1273, 1279, 1286 and 1299-301. Files on the early history of the WAAC and rates of pay for the Immobile Section.

HO 45/10891/356508. Deserters: Absentees from the Women's Army Auxiliary Corps. Proceedings against. (1918).

MEPO 2/1743. Women's Army Auxiliary Corps: absentees.

WO398. War Office: Women's (later Queen Mary's) Army Auxiliary Corps: Service Records, First World War 1917-1920 Documents Online.

WO95/84 and WO95/85. War Diaries Documents Online.

WO 32/5253. Women's Services: Women's Auxiliary Corps (Code 68(D)): Decisions reached concerning organisation on a civil or military basis (1917).

WO 32/5530. War Office and successors: Registered Files (General Series). Civil Staffs (Outstations): General (Code 47(A)): Introduction of female labour in all units at home; extension of Women's Army Auxiliary Corps (1917).

WO 32/5253. War Office and successors: Registered Files (General Series). Women's Services: Womens Auxiliary Corps (Code 68(D)): Decisions reached concerning organisation on a civil or military basis.

WO 32/5254. War Office and successors: Registered Files (General Series). Women's Services: Womens Auxiliary Corps (Code 68(D)): Administrative staff required; appointments, pay and conditions of service.

WO 32/5255. War Office and successors: Registered Files (General Series). Women's Services: General (Code 68(A)): Entitlement of members of Womens Corps to same compensation following disablement as that paid to servicemen under Royal Pension Warrant.

WO 32/5252. War Office and successors: Registered Files (General Series). Women's Services: Womens Auxiliary Corps (Code 68(D)): Proposals regarding uniform and badges to be worn by women holding positions equivalent to commissioned rank.

WO 32/5503. War Office and successors: Registered Files (General Series). Regimental Dress and Badges: Other Arms (Code 43(K)): Approval of design of hat or cap badge for members of Navy and Army Canteen Board Women's Corps.

WO 162/34. Commander-in-Chief and War Office: Adjutant General's Department: Papers. Women's Services. General. Recruitment of women for certain Corps with the United States Forces in France: Minutes of conferences.

WO 162/65. Recommendations for Honours etc. for Women's Auxiliary Army Corps (1918-1919).

WO 162/16. Incomplete nominal roll of the WAAC.

WO 162/62. List of women drivers employed by the Corps.

WO 162/56. Conference on the WAAC in June 1917.

WO 162/39, 47 and 63-4. Conditions in France for the WAAC, including hostels and accommodation, and various visits to WAAC and QMAAC units.

WO 162/51 and 53-4. Material on the discharge and demobilisation of members of the QMAAC and on possible post-war overseas resettlement.

WO 162/41. Report on the Women War Workers' Resettlement Committee, November 1918

WO 372. War Office:Service Medal and Award Rolls Index, First World War Documents Online.

NAM: Templar Research Centre

Online exhibition about WAACs can be read at: www.nam.ac.uk/exhibitions/online-exhibitions/waacs-war

The Portal catalogue to the NAM collection is through the Inventory catalogue: www.nam.ac.uk/inventory. The Inventory online catalogue can be searched using 'Queen Mary's Army Auxiliary Corps' or 'Women's Army Auxiliary Corps.' in the Regiment box.

The Royal Air Force Museum Library and Archive can be searched through Navigator http://navigator.rafmuseum.org/

Adjutant General's Corps Museum

curator@agcmuseum.co.uk
The Adjutant General's Corps museum includes records of the Women's Royal Army Corps, Auxiliary Territorial Service, Women's Army Auxiliary Corps.

Online

The diary of the 19 year old war correspondent turned undercover Sapper, *Sapper Dorothy Lawrence: The Only English Woman Soldier, Late Royal Engineers, Fifty-First Division 179th Tunneling Company* (J Lane, 1919) can be read online at http://archive.org/details/ sapperdorothyla00lawrgoog.

Women's Royal Naval Service (WRNS)

1917-1919 - download records from: www.nationalarchives.gov.uk/documentsonline/wrns.asp

WRNS officers' service records card and files up to circa 1929 can be searched online at: www.nationalarchives.gov.uk/documentsonline/navy-cards-and-files.asp

TNA

ADM 318/1-556. Personal Files of Short Service Officers: - files on those commissioned 1917-1919, does not include the records of those who resigned for personal reasons during 1918 Documents Online.

ADM 321/1-2. Registers of WRNS officers' appointments and promotions 1917-19 Documents Online.

ADM 336/1-22. Ratings' registers 1918-19 (alphabetical). Documents Online.

ADM 1/8615/197. 1921 Former members of WRNS were allowed to wear uniform when selling poppies in Trafalgar Square.

NATS 1/1304. Material on WRNS.

ADM 1/8425/181. Introduction of women clerks and other female workers to the Navy in June 1915. The formation of the WRNS.

ADM 1/8533/220. WRNS representation on courts of enquiry involving a members of the corps.

ADM 104. Records of QARNNS (nurses) and its reserve of civilian nurses who enlisted temporarily for the duration.

ADM 104/161. Medal awards.

ADM 104/162-5. QARRNS Reserve.

ADM 104/96 Nursing sisters' and wardmasters' establishment book 1912-27; includes names, ranks, and sates of appointment and discharge; there is an index to establishments, whether hospital or barracks.

ADM 318. Personal files of Short Service Officers are at TNA in series.

ADM 321. Registers of officers' appointments, promotions and resignations.

ADM 336. Registers of Service for Ratings are arranged by service number.

ADM 171/133. The WRNS campaign medal roll can be searched in pages 581-2.

ADM 116. Includes records of the creation of the WRNS, plus details of its uniform and organisation.

MT 9/1589. A roll of honour of women who died while serving in the mercantile marine.
WO 162/60. Recruitment of women workers attached to the RFC.
WO 162/44. Transfer of personnel WRNS and WRAF.

RNM
To book an appointment to see the WRNS Collection, contact the curator at the Royal Naval Museum.

WWI Women's RAF (WRAF)
AIR 80/1-268. Airwomen's Service Records Documents Online.
AIR 2/11/87/Instruction/404. Minutes of a joint committee of the Air Board and the Ministry of Munitions on training women for the RFC.
AIR 2/93/CW 1528, 94/CW 5788 AND CW 12318). Files on the creation of the WRAF and the RAFNS. Names of the first RAFNS nurses are also found in the AIR 2 series.
AIR 1/619.16/15/347. Some reference to WRAF constitution and regulations.
AIR 10. Series of Air Ministry publications.
AIR 1/106/15/9/284. Pay details of the WRAF.
AIR 10/18. Details of the voluntary transfer of personnel from the WRNS, WAAC and Women's Legion Motor Drivers to the WRAF.
AIR 2/943. 'Labour substitution of servicemen in all theatres in 1917 by women and coloured labourer'.
NATS 1/1280. Material on the WRAF.
AIR 2/122/b 9511. Papers on the demobilisation of WRAF.
AIR 80 (index AIR 78). Surviving service records for airwomen 1918-20.
MH 106/1497 sample medical records of WRAF women, which can include details of an ancestor whose service record no longer exists.
AIR 2/93/CW 66031. Files on the establishment of Nursing Service in 1923 (PMRAFNS).
T 1/12202. Air Ministry. Establishment of a separate nursing service for the Royal Air Force. (1918).

Medal Cards
MH 106/1187. Royal Air Force and Nursing Service Auxiliary (24 October 1917 - 26 March 1918). Some transferred from the TFNS.

Between the Wars

For this period, women's service records are retained by the Ministry of Defence.

Some women could be found at a hospital or other institution on www.ancestry.co.uk in the London electoral registers or in the British Library. These can help to confirm addresses and to show other adults at the same address as well as who lived nearby.

The Women's Library @ LSE
GB 106 1SOS. Records of the Society for the Overseas Settlement of British Women (1901-1964).

TNA

WO 32/13950. WOMENS SERVICES: Auxiliary Territorial Service (Code 68C): Formation of Officers Association by representatives of Officers Help Societies.

RECO 1 Papers of the Ministry of Reconstruction, of the two Reconstruction Committees of the Cabinet which preceded it, and of various committees and sub-committees appointed by them.

KV 2. Records of the Security Service: Personal Files - Communists and Suspected Communists, including Russian and Communist Sympathisers.

KV 5/112. The International Brigade Association and Friends of Republican Spain: list of persons who fought in Spain, 1936-1939; annotated list of people who fought in the Spanish Civil War. Includes a Roll of Honour of those killed. Documents Online.

FO 889. Foreign Office: Consulate, Valencia, Spain: Spanish Civil War Miscellanea 1936-1946.

Online

Records of the International Brigade are held at the Marx Memorial Library: www.marx-memorial-library.org

A good overview of the International Brigades can be found at: www.marx-memorial-library.org

Archives

Other archives of Communist or International Brigade material are the People's History Museum in Manchester, the Working Class Movement Library in Salford and the The Association of Jewish Ex-Servicemen and Women (AJEX) in London.

Second World War and the Emergence of New Roles

Online

www.bbc.co.uk/ww2peopleswar. BBC WW2 People's War: archive of wartime memories

www.londonscreenarchive.org.uk. Catalogue of more than 16000 films of twentieth century London from 1912 onwards; 1100 are available to view online; films can be searched by keyword, date and name of archive in which they were stored; Second World War films include those showing women at work in London.

www.homesweethomefront.co.uk. Background, details and images on the WLA: www.womenslandarmytribute.co.uk

www.bures.me.uk/wla/wla.htm

www.womenslandarmy.co.uk

http://landarmy.org.uk

www.wrvs.org. Women's (Royal) Volunteers Service (WVS/WRVS): www.fortunecity.co.uk/meltingpot/oxford/330/womenwar/wvs/wvs.html

English Heritage is working on a project to list every PoW camp from this time. The list so far can be found at: www.english-heritage.org.uk/publications/prisoner-of-war-camps/prisoner-of-war-camps.pdf.

www.kindertransport.org

TNA

MAF 421/1. Ministry of Food: Women's Land Army: Index to Service Records of the Second World War. Index A - Z. (1939-1948).

MAF 59. This series contains minutes of county committees, collections of photographs and recruiting posters and selected files, mostly from the period 1938 to 1950 relating to the Women's Land Army. (1916-1985).

MAF 900. Correspondence and papers selected to illustrate the day-to-day work of a County Agricultural Executive Committee, 1917 to 1919, Emergency Services, Wartime Meals, Salvage, Manpower and Food Advice Divisions of the Ministry of Food, the Women's Land Army 1939 to 1951, and the operation of the Improvement of Livestock (Licensing of Bulls) Act 1931. (1917-1968)

MAF 186. The series deals with the supply of labour for agriculture including the employment of aliens, school children, civil prisoners, prisoners of war, and policy matters relating to the Women's Land Army. (1940-1973).

HO 356/2. Home Office: Establishment Division: S GEN Files. Women's Voluntary Services (WVS): setting up; appointments; reports of activities; consideration of role of WVS and women's institutes after Second World War.

HO 186/2327. Ministry of Home Security: Air Raid Precautions (ARP GEN) Registered files. Women's Voluntary Services, WVS in wartime and co-operation with civil defence services: activities in Region No.2.

HO 186/574. Ministry of Home Security: Air Raid Precautions (ARP GEN) Registered files. Women's Voluntary Services, Extension of WVS activities to Northern Ireland.

CUST 106/452. War Registry: Registered Files. Release of imported goods without licence for Womens Voluntary service (WVS).

Government policy records on the evacuation can be found in TNA in references CAB series, HO 45, HO 158, HO 186 HO 199, HO 202, HO 204, HO 207, HLG 7, RG 23 and RG 40.

The Women's Library @ LSE

8SUF/B series. Contains some oral history interviews with members of the WRVS.

NAS

GD1/171/1. Records of Women's Voluntary Services (WVS) 1941-1945

GD193/32/1. Correspondence - Lady Steele-Maitland in her capacity as county organiser for the W.V.S. 1939.

Mass Observation Archive

SxMOA1/2/32/1/A/5. Statistics about women in the Womens Voluntary Service (WVS), Air Raid Precautions (ARP), Womens Land Army (WLA) and in industry.

SxMOA1/2/32/1/H/2. Correspondence between Tom Harrisson and senior members of the Womens Land Army about getting access to information about the WLA.

SxMOA1/2/32/1/H/5. Opinions on the organisation of the Womens Land Army from other WLA personnels.

IWM

Extensive holdings of objects relating to all the voluntary services and areas of war work. The collection of private papers relating to the WLA includes discharge document 1947, a pledge of service, Notification of training 1943, letters and memoirs.

Women Nurses, Doctors and Medical Services in the Second World War

QAIMNS, QAIMNSR and TANS service records are retained by the Ministry of Defence. A collection of records relating to 1,244 army nurses who served in France has been transcribed by Sue Light and can be searched at Findmypast.

Service records of VADs are held by British Red Cross, Museum and Archives department, 44 Moorfields, London EC2Y 9AL.

TNA

WO 177/14, 1157, 1199. War Office: Army Medical Services: War Diaries, Second World War. Middle East Forces. British Troops in Egypt. D.D.M.S.; War Office: Army Medical Services: War Diaries, Second World War. General Hospitals. 11 Gen. Hosp.; War Office: Army Medical Services: War Diaries, Second World War. General Hospitals. 18 Gen. Hosp. Findmypast.

WO 145/2. War Office: Registers of Recipients of the Royal Red Cross. Register of awards. Indexed. (1918-1943) Findmypast.

WO 145/3. War Office: Registers of Recipients of the Royal Red Cross. Register of awards. Indexed.

WO 222/1568. War Office: Medical Historians' Papers: First and Second World Wars. Reports and Returns. Miscellaneous. Location of British General Hospitals. Item open from 1972.

WO 361/320. War Office: Department of the Permanent Under Secretary of State: Casualties (L) Branch: Enquiries into Missing Personnel, 1939-45 War. Malaya: Queen Alexandra's Imperial Mililtary Nursing Service (QAIMNS); missing personnel including those missing after sinking of *SS Kuala* off Pom Pong.

WO 32/17626. War Office and successors: Registered Files (General Series). Proposal for a letter of appreciation to officers of Queen Alexandra's Imperial Military Nursing Service (QAIMNS) on retirement.

WO373/54/173. War Office and Ministry of Defence: Military Secretary's Department: Recommendations for Honours and Awards for Gallant and Distinguished Service (Army). Combatant Gallantry Awards. North West Europe. Name L'Estrange, Elizabeth Charlotte Rank: Acting Senior Sister Service No: 206271 Regiment: Queen Alexandra's.

WO 373/156/357. War Office and Ministry of Defence: Military Secretary's Department: Recommendations for Honours and Awards for Gallant and Distinguished Service (Army). Half-Yearly (New Year and Sovereign's Birthday) Awards. Name Edwards, Brenda Hazelby Rank: Sister QAIMNS Service No: 238151 Regiment: Queen Alexandra's.

IWM

Documents.2605. Private Papers of E M Stevenson (QAIMNS 1942-42).
Documents.6341. Private Papers of Mrs C M S Baker (QAIMNS from 1943).
Documents.147. Private Papers of Mrs A Radloff (QAIMN(R)).

Documents.12472. Private Papers of Miss F E Brown (QAIMNS from 1942).

Documents.174649. Private Papers of Ms P Salter (QAIMNS).

Documents.16686. Private Papers of Miss A K D Morgan (QAIMNS(R)).

Documents.6989. Private Papers of Mrs B Jenkins (VAD).

Documents.10904. Private Papers of Miss M V Norman (Naval VAD).

Documents.713. Private Papers of Mrs P Collins (VAD).

Documents.16749. Account written by a nurse who served in the First and Second World Wars (VAD).

Documents.13057. Private Papers of Mrs D Walters (VAD).

Documents.10791. Private Papers of Miss A Bird (VAD).

Documents.13132. Private Papers of Mrs E Thomas (VAD).

Documents.16840. Private Papers of Miss E O Bradley (VAD).

Documents.16965. Private Papers of F Smith (daughter, Norah, was a member TANS).

Auxiliary Territorial Service (ATS)

Service Records are retained by the Ministry of Defence.

FANY Records are held at FANY (PRVC), TA Centre, 95 Horseferry Road, London, SW1P 2DX.

TNA

WO 169. Series contains 145 War Diaries that refer to the ATS.

WO 32. War Office and successors: Registered Files (General Series).

There are over 400 records at TNA that relate specifically to the ATS. They can be found by searching on 'Auxiliary Territorial Service' via Discovery. A selection of these records include:

WO 32/4594. Women's Services: Auxiliary Territorial Service (Code 68(C)): Revised Terms of Service.

WO 32/10084. Women's Services: Auxiliary Territorial Service (Code 68(C)): Staff appointments; selections of ATS Officers.

WO 32/10034. Women's Services: Auxiliary Territorial Service (Code 68(C)): Employment of A.T.S. personnel.

WO 32/4705. Women's Services: Auxiliary Territorial Service (Code 68(C)): Uniform and badge.

WO 373/68/820. Recommendation for Award for Crowhurst, Vera Rank: Private.

WO 32/10044. Women's Services: Auxiliary Territorial Service (Code 68(C)): Titles and badges of rank.

WO 231/239. Army Training Memorandum No. 23. Individual training period, 1939-1940. Part I, instructions for higher training in 1939-1940. Part II, general training. Part III, individual training by arms. Part IV, developments in organisation and equipment. Part V, Territorial Army. Part VI, Auxiliary Territorial Service.

LAB 6/188. Ministry of Labour and National Service and Ministry of Labour: Military Recruitment: Registered Files. Recruitment of women for Auxiliary Territorial Service selection tests.

LAB 6/180. Ministry of Labour and National Service and Ministry of Labour: Military Recruitment: Registered Files. Recruitment of women for the Auxiliary Territorial Service.

LAB 8/388. Ministry of Labour and successors: Employment Policy, Registered Files (EM series and other series). Intensive recruiting campaign for the Auxiliary Territorial Service.

T 164/188/27. Treasury: Establishment Department, Superannuation Division: Registered Files (P, PC, PU and PS Series). Dawson, H: service in Auxiliary Territorial Service ignored in assessment of compensation to widow.

T 213/126. Reorganisation of the Auxiliary Territorial Service directorate (1941-1950).

NAM

ATS discharge books 1938-1949 (long list, volunteering/conscripted & discharged; rank and number).

IWM

Collections include 49 private papers, such as ATS letters, diaries and memoirs'. There are also reference works, films, oral histories and items of uniform. Documents relating to FANY are:

Documents.15349. Private Papers of Mrs M Pawley (FANY with SOE).

Documents.13552. Private Papers of Miss W J Holmes (Women's Transport Service (FANY) with SOE).

Documents.13337. Private Papers of Lady Pamela Niven (FANY with SOE).

Documents.12574. Private Papers of Miss B E Dawson (FANY).

Documents.12022. Private Papers of Miss S Cook (FANY with SOE).

Documents.9600. Private Papers of Junior Commander J E Peyman (ATS FANY).

Documents.6468. Private Papers of Mrs L Orde (ATS FANY).

Documents.12692. Private Papers of Junior Commander A Brocklebank (FANY/Women's Transport Service).

Mass Observation Archive

SxMOA1/1/6/10/35. 936 Summary Interim Report on ATS: Women's attitudes to conscription, propaganda, war work, women's services.

SxMOA1/1/6/11/10. 952 ATS Campaign Women's attitude to work and to war work: preferences for ARP nursing, munitions work, Land Army Services.

SxMOA1/1/6/11/13. 955 ATS: Attitudes towards women in the ATS p1 missing.

SxMOA1/1/6/11/27. 976 ATS Advertising (missing): Missing. See File Reports 952 (ATS Campaign), 955 (ATS).

SxMOA1/1/7/2/10. 1083 ATS Campaign: Attitudes and behaviour of women towards work conscription, the services and the ATS.

SxMOA1/2/17/12/D/11. Extract from Schuil Diary (M-O) 15.1.42 - impressions of the film & comment on girls in the ATS.

SxMOA1/2/42/6/C/66. Poster 66: 'Spare a Trinket' Fund, ATS, An Exhibition of Royal Gifts' 'Gifts given by Her Majesty the Queen and other members of the Royal Family, will be Exhibited...', ATS Trinket Fund, 221 Union St, Aberdeen (M). Printed for the ATS. Received by M-O 29.8.41 from MacPhail, Aberdeen.

SxMOA1/2/66/4/G/2. Handwritten general impression from ATS qq, tabulated results and explanation, 19-22.11.41.

SxMOA99/61/3/1. Papers from ATS training: bound notebook with lecture notes, typing tests, exam papers, examination answers, message forms and loose notations.

SxMOA99/61/3/6. ATS and VAD Release Book 26.03.1946. 1 stapled booklet.

SxMOA99/61/3/12. 'Class A releases (ATS and VAD members)' undated. 1 information sheet.

SxMOA1/2/32 TC32. Women in Wartime 1939-45: Much of the material in this collection, an investigation of wartime employment for women, results from the ATS Survey of 1941. There are detailed, inside reports on all aspects of WAAF life. A collection of letters from women munitions workers is included, together with material concerning employment in civil areas and information on women's organisations. This material is related to women's attitudes to war work and omits references to other areas of their lives, for which relevant Topic Collections should be consulted: Evacuation, Health, Industry, Personal Appearance, Sexual Behaviour, Shopping.

SxMOA99/30. Froom: This small collection holds slides of paintings painted by Mrs. Pamela Froom. The paintings portray the life of ATS/FANY.

SxMOA99/41. Hudson: Miss Hudson served in the ATS, Auxiliary Territorial Service, during the World War II.

SxMOA99/61. Richardson: Ida Richardson served in the ATS, Auxiliary Territorial Service, as a teleprinter operator.

SxMOA99/83. Watkins: This collection holds two notebooks from a 'Make and Mend' course attended by Pte King (later Mrs. Watkins) serving in the ATS in 1943.

SxMOA99/93. Muriel Mary Hill Papers. Served in the ATS and was posted to Bathford.

Online

List of resources and memories of former ATS personnel at: www.atsremembered.org.uk/
Violette Szabo Museum: www.violette-szabo-museum.co.uk
www.wracassociation.org.uk

Women's Auxiliary Air Force (WAAF) and the Air Transport Auxiliary (ATA)

WAAF Service Records are retained by the Ministry of Defence.

TNA

AIR 29/674. Air Ministry and Ministry of Defence: Operations Record Books, Miscellaneous Units. Mobile Field Hospitals. 2 WAAF Convalescent Depot, Dungaval (UK); became WAAF Convalescent Depot March 1943 and moved to Studley Priory January 1945; disbanded June 1946.

AIR 29/490. WAAF Depot. Formed at Innsworth, Gloucester (UK) in January 1940. Became 30 WAAF Recruit Centre Innsworth, Gloucester (UK) in November 1942. with appendices.

AIR 29/490. Air Ministry and Ministry of Defence: Operations Record Books, Miscellaneous Units. Air Crew Holding Units. 3 WAAF Depot, Morecambe (UK). Became 31 WAAF Recruit Centre, Morecambe (UK) in December 1942.

AIR 21/5. Judge Advocate General's Office: Royal Air Force Courts Martial Registers. District Courts Martial, WAAF, Home and Abroad.

AIR 29/767. Air Ministry and Ministry of Defence: Operations Record Books, Miscellaneous Units. Mobile Field Hospitals. WAAF Hospital Uxbridge, became RAF Station Hospital Uxbridge, July 1941 (UK).

AIR 2/8793. Air Ministry and Ministry of Defence: Registered Files. Women's Auxiliary Air Force: Organisation (Code B, 77/2): WAAF Advisory Council.

AIR 29/589 1 Air Gunners School, Pembrey. Includes four photographs of a WAAF parade, and three of WAAF parade, and three of the funeral of a German airman; all dated 1942 (AGS UK). with appendices.

AIR 29/764. Air Ministry and Ministry of Defence: Operations Record Books, Miscellaneous Units. Mobile Field Hospitals. 11 WAAF Convalescent Depot, Alexandria (Egypt) formed December 1944; moved to Port Fouad, Port Said, December 1946. With appendices.

AIR 29/490. RAF Reception Depot, West Drayton (UK). Formed in September 1924. Became WAAF Depot West Drayton (UK) in October 1939. Moved to Harrogate (UK) in September 1940. Became 1 WAAF Depot, Harrogate (UK) in February 1941. Moved to Bridgnorth (UK) in May 1941. with appendices.

AIR 29/752. WAAF Officers School; formed at Reading July 1940, moved to Gerrards Cross November 1940, moved to Gerrards Cross November 1940 as WAAF Disciplinary School, moved to Loughborough July 1941, then to Windermere November 1942, then to Stratford-on-Avon July 1944 (UK). With appendices.

AIR 2/10919. Air Ministry and Ministry of Defence: Registered Files. Women's Auxiliary Air Force: Personnel (Code B, 77/1): Officers and other ranks (including WAAF) consorting in public: draft amendment to King's Regulations and Air Council Instructions.

AIR 21/4B. Judge Advocate General's Office: Royal Air Force Courts Martial Registers. District Courts Martial, WAAF, Home.

AIR 29/490. Air Ministry and Ministry of Defence: Operations Record Books, Miscellaneous Units. Air Crew Holding Units. WAAF Headquarters.

AIR 29/717. Air Ministry and Ministry of Defence: Operations Record Books, Miscellaneous Units. Operational Training Units. WAAF School of Physical Training, Loughborough, Uxbridge and Halton (UK).

AIR 2/12604. Air Ministry and Ministry of Defence: Registered Files. WAAF (later WRAF), Organisation (Code B, 77/2): Administrative staff: complements and policy.

AIR 29/687. 84 Operational Training Unit (OTU). Formed at Desborough (UK), September 1943, with satellite at Harrington (UK) in Record Books, Miscellaneous Units. Operational Training Units. Contains photographs of a handicraft exhibition, 'Brains Trust' room, presentation of the Thorold Cup, station facilities, WAAF.

AIR 29/714. Air Ministry and Ministry of Defence: Operations Record Books, Miscellaneous Units. Operational Training Units. Plotter School, Leighton Buzzard, UK. Includes correspondence on the Women's Auxiliary Air Force (WAAF) accommodation. with appendices.

AIR 29/481. Womens Auxiliary Air Force (WAAF), Advisory Officer, Northwest African Air Forces (NAAF). Formed at Algiers (Algeria) in May 1943. Moved to La Marsa (Tunisia) in August 1943.

AIR 29/590. Air Ministry and Ministry of Defence: Operations Record Books, Miscellaneous Units. Training Units. 4 Air Gunners School, Morpeth; includes six photographs of personnel and a 1944 WAAF anniversary programme (AGS UK). With appendices.

AIR 29/481 Air Ministry and Ministry of Defence: Operations Record Books, Miscellaneous Units. Air Crew Holding Units. Womens Auxiliary Air Force (WAAF), South African Air Force. Based at Cairo (Egypt) in May 1943. With appendices.

AIR 29/764. Air Ministry and Ministry of Defence: Operations Record Books, Miscellaneous Units. Mobile Field Hospitals. 1 WAAF Convalescent Depot, Torquay (UK); disbanded December 1942.

Mass Observation Archive

SxMOA1/2/32/3/1. WAAF: Women's Auxiliary Air Force - Personal reports, descriptions of WAAF exhibitions, and an article entitled 'WAAF' by Mrs G Barker of the Ministry of Information, (US Division), 17.3.42.

SxMOA1/2/32/3/2. WAAF: Reports from an Observer 1941-2 - WAAF: Reports from an Observer 1941-2.

SxMOA1/1/5/8/7 **323**. WAAF Exhibition (Celia Fremlin).

SxMOA1/1/6/6/34 **757**. General Picture of WAAF Life.

SxMOA1/1/7/1/7 **1029**. WAAF Observer.

SxMOA1/1/7/2/17 **1091**. WAAF Morale.

SxMOA1/1/8/3/7 **1620**. After the War - Feelings in the WAAF.

SxMOA1/2/20/7/A/19. WAAF Library Interviews (19.4.42, 14 small pp, hw).

SxMOA1/2/32/1/E/3. Observations and overheard comments on the Auxiliary Territorial Service and the Women's Auxiliary Air Force.

SxMOA1/2/32/1/F/3. Replies from male members of the Panel in the Army and in the Royal Air Force: attitudes towards the Auxiliary Territorial Service (Auxiliary Territorial Service) and the Womens Auxiliary Air Force (WAAF) respectively, Oct 1941.

SxMOA1/2/32/1/G/5. Recruitment literature for the WAAF.

SxMOA1/2/65/3/G/1. Work in wartime; WAAF; sleep during raids; social life and air raids; behaviour during warnings; personal and domestic life; pacifists; RAF achievements.

WAAF Association: www.waafassociation.org.uk

Detailed information on WAAFs from the RAF Museum - features copies of documents: www.rafmuseum.org.uk/online-exhibitions/women-of-the-air-force/waaf-1939-1949-part1.cfm

Air Ministry pamphlets - these useful documents list trades of WAAFs.

Surviving personnel files, aircrew logbooks and private papers of ATA members cam be found at the RAF Museum Archive: www.rafmuseum.org.uk/london/collections/archive/

IWM has 70 sets of private papers relating to WAAFs in the Second World War. These can be identified in the Documents section of the Collections catalogue.

The Women's Royal Naval Service and women of the Merchant Navy in the Second World War

WRNS commissioned officers can be found in contemporary copies of *The Navy List.*

Service records of all WRNS 1939-1955 can be obtained from the Ministry of Defence or by writing to the Director of Naval Personnel, Navy Search, TNT Records Management, PO Box 7814, Tenton Point, William Nadin Way, Swadlincote, Derbyshire DE11 1EG (Tel: 01283 227912 or 227913).

TNA
The National Archives holds over 200 records relating to the WRNS between 1925 and 1949. These cover a broad range of subjects, including correspondence, reports on living conditions in the Tropics, details of training schemes, pilots/ Flying Control Officers in the WRNS, rates of pay, the WRNS badge, officers' servants, awards of commendation, accommodation of ratings and disciplinary hearings.

Women also served on merchant shipping. Several of these women received medals for their contribution to the war effort and these records can be searched via TNA website: www.nationalarchives.gov.uk/documentsonline/seamens-medals.asp?WT.hp=Medals%20issued%20to%20Merchant%20Seamen

RNM
Royal Naval Museum, Portsmouth holds the WRNS Historic Collection of around 5,000 photographs, manuscripts, uniforms, paintings, drawings and other items. These include items from both world wars and up to 1993.
www.royalnavalmuseum.org

IWM has 43 collections of private papers relating the WRNS, including letters, diaries and memoirs.

Mass Observation Archive
SxMOA1/2/32/1/G/3. Recruitment literature for the Women's Royal Naval Service (WRNS).
SxMOA99/91. Beryl Wood Archive - includes letters written by M E Hiller of the WRNS.

Online
www.seayourhistory.org.uk. Sea Your History: twentieth century Royal Navy history. Items from the WRNS Historic Collection can be viewed here.
www.wrens.org.uk. Association of Wrens - supporting the WRNS Benevolent Trust.

SPIES & INTELLIGENCE WORK

Service records are retained by the relevant section of the Ministry of Defence. Further details can be obtained from the Veterans' Agency via their website www.veteransuk.info/service_records/service_records.html or by writing to Service Personnel and Veterans Agency, Norcross, Blackpool FY5 3WP.

No full list of Bletchley staff survives, but there is a December 1940 list at TNA series HW 14/9. Other names may be found in series HW/16, HW14/36, and HW 41/219.

Further staff lists, personnel cards and other records can be found at Bletchley Park archives, which are currently being digitised. More information on them can be found at: www.bletchleypark.org.uk/edu/archives

There is also a Roll of Honour for veterans, which gives details of further sources: www.bletchleypark.org.uk/content/hist/history/RollofHonour.rhtm

Service records for those in intelligence can be ordered in the same way as those in other units. Clues to the secret nature of their work may be mentioned in notes and acronyms, like SLU (Special Liaison Units) or FSIU (Field Signals Intelligence Units).

Records from the camps include correspondence with the War Office or PoW cards. Some women can be found in the WO 367 registers of 13,500 military and civilian internees in Singapore.

The International Committee of the Red Cross (ICRC) retain incomplete lists of all known PoWs and civilian internees. Those seeking information on an individual affected by a twentieth - century conflict can fill in an online questionnaire via their Archives website: www.icrc.org/eng/resources/icrc-archives/index.jsp

TNA. holds the liberation questionnaires that prisoners completed after the war. These are held in WO 3444.

WO 78. Maps and Plans 1627-1953. Includes maps drawn up from intelligence gathering operations.

WO 208. Directorate of Military Intelligence 1917-1974. Contains intelligence material and interrogation reports for the Second World War.

ADM 223. Naval intelligence papers 1914-1978.

DEFE 3. Intelligence from Enemy Communications, 1941-1945. Translations of decrypted signals and summaries of intelligence from signals.

HW 1. Government Code and Cypher School Signals Intelligence passed to the Prime Minister, Messages and Correspondence, 1940-1946.

HD 5/1. Outlines the establishment and history of the Polish 'Deuxieme Bureau' network in France during the Second World War.

HS 1. SOE operations: The Far East.

HS 2. SOE operations: Scandinavia.

HS 3. SOE operations: Africa and the Middle East.

HS 4. SOE operations: Eastern Europe.

HS 5. SOE operations: Balkans.

HS 6. SOE operations: Western Europe.

HS 7. SOE Histories and War Diaries.

HS 8. SOE headquarters records.

HS 9. SOE Personnel Files (parts of these files remain confidential and unavailable).

HS 10. Photographs of equipment developed by SOE Station 15b for covert operations behind enemy lines.

HS 11. SOE Registry: General Nominal and Subject file index 1939-1946.

HS 12. SOE Registry: Index of Honours and Awards, 1939-1946 (an ancestor may be found here, even if a personnel file does not survive].

HS 13. SOE Registry: France Nominal Index, 1940-1946.

HS 14. SOE Registry: Belgium (including some Dutch) Nominal Index, 1939-1946.

HS 15. SOE Italian Section and Middle Eastern and Greek Section Agent Particulars Nominal Index, 1939-1946.

HS 16. SOE Playfair and Wireless Operators Codes Nominal Code Index, 1940-1946.

HS 17. SOE Registry: Scandinavia Nominal Index Cards, 1940-1946.

HS 18. SOE Registry: Iberian Nominal Card Index, 1940-1946.

HS 19. SOE Staff Income Tax Nominal Index Cards, 1940-1946.

HS 20. SOE Registry: Miscellaneous Nominal Card Index, 1940-1946.

Some files of SOE agents can be found in reference **KV 2** Personal (PF Series) files, 1913-1979.

HW 1. Signals Intelligence Passed to the Prime Minister, Messages and Correspondence.

HW 4. Far East Combined Bureau, Signals Intelligence Centre in the Far East (*HMS Anderson*): Records, 1940-1945.

HW 5. German Section: Reports of German Army and Air Force High Grade Machine Decrypts (CX/FJ, CX/JQ and CX/MSS Reports), 1940-1945.

HW 7. Room 40 and successors: World War I Official Histories, 1914-1923.

HW 12. Diplomatic Section and predecessors: Decrypts of Intercepted Diplomatic Communications (BJ Series), 1919-1945.

HW 15. Venona Project: Record, 1940-1949.

HW 16. German Police Section: Decrypts of German Police Communications during Second World War, 1939-1945.

HW 17/1-33. Decrypts of Communist International (COMINTERN) Messages, 1930-1945.

HW 25. Cryptographic Studies, 1920-1978.

HW 48. Hut 3: Intelligence Reports on German Plans for the Sea-born Invasion of Britain (Operation Smith/Sea Lion), 1940-1941.

HW 73. German Signals Intelligence in the Second World War: Studies, 1934-1945.

IWM holds 143 collections of private papers relating to men and women in SOE during the Second World War. The wider collections include uniform, medals and other items belonging to SOE officers, such as Violette Szabo, and film and sound recordings. The library has extensive holdings.

Our Secret War oral interviews: www.our-secret-war.org

British Women in the Empire

The National Archives holds a large volume of records on British Prisoner of War camps 1939-1948.

CO 875/16/12. Women's Periodicals: work of women in Africa, the West Indies, Malta, for the war effort (1942-1944).

CO 968/81/4. Recruitment of women: West Indies.

WO 32/10607. War Office and successors: Registered Files (General Series). Bands and Music: Regimental Marches (Code 62(B)): Canadian Women's Army Corps.

WO 32/10607. War Office and successors: Registered Files (General Series). Overseas: Canada (Code 0(F)): Canadian Womens Army Corps: Regimental Pipe Air.

WO 179/2547. War Office: Canadian, South African, New Zealand and Indian (United Kingdom) Forces (Dominion Forces): War Diaries, Second World War. Canadian Forces. Canadian Womens Army Corps. 43 Coy.

WO 179/2546. War Office: Canadian, South African, New Zealand and Indian (United Kingdom) Forces (Dominion Forces): War Diaries, Second World War. Canadian Forces. Canadian Womens Army Corps. 42 Coy.

WO 179/2545. War Office: Canadian, South African, New Zealand and Indian (United Kingdom) Forces (Dominion Forces): War Diaries, Second World War. Canadian Forces. Canadian Womens Army Corps. 41 Coy.

WO 179/2548. War Office: Canadian, South African, New Zealand and Indian (United Kingdom) Forces (Dominion Forces): War Diaries, Second World War. Canadian Forces. Canadian Womens Army Corps. 200 Coy.

WO 373/85/623. Recommendation for Award for Vivash, Irene Miawa Rank: Acting Quarter Master Sergeant.

WO 373/65/2475. Order of the British Empire of Major Margaret Joan Spencer of the Australian Women's Army Service.

CO 968/39/7. Colonial Office and Commonwealth Office: Defence Department and successors: Original Correspondence. East Africa: Women's Territorial Service.

CO 968/74/11. Colonial Office and Commonwealth Office: Defence Department and successors: Original Correspondence. Manpower. East Africa: Women's Territorial Service.

WO 169/14422. War Office: British Forces, Middle East: War Diaries, Second World War. East Africa Command. Womens Services. Womens Territorial Service.

WO 169/18556. War Office: British Forces, Middle East: War Diaries, Second World War. East Africa Command. Auxiliary Territorial Service. Womens Territorial Services.

WO 169/22027. War Office: British Forces, Middle East: War Diaries, Second World War. East Africa Command. Auxiliary Territorial Service. Womens Territorial Service.

WO 169/3223. War Office: British Forces, Middle East: War Diaries, Second World War. East Africa. Miscellaneous. Womens Territorial Service.

WO 169/7256. War Office: British Forces, Middle East: War Diaries, Second World War. East Africa Command. Auxiliary Territorial Service. Womens T.A.E.A.

WO 373/100/761. The London Omnibus List for Gallant and Distinguished Services in the Field. Name Baird, Kathleen Mary Rank: Nurse Service No: 81706 Regiment: New Zealand Women's Auxiliary Army Corps Medium Division.

DO 35/1008/2. Dominions Office and Commonwealth Relations Office: Original Correspondence. War-General. Establishment of Women's Royal Naval Service: New Zealand.

AIR 54/156. South Africa Air Force: Operations Record Books. AIR 54. South African Womens Auxiliary Air Force, Middle East.

AIR 54/135. South Africa Air Force: Operations Record Books. AIR 54. Womens Auxiliary Air Force.

AIR 54/199. South Africa Air Force: Operations Record Books. Womens Auxiliary Air Force, Mediterranean Allied Air Forces.

AIR 54/134. South Africa Air Force: Operations Record Books. Womens Auxiliary Air Force.

AIR 54/135. South Africa Air Force: Operations Record Books. Womens Auxiliary Air Force.

AIR 54/155. South Africa Air Force: Operations Record Books. South African Womens Auxiliary Air Force, East Africa.

AIR 54/156. South Africa Air Force: Operations Record Books. South African Womens Auxiliary Air Force, Middle East.

AIR 54/155. South Africa Air Force: Operations Record Books. South African Womens Auxiliary Air Force, Middle East.

WO 32/10664. War Office and successors: Registered Files (General Series). Womens Services: Womens Auxiliary Corps (Code 68(D)): Womens Auxiliary Corps, India: formation.

WO 32/10664. War Office and successors: Registered Files (General Series). Overseas: India (Code 0(Z)): Womens Auxiliary Corps, India: formation.

WO 373/157/371. Recommendation for Award for May, James Eleanor Rank: Chief Commander Regiment: Women Auxiliary Corps, India.

AIR 23/2217. Air Ministry and Ministry of Defence: Royal Air Force Overseas Commands: Reports and Correspondence. Air Forces in India and Air Command South-East Asia. Womens Auxiliary Air Force in India and Ceylon: organisation and policy.

AIR 23/4986. Air Ministry and Ministry of Defence: Royal Air Force Overseas Commands: Reports and Correspondence. Air Command South-East Asia. Womens Auxiliary Air Force in India: conditions.

WO 203/780. War Office: South East Asia Command: Military Headquarters Papers, Second World War. Allied Land Forces South East Asia. Women's Auxiliary Service Burma: brief history.

FO 643/37. Burma Office, Burma Secretariat, and Foreign Office, Embassy, Rangoon, Burma: General Correspondence. Internal Affairs, Associations and Societies: Women's Auxiliary Service (Burma).

WO 373/79/325. Meritorious Service Awards. Various Theatres. Name Taylor, Ninian Regiment: Women's Auxiliary Service Burma Theatre of Combat or Operation: Burma Award: Member of the Most Excellent Order of the British Empire.

WO 373/81/355. Meritorious Service Awards. Various Theatres. Name Tucker, Mabel Grace Rank: Major Service No: 4 Regiment: Women's Auxiliary Services Theatre of Combat or Operation: Burma Award: Member of the Most Excellent Order of the British Empire.

WO 373/81/303. Meritorious Service Awards. Various Theatres. Name Morton, Joan Margaret Rank: Major Regiment: Women's Auxiliary Services Theatre of Combat or Operation: Burma Award: Member of the Most Excellent Order of the British Empire.

WO 373/81/339. Meritorious Service Awards. Various Theatres. Name St John, Lois Irene Rank: Major Service No: 2 Regiment: Women's Auxiliary Services Theatre of Combat or Operation: Burma Award: Member of the Most Excellent Order of the British Empire.

ADM 1/17377. Naval Stations (Code 50). Foreign Countries (52): Report of Royal Indian Navy 1943-1944. Formation of Womens' Royal Indian Naval Service: installation of a Royal Indian Naval Hospital at Bombay.

CO 850/192/23. Colonial Office: Personnel: Original Correspondence. Colonial Nursing Service: recruitment of nursing sisters outside the UK.

CO 850/169/17. Colonial Office: Personnel: Original Correspondence. Colonial Nursing Service. Overseas Nursing Association: applications for appointment from coloured nurses.

CO 850/175/17. Colonial Office: Personnel: Original Correspondence. Colonial Nursing Service: conditions of service, Palestine.

CO 850/175/16. Colonial Office: Personnel: Original Correspondence. Colonial Nursing Service: summaries of conditions of service.

CO 850/157/18. Colonial Office: Personnel: Original Correspondence. National Service Scheme. Re-employment of retired officers. Colonial Nursing Service.

CO 850/175/15. Colonial Office: Personnel: Original Correspondence. Colonial Nursing Service: seniority on transfer.

CO 877/26/2. Colonial Office: Appointments Department: Registered Files. Post-war recruitment: Colonial Nursing Service.

CO 850/212/12. Colonial Office: Personnel: Original Correspondence. Colonial Nursing Service: wartime recruitment.

CO 850/174/17. Colonial Office: Personnel: Original Correspondence. Annual confidential reports on officers: revision and inclusion of Colonial Nursing Service.

CO 850/204/3. Colonial Office: Personnel: Original Correspondence. Pensions. Colonial Nursing Service: pension and superannuation arrangements.

CO 850/151/23. Colonial Office: Personnel: Original Correspondence. Creation of a unified colonial nursing service.

CO 850/84/12. Colonial Office: Personnel: Original Correspondence. Establishment of a colonial nursing service.

CO 850/133/10. Colonial Office: Personnel: Original Correspondence. Constitution and composition of the Colonial Nursing Service.

CO 850/192/24. Colonial Office: Personnel: Original Correspondence. Colonial Nursing Service: recruitment in wartime.

CO 850/169/19. Colonial Office: Personnel: Original Correspondence. Colonial Nursing Service. Nurses confirmed in their appointments.

CO 850/169/15. Colonial Office: Personnel: Original Correspondence. Colonial Nursing Service. Miscellaneous enquiries.

CO 850/169/16. Colonial Office: Personnel: Original Correspondence. Colonial Nursing Service. Revised form of agreement: strict interpretation of passage clause by British Guiana in event of officer resigning for marriage.

CO 850/169/18. Colonial Office: Personnel: Original Correspondence. Colonial Nursing Service. Recruitment policy.

IWM holds many PoW records, including papers, books, images and oral interviews.

AP 14372D. A group of West Indian women, recruited to join the ATS, wait for transport to take them to their training camp, 10 November 1943.

PL 14369D. Three women from Trinidad, who volunteered for service in the ATS, are seen looking at a poster showing English countryside, 10 November 1943.

CP 13937D. A group of West Indian ATS recruits just arrived at camp in an army car, November 1943.

D 21328. Garden party of West Indian ATS: women working in one of Britain's Ordnance depots attend a party given in their honour by members of the WVS and the British Legion Women's section at Bicester.

D 21361. A tea party for 28 ATS women from the West Indies held at the Colonial Office by the Duke of Devonshire, Parliamentary Under Secretary of State for the Colonies.

PLP 3836D. Four Jamaican volunteers for the WAAF are seen leaving the Colonial Centre in Russell Square, London, 17 February 1943.

CH 11677. A portrait of WAAF from Kingston, Jamaica, 3 December 1943.

D 15033. A WAAF recruit from Trinidad, West Indies, pictured walking in a British park.

HU 53753. Leading Aircraftwoman Lilian Bader, the first WAAF to be trained as an Instrument Repairer. (NB: The Imperial War Museum's Department of Documents holds the memoirs of Mrs L M Bader).

PL 9610F. Under a scheme run by the Colonial Officer nurses from the West Indies underwent training at a London hospital. This photograph shows a nurse from Grenada taking a patient's temperature in a ward of a Fulham (London County Council) hospital, 14 March 1945.

PL 9609F. Student nurses from Grenada pictured together at a Fulham hospital, 14 March 1945.

WO 345. War Office: Japanese Index Cards of Allied Prisoners of War and Internees, Second World War.

WO 367. War Office: Japanese Registers of Allied Prisoners of War and Civilian Internees held in Camps in Singapore, Second World Wars.

WO 344. War Office: Directorate of Military Intelligence: Liberated Prisoner of War Interrogation Questionnaires.

WO 392. War Office: Directorate of Prisoners of War: Prisoners of War Lists, Second World War.

WO 361. War Office: Directorate of Prisoners of War: Prisoners of War Lists, Second World War.

CO 980. Colonial Office: Prisoners of War and Civilian Internees Department.

HO 215. Home Office: Internment, General Files.

RG 32. (Online at: www.bmdregisters.co.uk) Notifications of Prisoner of War Deaths.

Online (PoW Research)

www.captivememories.org.uk
www.malayanvolunteersgroup.org.uk
www.cofepow.org.uk
www.researchingfepowhistory.org.uk
www.mansell.com

Australia

National Archives of Australia: www.naa.gov.au/
Trove: http://trove.nla.gov.au/
Australian Women's Register: www.womenaustralia.info/
Australian Department of Defence: www.defence.gov.au/footer/contacts
World War Two nominal Roll: www.ww2roll.gov.au

Canada

Library and Archives Canada: www.collectionscanada.gc.ca
Second World War Service Files: Canadian Armed Forces War Dead: www.collectionscanada.gc.ca/databases/war-dead/001056-100.01-e.php
CFB Esquimalt Naval & Military Museum: www.navalandmilitarymuseum.org/index.asp
Canada at War: www.canadaatwar.ca/index.php
Canadian War Museum: www.warmuseum.ca/home
Canadian Newspapers and the Second World War: www.warmuseum.ca/cwm/exhibitions/newspapers/intro_e.shtmls

New Zealand

NZDF Archives www.nzdf.mil.nz/personnel%2Drecords/nzdf-archives/default.htm

South Africa

South African National Defence Forces
Documentation Service Directorate, (Personnel Division)
Private Bag X289, Pretoria, 0001, South Africa:
fax: +27 12 323 5613
(Mail or fax inquiries only)

Zimbabwe (formerly Rhodesia)

The National Archives of Zimbabwe: www.archives.gov.zw/

Most records relating to women serving in India in the Second World war are held in the India Office Records at the British Library. These include:

IOR:L/AG/20/39/1. Contains release leave accounts and records of the payment of gratuities to members of the Indian Army Nursing Services

IOR:L/AG/21/13/97. Includes service pensions paid to retired members of the Indian Military Nursing service in the UK.

IOR: L/MIL/14. Personal Files relating to VADS who served in India.

IOR:L/AG/20/41/1-4. Payment books on appointment.

IOR:L/AG/20/41/5-6. Records of VADs released in the UK 1946-1947.

End of War and Demobilisation

www.forcesreunited.org.uk. The largest British Armed Forces Community on the web and can help to connect veterans or to find a former colleague of an ancestor.

Regimental and veterans' associations can be similarly useful. Bletchley Parks holds an annual Veterans' Day.

IWM
Documents.8973. Release certificate issued by the Women's Land Army to Miss L D Dave in April 1946.

There are over 30 other examples of release certificates in the Documents collection. IWM has a good collection of papers, photographs and other material relating to demobilisation of women's services.

NAM
WRAC trace cards 1949-1985 (the official number is required).

ITN Source (archive footage): www.itnsource.com/en/
WRAC Association: www.wracassociation.org.uk
WRVS: www.wrvs.org.uk
FANY: www.fany.org.uk

Chronology of events and formation of organisations featured in the book

1638-1641	The Scottish (Bishops') Wars.
1642-1646	The First Civil War.
10 Jul 1642	First Siege of Hull.
24 Sep - 1 Oct 1642	Manchester and Salford.
2 Sep - 11 Oct 1643	2nd Siege of Hull .
1642-1645	Siege of Skipton Castle.
1642-1645	Siege of Leicester.
23 Oct 1642	Battle of Edgehill.
1642	First Siege of Exeter.
4 Nov 1642 - 25 Apr 1643	Siege of Reading and Chalgrove Field.
May 1643	Siege of Wardour Castle - defended in vain by Lady Blanche Arundell.
30 Jun 1643	Battle of Adwalton Moor.
13 Jul 1643	Battle of Roundaway Down.
23-26 Jul 1643	Siege of Bristol.
1643	Second Siege of Exeter.
10 Aug - 5 Sep 1643	Siege of Gloucester.
20 Sep 1643	First Battle of Newbury.
21 Nov 1643 - 25 Feb 1644	Siege of Wythenshawe Hall.
Dec 1643	Siege of Arundel Castle.
25 Jan 1644	Battle of Nantwich.
29 Feb - 21 Mar 1644	First Siege of Newark.
5-6 Mar 1644	Siege of Hemyock Castle.
1644	Siege of Lyme Regis.
1644	Siege of Oxford.
1644	Siege of Newcastle-on-Tyne.
1644	Siege of Plymouth.
1644	Siege of Beeston Castle.
1644	Siege of Lathom House.

1644	Second Siege of Newark.
22 Apr - 16 Jul 1644	Siege of York.
Jun 1644	Battle of Marston Moor.
Jul 1644 - Jul 1645	Siege of Taunton.
27 Oct 1644	Second Battle of Newbury.
Feb 1645 - Jan 1646	Siege of Chester.
14 Jun 1645	Battle of Naseby.
26 Nov 1645 - 8 May 1646	Third Siege of Newark.
1645	Third Siege of Exeter.
1646	Siege of Pendennis Castle.
1648-1649	The Second Civil War.
1648	Siege of Colchester.
May - Jul 1648	Siege of Pembroke.
1649-1651	The Third Civil War.
24 Mar 1649	Pontefract and Scarborough - Lady Cholmley of Scarborough Castle nursed the sick during the siege; usually local women as difficult to move 'hospitals'.
1652-1654	Dutch War.
1756-1763	Seven Years' War.
1799-1815	Napoleonic Wars.
1813	EIC monopoly ends.
1853-1856	Crimean War.
March 1854	Britain, France and Turkey declare war on Russia; Florence Nightingale is recruited to oversee the introduction of female nurses into the military hospitals in Turkey.
November 1854	Battle of Inkerman.
1855	Mary Seacole arrives in the Crimea.
1857-1858	Indian Mutiny.
1870	British National Society for Aid to the Sick and Wounded in War founded.
1870-1871	Franco-Prussian War.
1876	Turco-Servian War.
1877-1878	Russo-Turkish War.
1878-1880	Afghan Wars.
1879	Zulu War.
1880-1881	First Boer War.
1882	Anglo-Egyptian War
1883	Queen Victoria awards Florence Nightingale the Royal Red Cross.
1884-1885	Egyptian Campaign (Sudan War).
1885	Qualified midwife matrons for soldiers' wives and children.

1892	Matabele War.
1898	Battle of Omdurman; Sudan expedition.
1899-1902	Second Anglo-Boer War (South African War).
1903	QAIMNS replaced ANS.
1905	The British National Society for Aid to the Sick and Wounded in War became known as the British Red Cross Society.
1907	Florence Nightingale is the first woman to receive the Order of Merit.
1907	Territorial and Reserve Forces Act introduced a scheme for Voluntary Aid: 'trained volunteers were to be organised into Voluntary Aid Detachments which could be attached to either the British Red Cross Society, the Order of St John or the Territorial Forces Association'.
1908	QAIMNSR formed.
1908	Territorial Force Nursing Service formed.
1911	UK census.
1912-1913	Balkan Wars.
4 Aug 1914	Britain declares war on Germany.
10 Aug 1914	Suffragettes in prison are offered amnesty.
Sep 1914	Women's Volunteer Reserve and Women's Defence Relief Corps established.
1 Feb 1915	Endell Street Military Hospital opens.
Apr 1915	Bombs fall on London.
May 1915	Coalition government came into force.
Mar 1915	Ministry of Munitions established; War Service Register opens.
17 Jul 1915	Women's 'Right to Serve' march in London.
Aug 1915	National Register for men and women between the ages of 16 and 65 established.
27 Jan 1916	Conscription introduced for unmarried men (First Military Service Bill).
Mar 1916	Women's National Land Service Corps established.
May 1916	Universal military conscription of men (aged 18-41).
1 Dec 1916	Women's Army Auxiliary Corps (WAAC) established.
7 Dec 1916	Asquith ousted from the Coalition Government.
7 Dec 1916	Lloyd George Coalition Government established; begins more efficient organisation of the Home war effort.
1916	Women's Auxiliary Military Services established.
3 Mar 1916	WAAC enrols first members.
Mar 1916	Military Medal was created.
Jul 1916	The first award of the Military Medal was made to a French Nurse Mlle E Moeau 'for gallantry'.

Sep 1916	Lady Dorothie Feilding was the first Englishwoman recipient of the Military Medal 'for bravery as an ambulance driver'.
Jan 1917	Miss D Eden was the first woman to be mentioned in despatches for bravery while nursing.
Jun 1917	King George V created the Order of the British Empire, and the Order of the Companions of Honour - both for men and women.
29 Nov 1917	Women's Royal Naval Service (WRNS) established.
1 Jan 1918	Food rationing (of sugar) is introduced in Britain.
6 Feb 1918	Representation of the People Act extends the franchise to most women over the age of 30.
1 Apr 1918	Women's Royal Air Force (WRAF) established.
9 Apr 1918	WAAC is renamed Queen Mary's Army Auxiliary Corps (QMAAC).
19 May 1918	Last air raid on London.
11 Nov 1918	Armistice is signed.
10 Feb 1919	Conference of Allied Women attends Peace Conference.
28 Nov 1919	Nancy Astor elected first female MP.
23 Dec 1919	British Sex Disqualification Removal Act - women can enter trades and professions.
1920	WRAF disbanded.
1923	The RAF Nursing Service was renamed Princess Mary's Royal Air Force Nursing Service.
1937	Air Raid Precautions Act imposed ARP duties on local authorities.
9 Sep 1938	Auxiliary Territorial Service (ATS) established.
30 Sep 1938	Munich Agreement signed.
Apr 1939	Women's Royal Naval Service reformed.
28 Jun 1939	Women's Auxiliary Air Force (WAAF) formed.
1 Jul 1939	Women's Land Army is formed.
1 Sep 1939	Mass evacuation of towns and cities; WVS assists.
2 Sep 1939	National Service (Armed Forces) Act passed enabling all men 18-41 to be called up.
3 Sep 1939	Britain and France declare war on Germany.
1939-1945	Second World War.
Oct 1939	Males aged 20-23 had to register for one of the armed forces.
22 Dec 1939	First WAAF regulation issued.
8 Jan 1940	Food rationing is re-introduced, beginning with bacon, butter and sugar.
14 May 1940	Local Defence Volunteers (LDV) was created.

May 1940	Evacuation of British troops and women's services from Dunkirk.
24 Aug 1940	First daylight air raid on London.
Sep 1940	First women are trained to work anti-aircraft guns.
7 Sep 1940	Blitz begins: mass evacuation of women and children from some urban areas.
Apr 1941	Women trained to operate searchlights.
25 Apr 1941	Defence (Women's Forces) Regulations declared all personnel enrolled in the ATS and the WAAF members of the Armed Forces of the Crown.
19 Jun 1941	First non-training flights of the women's section of the Air Transport Auxiliary (ATA).
Aug 1941	National Fire Service (NFS) formed out of the AFS and local authority fire brigades.
7 Dec 1941	Japan bombs the US Military Base at Pearl Harbor
18 Dec 1941	National Service Act No 2 (enacted 1942) - calls up single women aged 20-30 years, and widows with no children; women could choose to enter the armed forces or to perform vital war work in farming or industry.
Spring 1942	Age limit expanded to include women between 19 and 43 years old.
Apr 1942	Women's Timber Corps formed.
May 1942	Fall of Singapore.
1943	9/10 single women and 8/10 of married women, aged 18-40, are serving in the armed forces or working in industry.
4 Oct 1943	Air Commandant Lady Mary Welsh appointed Director of the WAAF.
8 May 1945	VE Day - Victory in Europe: Germany surrenders to the Western Allies and Russia.
15 Aug 1945	VJ Day - Victory in Japan: Japan surrenders to the Allies.
1946	APR disbanded.
8 Jun 1946	Victory Day parade in London.
Aug 1946	Women's Timber Corps disbanded.
1948	Army and Air Force (Women's Service) Act.
1948	National Fire Service disbanded.
1948	Introduction of the National Health Service (NHS).
1949	QAIMNS becomes QARANC.
1949	WRNS becomes permanent service.
1949	Civil Defence Corps.
1949	ATS becomes WRAC.

1949	Women's Royal Air Force (WRAF) established within the RAF (Director Dame Felicity Peake).
1950	Women's Land Army is disbanded.
1950-1953	Korean War.
1966	WVS becomes WRVS.
1977	Naval Disciplines Act formalises WRNS as part of the Royal Navy.
1992	Women are incorporated into the armed forces.
1994	WRAF merged with RAF.
2000	QARNNS officially becomes part of the Royal Navy.
9 Jul 2005	Memorial to the Women of World War Two unveiled.

Female Recipients of the George Cross

This is the civilian counterpart of the Victoria Cross (AM = Albert Medal; EM = Edward Medal; EGM = Empire Gallantry Medals which were exchanged for the George Cross).

ALLEN, Florence Alice Miss. Children's Nurse, Earthquake rescue 19 Nov 1935 (originally awarded the AM).

ASHBURNHAM, Doreen Miss. 11 year-old girl, Fighting off a cougar 20 Dec 1917 (originally awarded the AM).

ASHRAF-un-NISA Begum. Begum of Hyderabad, Fire rescue 1 Feb 1937 EGM.

FRASER, Harriet Elizabeth. (later Mrs. BARRY) Miss. Staff Nurse, Terr. Force Nursing Service, Hospital fire rescue 31 Jan 1919 (originally awarded the AM).

HARRISON, Barbara Jane (BOAC air stewardess, 1968) - Airplane rescue 8 Aug 1969 GC.

KHAN, Noor Inayat (WAAF) - INAYAT-KHAN, Noor Asst. Sect. Off. WAAF, secd. to FANY Espionage 5 Apr 1949 GC.

SANSOM, Odette (FANY) - SANSOM, Odette Marie Celine Mrs. Women's Transport Service (FANY), Espionage and PoW 20 Aug 1946 GC.

SZABO, Violette (ATS) - SZABO, Violette Reine Elizabeth Ensign, Women's Transport Service (FANY), Espionage 17 Dec 1946 GC.

THOMAS, Dorothy Louise Miss. Nurse, Middlesex Hosp., London Explosion averted 2 Mar 1934 EGM.

TOWNSEND, Emma Jose Miss. Schoolgirl, Fighting off a murderer 6 Sep 1932 EGM

VAUGHAN, Margaret (later Mrs. PURVES) Miss. 14 year-old Schoolgirl, Tidal rescue 1 Nov 1949 (originally awarded the AM).

WOLSEY, Hilda Elizabeth Miss. Nurse, Hanwell Asylum, Lunatic asylum rescue 28 Mar 1911 (originally awarded the AM).

To date there have been no female recipients of the Victoria Cross, although it is possible for women to receive this award.

In 2011, the British Prime Minister David Cameron announced the return of the British Empire Medal (BEM), which had been founded in 1917 but was stopped in 1993. It was awarded for 'meritorious' actions whether by civilians or military personnel.

The twelve panels on the oak screen in York Minster, each bearing the appropriate insignia, open to reveal the 'THE NAMES OF THE WOMEN OF THE EMPIRE WHO GAVE THEIR LIVES IN THE WAR 1914 - 1918 TO WHOSE MEMORY THE FIVE SISTERS WINDOW WAS RESTORED'. The memorial was unveiled on 24 June 1925. All names of those commemorated on the Women's Screens are reproduced here with the permission of David Vickers of: www.forthefallen.co.uk, who transcribed them from photographs he took in 2010.

Women's Screen One
York Minster
Queen Alexandra's Royal Naval Nursing Service

AINSWORTH Grace G
BEARD Eva G
CHAMBERLAIN Louisa

EDWARDS Caroline M
ELVINS Eliza M
GRIGSON Mabel E
PREVOST Annette M

ROBINS Mary J
ROWLATT Olive K
WILSON Annie

Women's Royal Naval Service

Officers

MACKINTOSH Evelyn M

Ratings

BEARDSALL E
BOWMAN Hilda May
CARE Margaret L
CARR Josephine
CLARKE Lucy Emma
COURT Helen I
DAVIES Caroline J
DRYSDALE Georgina

DREWRY Harriet H
DUKE Charlotte
ELDER Mrs E G
FLANNERY Mrs A M
HALL Mrs Sarah A
HUNTER Bessie Sim
HUNTER Lucy A
KNOWLES Alice

LOCKHART Mabel
O'KEEFE Sara
PEARSON Mabel C
READMAN Lucy
SKINNER Phyllis A
WHITE Dorothy M
WILLS Mrs Susan S
WOODRUFF Mary

Women's Screen Two
York Minster
Queen Alexandra's Imperial Military Nursing Service

ANDREWS Ellen
ARMSTRONG Ellen
ASTELL Ethel F
BATES Frances M
BEAUFOY Kate
BENNETT Helena S
BERESFORD Rebecca R
BERRIE Charlotte
BLACKLOCK Alice M
BLAKE Edith
BLENCOWE Mabel E
BOLGER Kathleen
BOND Ella Maude
BRACE Frances E
BRETT Norah V
BRINTON Gertrude
BROWN Euphemia L
BUCKLER Elinor
BUTLER Sarah E
CALLIER Ethel F M
CAMMACK Edith M
CHALLINOR E Annie
CHANDLER Dorothy M
CLIMIE Agnes M
CLOUGH Mary
COLE Dorothy H
COLE Emily Helena
COMPTON F D'Oyley
CONSTERDINE V C
COOKE Ella Kate
COX Annie
CROYSDALE Marjorie
CRUICKSHANK I
DALTON Joan G
DANAHER Mary
DAWES Emily
DAWSON Eveline M

DEWAR Margaret S
DOHERTY Mary A
DONOVAN Bridget
DUCKERS M E
DUNCAN I L M
EDGAR Elizabeth
ELIFFE Margaret
ELLIOTT E
EVANS Jane
FARLEY Martha
FERNLEY Ethel
FERGUSON Rachel
FLINTOFF Alice
FORBES B G F
FOYSTER Ellen L
GARLICK Hilda
GARNER A E C
GASKELL Lily
GLADSTONE E M
GLEDHILL Annie
GOLDSMITH A A V
GRANT May
GORBUTT Martha
GRAY Emily
GREENWOOD HOPPER J E
GREATOREX Janet
GRIFFIN Lillian
GRIFFITHS Janet L
GROVER Alice Jane
GURNEY Elizabeth
HALL Frances Mary
HAMILTON Margaret
HANNAFORD Ida D
HARKNESS Bessie
HASTINGS Helen M
HAWLEY Florence
HAWLEY Nellie

HENRY Charlotte E
HILLING Sophie
HILLS Maud Ellen
HOBBES Narrelle
HODGSON Eveline M
HOOK Florence M L
HOWARD Florence G
HUGHES Gladys C
IRWIN Winifred H
JACK Christina
JAMIESON Jessie S
JOHNSTON M Hessie
JONES Gertrude E
JONES Hilda Lilian
KEMP Christina M F
KEMP Elise Margaret
KENDALL Rose E
KYNOCK Alison G
LANCASTER Alice H
LEA Hilda
MANN Agnes Grieg
MACBETH M Ann
MACGILL Mary
MACKENZIE I
MACKINNON M
MCALLISTER C
MCCOMBIE C
MCDONALD E
MCGIBBON Rose
MCROBBIE J E
MARK Hannah D
MARLEY Grace M
MARMION M
MARNOCH M B
MARSHALL M B
MASON Fanny M
MELDRUM Isabel

MILLER Catherine
MILLER Frances
MILNE Helen
MILNE Mabel
MORETON Ada
MURRAY Mabel
NICOL Christina
O'BRIEN Moyra
ROBERTS Eleanor
O'GORMAN Eileen M
PARKER Elsie K D
PATTERSON Jessie J
PEARSE Phyllis Ada
PEPPER Edith D
PHILIPS Jessie J
PILLING Doris
RADCLIFFE Ethel B
REID Annie C
RITCHIE Jessie
ROBERTS Anne L
ROBERTS Jane
ROBERTS Margaret D
ROBINETTE Caroline

ROBINSON Elizabeth
RODWELL Mary
ROWLANDS Helena M
RUSSELL Alice M
SAXON Ethel
SEYMOUR C Mary
SIMPSON Edith
SIMPSON Elizabeth
SMITH Frances F
SMITH Jeanie B
SMITHIES Ettie L
SPINDLER Nellie
STACEY Dorothy L
STANLEY Ada
STEPHENSON G Annie
STEVENS Lottie M
STEWART E Grace
STEWART Wilma B
STURT Kate Rosina
SWAIN Lucy Melton
TEGGIN Eugenie
THOMAS Lilian
THOMAS M E

THOMSON E R
THOMSON Kerr M
TINDALL Fanny
TOWNSEND M
TREVITHAN Rita
TULLOCH Edith
TURTON Alice M
VINTER Bertha
WAKEFIELD J
WALLACE E
WALSHE Mary A
WATSON D M
WATSON E H
WATSON Mary
WELFORD Alice
WHEATLEY Annie
WILLS Mary E
WILLISON Nellie
WILSON C M
WILSON Myrtle E
WOODLEY Ada
WRIGHT Hannah E
MANNELL Dorothy W

Queen Alexandra's Military Nursing Service For India

JAY K Christine   KEARNEY I

Women's Screen Three
York Minster
Queen Mary's Auxiliary Army Corps

ABSOLOM W E
ASPDEN Dorothy
BAILEY Ethel M
BALL C C
BARFORD Edith
BARHAM Ethel A
BARROW M A
BENOY Florence E
BILLINGTON Sarah
BLAIKLEY Mary M
BOTTOMS L A G
BRADLEY Jane
BRANNIGAN Nellie
BREWER Kate S A
BROWN May F
BULL Mary
CAMPBELL B
CARPENTER E V
CARROLL K
CARY Bessie
CARY Hilda
CASWELL M
CHAMBERS Mary M
CLARKSON E G
CLITHEROE Mary
COBB Gladys H
CONNOR Catherine
COOMBES Violet G
COOPER Harriet
CORCORAN Annie

HARLAND Eva M
HARRICK M K
HARRINGTON Lena
HARRIS Sarah L
HARROLD Helen C
HODGSON F C
HOLBOROW Rose M
HOOPER K E A
HOPE Florence E
HORNER Violet M
HOWELL Emma
HYDE Pattie
ING Elsie V
INGLIS Kathleen
JOHNCOCK F M
JOHNS Mildred M
JOHNSON Minnie
JOHNSTON E S
JONES Annie E
JORDAN Lois
KNOX Jane
LAST Julia
LATHAM Louisa
LEE Elsie May
LESSER Ada
LORD Winifred J
LUKER D M
LUND Minnie W
MACMAHON Agnes
MADDOCKS D B

PETTER Ellen M
PRIESTLEY Elsie
QUANE Doris
RAULT Nelly F R
REED Dorothy A
REEVES Eliza J
RICHARDSON Maud
ROBERTS Jean
RODGERS C H
ROGERS Marie L
ROUTLEDGE G H
ROWLAND Mary M
RUSSELL Eleanor
SAINT Lucy Jane
SHAYLER Nellie E
SIMMONS C M
SMITH Annie T
SMITH A W M
SMITH Brunetta
SMITH Diana R
SMITH Mary E
SMYTH Mary
SOLLIS K R
SPEIGHT Louie
SPITTLE Anne
STEELE W M
STEPHENS I D
STIEBEL Marie L
TAIT E E
TARR Mabel

COTTON Rose
CROZIER Clara
DALY Mary E
DAVIES Madge
DAVIS E S
DAW Winifred
DUNNE Sheila
DYER G W A
ELLIES Esther
EVANS Mary A
EVANS Jane
FERGUSON Mary
FOULKES Elsie
FRANSHAW Agnes N
GALLEY Amy C
GEOGHEGAN B E
GERRARD Nellie
GIBSON M A C
GOODING F
GOSLING Clara
GRANT Jeannie M
GRANT Jessie
GREEN Ethel
HALL A
HAMER Ellen B
HARDING Violet N

MADDOCKS S E
MARTIN Eleanor
MARTIN M T
MASSEY F E M
MATTHEWS M M
MAUNDER N M
MAYERS May
MAYNE Gertrude
MILLER Annie C
MITCHELL F H
MOORE B V
MOORE Sara M
MOORES Annie E
NATTRESS E A
NUTLEY Catherine
O'NEILL N T
O'REILLY Marion
PAGE B A
PARKER Ethel F M
PARNELL Elsie
PATRICK Lilian P
PEAKE Susan
PHILLIPS Violet
PICKERING Edith
POOLEY Beatrice
LONG V A Lambton
STEVENSON M M

THOMAS Olive G
THOMASSON Alice
THOMSON Ellen
THORNTON D M
TODD Barbara R
TOOBY Frances
TWADELL Maud E
TWELLS Alice
WALCROFT Kitty
WALKER W L
WALLACE Mary
WALSH Betsy M
WATSON Jeannie
WATT Alicia
WELLER Ada E
WESTWELL Mary
WHALL A M
WHITCOMBE Amy L
WHITTAKER E
WHITWORTH N
WILLS Beatrice L
WILSON Jemina
WRIGHT Elsie M
WRIGHT Jennie
WRIGHT Maud
WYLIE May

AITKEN Mary
ALLEN Louisa
AMBROSE Blanche A
ANDERSON Hastie J
ANSCOMBE Daisy M
ARMER Alice Ruth
ASHLEY Dora
BADCOCK Dorothy
BLACKBURN Elizabeth
BRIGNELL Alice
BROAD Netta Ellen
CHALMERS M H
CHURCH Rose Maria
CLARKE Ellen
COLLINS Grace Z
CONNER Annie
COOME Agnes Hilda
CRAIK Annie
CROSS Amelia
DALY Alice
DAVEY Violet E
DAVIS Marjorie E
DAY Charlotte A
DYE Mabel
ELLIS F Mary
EVANS Nellie
FITZGERALD M L
GIBSON Susan
GOODSELL Lily S
GOODWIN B
BACKHURST K A
CALDER Mary M
HOLMES Lily C

GRAY Florence
HARPER Lilian F
HARRIS Lucy
HARRIS Marianne B
HIBBERD Ivy M P
HOLLIDAY Elizabeth
HORTON Amy
HOWELL Eunice
HUDSON Daisy
HUDSON Francis L
HUGHES Ada Styles
KENNARD Fanny A
LAMBERT Emmie
LAPISH Marian
LLEWELLYN JONES F M D
LOOKER Nesta Mary
MACKENZIE Helen
MARSH Lilian Maud
MARTIN Ada E
MCNEIL Catherine M
MCTAGGART Jessie
MOORE Emily
MURRELL E I
NEAL Rose Edith
NICHOLSON M P
NUTLEY May A
O'DONNELL P E
PAYNE M G
PHILLIPS Ethel A
LYALL Annie
PARRATT B L
REEKS Edith Jane
SELBY Lily
SISSENS Lily

PIGGETT Annie L
PIGOTT Alice
PLANT Lilian
PORTER Violet M
PURDY Phyllis
RAMSDEN Clara
RICHARDS Ethel
ROBERTS Annie
ROBERTS Elizabeth
ROE Annie
SCAMMELL Lily
SHAW May Elizabeth
SILLITOE Ada F V
SIMMONS Annie
SMITH Annie G
SMITH Fanny
SMITHERS Dorothy M
SPARKES Florence
SPOONER Isabella J
STANLEY Mary Ann
STOKES Emily
TAYLOR Lilian A M
TOWNSEND F
TUCKER M Annie
TURMAINE Rose J
WALTER Gladys
WATFORD Nellie
WILLIAMS E O
WILSON Alice F
WOODCOCK M
STENNING Annie
VASS Lily F
WOOD Annie E

Women's Screen Five
York Minster
Order of Saint John and the British Red Cross

BAIN Annie Watson
GOLDING Bessie

MCDONALD I K M

MONTGOMERY M E
WHITEHEAD Ida K

Members of Voluntary Aid Detachments
Who Lost Their Lives On Active Service

ABBEY Agnes
ACLAND HOOD M
ADAMSON Annie
ADDS Florence B
ALLEN Emma
ALLOM Marjorie
ALLWOOD M
ANDERSON M
ARMSTRONG S J
ARNOLD Mary T
BAILY W Mrs
BALL Catherine
BARKER Edith F
BARLOW F Mrs
BARON Margaret A
BARRETT Violet
BARRY Anna M G
BARTON Mrs
BATES Madeline E
BATTERSBY Mary
BEETHAM Mrs
BENNETT H Mrs
BENNETT K C F
BENNETT O L
BICKERSTETH Joan
BLACKBURN Zina
BOUSFIELD Mary C
BOWSER Thekla
BRAITHWAITE M D
BRAMALL Ethel

CASS Mary E
CHADWICK Hilda F
CHADWICK Mabel E
CHAPMAN Marion D
CHINN Lilian E
CLEMENTS Sarah
COATES Winifred S
COCK Beatrice Mrs
COLES Daisy H M
COLTON Dorcas
COULDREY Mary
COX Frances
COUSINS Isabella D
CREWDSON D M L
CRIGHTON Dorothy
CRILLY J Mary
CRONEEN B Mrs
CURTEIS Rosamund
CURTIS Amy Mrs
DABNER Eleanor
DACOMBE A Mary
DANGERFIELD Ivy
DANN Maud
DAVIDSON Margaret
DAVIES Eva
DAWSON Alice Mary
DENISON Florence
DICKSON Esther
DICKSON Mary C
DIXON Dorothy

FEENEY Mildred
FENTON May Mrs
FERGUSON M M
FITZGERALD C
FLINT Doreen
FOX Dorothy
FURLONG Winifred
GAILEY Laura M
GARFORTH S
GASH S Mabel
GAWTHORNE L R Mrs
GAY Kate
GEM Gertrude Mrs
GILTMAN Gertrude
GLEADOW Doris
GLOVER Florence G
GOLDSON Lilian
GOOCH Phyllis
GOODLIFFE Ada
GOODMAN Dorothy
GORDON E M
GORDON-JONES G
GOULD Emily M
GRANT Elsie May
GRAY Mary B
GRIFFITHS J L
GRUNDY Marjorie A
GUILLEMARD P
GUNTON Effie R
GURNEY Sylvia

BRAMFITT M E
BRANFORD Mary
BRENT Y R H A D
BREWIS E
BRIDGEFORD M
BRIGGS Dorothy
BROSTER Sister
BROWN E Gladys
BROWN Winifred
BRUCE B J
BRYAN-DAUNT Z K
BUCKLEY Florence
BULMER Rose
BURGESS Meta
BURTENSHAW W H
BUTLER K B Mrs
BYTHEWAY Gertrude
CAMPION Eleanor L
CAREW Margaret
CARRICK W E
CARTER Ileene M
CARTER Vera L
CLIBBENS B L

DODD Emma Mrs
DODD Josephine
DOLAN Mary
DOWNS Sybil B
DRAGGE Doris May
DUGAN Norah
DUNCANSON Una
DUNNING Ethel
DUNNINGHAM A
DURNO M I K
EARLE Elspeth
EDWARDS M E M
ELGER Cicely Mrs
ELLISTON E K
ELWES Emily Mary
ENGLISH Winifred
EVANS Margaret E
EVANS Margaret M
FAITHFULL F May
FANNING B B
FARR Mabel
FAWKES Olive
GERARD M Lady
BLEEK Mildred J

HACKETT V C H
HAINES Jessie M
HALLAM Alice V
HALLEY M Mrs
HAMILTON Lily
HANDY A
HARDING Isabel L
HARTMAN Emily
HARVEY A F
HASNIP Mary
HASSE M Helen
HEATHCOTE M J
HEDGES Edith D
HELLYER Edythe C
HEMINGWAY Bessie
HERBERT Julia H
HILL Eleanor F
HODGE D
HOGG Florence
HOLDER Beatrice
HOLLIS K Mary
HOOD Ada Annie
HUFFAM Olive S
ALEXANDER Anne

HOOPER N L Mrs
HOPE Isabel
HORNSEY Sarah J
HORRELL D M
HUTTON Eva
IMESON Amy E
INGHAM Daisy
INGLIS Annie
INGRIM Edith
JOHNSTON Annie
JONES Ada
JONES D May
JONES Gladys
JONES Lilian
JONES Martin Mrs
KENTISH Edith M

NEISH Annie
NOEL Mrs
O'DONNELL J
OGG Kate E
OLPHERT F B
ORFORD Eleanor F
ORME Alice Mrs
OWEN Meriel G B
PAGE Doris
PAINE Phyllis
PARISH Maud Mrs
PARKER Lilian L
PARRY Ada B Mrs
PAVLIN Anne
PEARCE L N
PEARE Hilda F

SPARGO M Mrs
SQUIRE Dorothy J
STALLARD Alice M
STEPHENSON M S
STEVENS L Mrs
STEWART C
ST JOHN Esmee
STRANGE Alice M
SUTCLIFFE Zoe
SWAN Ethel Mrs
SYM Elsie
TAPSELL K Mary
TATE Ethel
TAYLOR Edith E
TAYLOR Ethel L
TAYLOR Gertrude

KERSHAW Annie
KING Dorothy
KING Nita M
KINNEAR K F
KIRK Jane M
LAMBARDE B A
LANGDALE Mary A
LARNER Bertha
LEDIARD H A
LEE E M
LEE Jeannie S
LEEPER Mildred
LEWIS Agnes
LIDDEL Lily
LINDSAY M Hon Mrs
LLEWELLYN G V
MACAN E
MALTBY Phyllis
MARTIN G M
MATTHEWS H Mrs
MACINTOSH M G R
MARSH Mary A
MATHIAS Florence
MAUNSELL Minnie
MCCALL K M
MCDOUGALL Mrs
MCGRIGOR L A M
MCLAUGHLIN E W
MCLAUGHLIN M M
MEADOWS P E
MEARES Ellen
MENELAWES Diana
MIDWOOD Lilian
MILLER Minnie D
MILLER T Mary
MILLES Maud Mrs
MOBERLEY Violet
MOORBY Hilda
MORGAN Hilda
MUNRO Minnie
MURDOCH Alice

PEEL Helen M
PINK Margery S
PLUMER A
POOLE Dorothy
PROCTOR Doris J
QUICK Lucy
RADFORD Edith
RANSOME Enid M
REID M
RICHARDS Ella
RIGBY Betsy Ann
ROBERTS A Mary
ROBERTS K H
ROBERTS H Mrs
ROGERS H Angela
ROLASON Mary
ROOKE Ellen M
ROPER Olive T
ROSKELL G L
ROY Louise I
ROW-FOGO G
RUNTO Gladys
RUTHERFORD A
RYLANCE Olive
SAMUELSON L Lady
SAUNDERS Emily
SELLAR Olive M
SETTLE F J
SEYMOUR C E M
SHAW Ellen M H
SHAW Lena
SHAW Nancy
SHEPHERD W
SHIMMIN Mona
SHORLT Fanny
SMALES F Emily
SMITH Mabel E
SMITH Mary C
SNELLING G
SNOW Edith Mrs
SOMERSET Alice

TAYLOR H B Mrs
TAYLOR Nellie
TEMPLE E Stella
THOMPSON H D M
THOMSON E
THOREN M O DE S DE
THURBY Lucy
TICHBORNE M E F
TINDALL Mary
TONKIN Edith M
TOUGH Helen F
TOZER Mrs
TROLLOPE Jessie
VAUGHAN Elsie M
WALKER Jennie
WALKER Sara
WALLACE D Mrs
WALLADGE Hilda
WALSH Sara
WARNOCK E
WARREN Florence
WATSON Helen
WATSON Hilda
WATSON Tamar
WHITE D M
WHITE V C B
WHITE-JERVIS D J
WILDASH Frances
WILDER A
WILLEY Olive J
WILLIAMS Irene
WILLIAMS Jennie
WILLIAMSON M Mrs
WILLIS Eliza Mrs
WOLFREYS Edith
WOOD Margaret (Yorks)
WOOD Margaret (Beds)
WRIGHT Amelia B
YEOMAN Eva D
YOUNG Ada E
YOUNG M C

MURPHY Rosina C
BURGESS M K

SOMERVILLE J A
BURTON F M
STEWART Kathleen

YOUNG Mary A E
GUBBINS J M

Women's Screen Six
York Minster
Medical Women

FORSTER Laura Dr
IMPEY Elsie A Dr

LEWIS Sybil L Dr
ROSS Elizabeth Dr

TATE Isobel A Dr
WILSON Marion Dr

Scottish Women's Hospitals

INGLIS E M Dr (Founder)
BURT Mary A DE B
CATON Florence
DUNLOP Jessie H L
EARLE Agnes
FANNIN Teresa

FRASER Madge N
GRAY Mary S B
GUY Alice Annie
JORDAN Louisa
LEIGHTON Clara

MCDOWELL M
MINSHULL Augusta
SMITH Olive
SUTHERLAND B G
TOUGHILL C M F R Mrs
UNDERWOOD E J Mrs

Endell Street Military Hospital

WOODCOCK L Dr
GRAHAM Mary R R C

MORRISON Gladys E
PALMES Joan M G

PRIOR Eva Graham
WILKES Helen

Auxiliary Hospitals

ADDISON C
AKED Adelaide B
ALLEN Alice M Mrs
ASHWORTH O L H
ATKINSON W E D
BALL Clare
BAXTER M Mrs
BERESFORD Hilda
BIRKETT M J
BLAKE M S
BOOKER Ellen M
BOSTOCK Ida M
BRADSHAW F M M Mrs
BRIDGE Jessie

HARDING K Mrs
HETTERLEY H C
HODGES C Mary
HOLDEN Ruth
HOMER Hilda
INGHAM Sarah L
JACKSON D V M
JAGGARD Jessie B
JEFFERSON F
JENKINS Emily
JOHNS Lisle
JOHNSON C
JOHNSON Gladys
JOWETT B Mrs

POPE Helen
PRESTON E
PRIDEAUX Lily J
RAINSFORD F E
REDFERN Esther
RICHARDSON Gwen
RHODES Amy Mrs
ROBERTS Jennie
ROBERTSON A S V Mrs
ROBINSON M Mrs
SALTMARSH M E
SENIOR Mary Mrs
SHAW Evelyn F
SMITH Margaret

BROUGHTON E D Mrs
BROWN L Mrs
BUCKERIDGE K Mrs
BUCKINGHAM M A
BUTCHART Amy K
CARTER E M Mrs
CAVELL Edith
CORFIELD A B
CRAGGS Olive
CULL Dorothy C
DEERE Kate
DIGBY Elsie Mrs
EDE Dorothy
EDLIN Mary Mrs
EVANS Katie
FALCONER-GRANT L W
FALKNER M L Mrs
FISHER Mabel Mrs
FLOWER H M P
GIBSON Marjorie
GILBERT Ada
GILLER Gladys
GORDON Agnes

KLINDWORTH F
LEVER B H Lady
LEWIS Flossie
LLOYD Alys
LOW Isabella
LYE Marjery
LYON Esme
MCNAUGHTEN S
MARCHENT Ethel
MARSHAM C
MARTIN Ida
MAYNE Margaret
MCNALLY Clare E
MEW Fanny
MILLS Rose L Mrs
MORGAN Jane
MORTON Helen
PAGET Isabella Mrs
PALMEIRI Alice Mrs
PEARSON Nelly Mrs
PECK Mary Mrs
PENROSE Esme K
PETER Mary
MACKINTOSH Isabel

SMITH Olive
SMITH S M C
SPINDLER Nellie
STEELL C M
STEVENS E A Mrs
STEVENSON D
STIRLING Lydia
SWINTON Ethel M
THOMAS B J B
THOMPSON M B
TODD Florence
TOUGH E Mrs
TUCKER Mary J
WALFORD Emma
WALLS Emma Mrs
WHITTINGTON M
WILKINS Frances
WILTON Mary
WOOD Margaret
WOLLACOTT E
WORLEDGE M E
WRIGHT Rose Mrs
YOULE Mildred

BARNES M
BELL G
BENNETT Willmott
BIRD L E
BOARDMAN M
CARE M L
CHAMBERS R
CLARKSON D R
COX F
CROFTON N
CROWTHER L
CROXTON N
DENHAM F M
HALL M A
HARRISON W M
HARROWER A

HUGHES Edith
HUMBY F M
JACKSON W N
JINKS Mary
JOHNSON A M
KIDD E
LALOR W M
LEE Beatrice
LEE R
LORAM Ruth
MCKAY G B C
MEIKLE N C
MITCHELL A M R
NEWBY F
NODDER R A
NOWELL R E

PORTER V M
RATHMELL E
REEVES L A
RICHARDS E
ROBSON E M
RUSSELL E C
RYLE M C
SALMON L
SALVATOR Sister
SINCLAIR C
SMITH-SLIGO W M G
SMITH C
SMITH Helen
SMYTH P G
SPIERS M E
SQUIRES E

HAWKES F
HERITAGE Audrey
HODSKINSON A
HOLLISTER N
HOWELL E
IM THURN Gladys

PARRATT B L
PATERSON D M
PAYNE M G
PICKARD R Mrs
POPE C M LEGH
PORTER A E

THOMPSON M
TITLEY M G
TORAN M
WILLIAMS C
WILSON Ruth
RYLE Margaret C C

British Committee of the French Red Cross

CRYAN Edith Maud
DAVIS M E
INMAN D M

KING Grace
MCDONALD Mina

NIVEN J C
PETTIT A Madame
STEVENS Beatrice

Women's Screen Seven
York Minster
Canadian Army Nursing Service

Matrons

JAGGARD Jessie B   FRASER Margaret Marjory

Nursing Sisters

BAKER Miriam E
BALDWIN D M Y
BOLTON Grace E
CAMPBELL Christina
DAGG Ainslie St C
DAVIS Lena Aloa
DOUGLAS Carola J
DUSSAULT Alexina
FOLLETTE Minnie A
FORNERI Agnes F
FORTESCUE M Jane
GALLAHER Minnie K
GARBUTT Sarah E
GREEN Matilda E

HENNAN Victoria B
JENNER Lenna Mae
KEALY Ida Lilian
KING Jessie Nelson
LOWE Margaret
MELLETT Henrietta
MUNRO M E E
MACDONALD K M
MACKENZIE Clare
MCDIARMID Jessie M
MCINTOSH Rebecca
MCKAY Evelyn V
MCKENZIE Mary A
MCLEAN Rena

MACPHERSON Agnes
PEEL Aileen Powers
PRINGLE Eden Lyal
ROSS Ada J
SAMPSON Mae Belle
SARE Gladys Irene
SPARKS Etta
STAMERS Anna J
TEMPLEMAN Jean
TUPPER Addie A
TWIST Dorothy P
WAKE Gladys M M
WHITELEY Anna E
WOOD Alice A Mrs

Dominion of Newfoundland

BARTLETT Bertha (of Brigus)

Women's Screen Eight
York Minster
Australian Army Nursing Service

Matron

WALKER R R C   MILES Jean

Sisters

KNOX Hilda Mary
MOORHOUSE Edith A

MOWBRAY Norma V
MUNRO Gertrude Evelyn
PORTER K L, R R C

TYSON Fanny I O
WILLIAMS Blodwyn

Staff Nurses

BICKNELL Louisa
CLARE Emily
DICKINSON Ruby
HENNESSY Ada May

MORETON Letitia G
O'GRADY Amy Veda
O'KANE Rosa
POWER Kathleen M
RIDGWAY Doris A

ROTHERY Elizabeth
STAFFORD Mary F
THOMPSON Ada Mildred
WATSON Beatrice M

Australian Red Cross Society

BRENNAN Adelle

GRANT Lydia W F
MCBRYDE N Mrs

RIGGALL L B

New South Wales

DICKSON May
GOODMAN Pearl
HIRST Amy D

NUGENT Lillie
REED Amelia

ROPER Ursula
STARLING Winifred
STEADMAN Annie

Sisters

BROWN Marion
CLARK Isabel
COOKE Ella
FOX Catherine
GORMAN Mary
BARNES E H

HAWKEN Ada
HILDYARD Nora
ISDELL Helena
JAMIESON Mabel
LIND Lily
RAE Mary

RATTRAY Lorna
ROGERS Margaret
TUBMAN Esther
WHISHAW Mabel
SPEEDY Miss L E
REYNOLDS P M

Attached

BENNETT Wilmot

FOLLIOTT Amy Charlotte Melora
THOMPSON M H

Women's Screen Ten
York Minster
Union of South Africa Army Nursing Service

BAKER Edith A
BEAUFORT Kaloolah
BERNSTEIN Dora
BLACK Eleanor E
BOLUS Dorothea K
ADDISON Corrie
BAIN Annie

DUNN Gertrude E
EDGAR E
EDMEADES C A
ERSKINE M M E
FITZHENRY Daisy A
HEARNS Beatrice
FREUN Elizabeth

HOCKEY Olive
MUNROW Annie W
PAFF Pauline H E
WARDLE Ida
WATKINS Julia K
MACDONALD Mina

Colonial Nursing Association

GRAHAM Marion

POULTON Maude

WINCHESTER Julia

Women's Screen
York Minster
Mercantile Marine Stewardesses

AMBLER J M
ARNOTT Sarah
BRUCE M

HAFKIN Sarah
HENRY Olivia
HIRD Agnes

OLIPHANT M E
OWEN Hannah
PALMER A

BURTON W
CAMPBELL A G
CARROLL A M
CASSELS Norah
COCHRANE E B
COSTER J
CREEGHAN Maggie
DODWELL Eleanor
DUNCAN Christina
ELBRA L
ENGLAND F J
FITZPATRICK Mary
FOULKES M
GREEN Mary

HOWDLE J E
IRVINE C
JOHNSTONE J
JONES Mary E
KENNEDY Eliza
MABERLY E
MCCORMACK M
MACDONALD M
MCGREGOR Agnes
MCLEAN Elizabeth
MCMILLAM Clara
NEWTON E
O'CALLAGHAN A

PARRY Louisa
PHELAN E A
RICHARDSON A
ROBERTS A
ROBERTSON Jean
SEYMOUR E
SHEAD Clara
SMITH A E
STUBBINGTON M
SOMERFIELD Ann
TOPP S
TRENERRY B
WEIR M
JOHNSON Jane

Munition Workers

ABBOTT Mrs
ALDERSON M
ALLEN Mabel
ALLISON Mary
ANDERSON E
ARMSTRONG Mary
ARMSTRONG Maud
ATHERLEY Mrs
ATKINSON E M
BAINBRIDGE K
BAKER Emily
BAMBER Diannah
BARBER Mildred
BARKER Maggie
BARRETT Bridget
BARON Annie E
BASHFORD Nellie
BATES Norah
BECKETT Helena
BEECH Martha
BELL Annie
BENSON Annie
BENTON F
BLACKAMORE J

BRADSHAW M A
BRANNON Emily
BRIDGET Couroy
BROOKS Violet M
BROWN Agnes (York)
BROWN A (Garston)
BROWN Dorothy
BROWN E
BROWN Elizabeth
BRUCE Elsie
BUCKLEY Gladys
BUNCE M
BUTTERWORTH S
CAMERON Margaret
CARTER F K
CARTER Mary E
CARRUTHERS I
CASHIN Bridget
CASH Elsie
CHANDLER Florrie
CHAPLIN Lovie
CHAPMAN Katie
CLARK Nellie
CLARKE E C

COPHAM Edith
COTSFORD Alice
CROWTHER Dolly
CROSSLAND Mary
CURRY Mrs
CURSLEY Gertrude
CURTIS Ada F
DAVIES Rosetta
DAWBER Mary
DAWSON Emily
DEANE Agnes
DEVONALD Esther
DILLON Edith
EADY Ciceley
EASTIDE Emily
EASTMENT K
EATON L M
ECCLES Margaret
EDDY Leah
ELLIOTT Lily
ELLIOTT Mary E
ELLIS Edith
ELLIS Lilian
ELSTONE Jane

BLACKSTONE M J

BLAND Sarah E

BOLTON Grace

BOTTERILL A

BOOTH Polly

BRADLY Irene

CLARKE Fanny

CLIPPELIER M

CLURE Mrs

COLE A

COOPER Clara

COOPER Sarah

ENGLAND Mrs

FARMER Annie

FARMER Ethel

FARRAR Elizabeth

FERGUSON Agnes

FETTIS Hilda

FEW Jane

FITZMAURICE M

FLYNN Maggie

FOLEY Mrs

FOUNTAIN C

FOX Charlotte

FREEMAN Annie

FREER Hannah

FROST Annie

FROST Clara

GARMAN M

GARRETT E M

GAVIN Helen

GIBBS E Lavinia

GIBSON Mary

GIBSON Mrs

GLEAVE Florence

GORRILL Ethel

GRANT Eliza

GLASSBY Ada

HAINSWORTH V

HALEY Edith

HALL Nellie

HAVERTY Marie

HAWKINS Ethel

HAYDEN Gladys

HEFFERNAN A

HENDERSON L

HERRIDGE C

HILL Kate

HILTON Elsie

HODGKINS F A R

HOLLINSHEAD A

HOLMES Annie

KEYWORTH M

KING Mrs

KNIGHT G

LAZENBY Mary

LEAVER Lily M

LEONARD Ann

LEVITT Edith

LINDLEY F H

LING Dorothy

LOMAS Florence

LOTTINGA M C

LUMLEY Mrs

LYONS M

MACEY E

MARSH W B

MASKELL Mrs

MASON E

MASSEY C

MCINTOSH B

MEAD Lottie

MELVILLE Amy

METCALF Annie

MORGAN M

MORRIS Lily

MORRISON A G

MOULDS Nellie

NEWSOME Annie

OATES Elsie

OWEN Mary

PANNELL Mrs

PARRAGREEN E J

PAYNE S

PEAKER Sarah

PERKINS Edith

RUSHTON Ethel

ROWLEY Mary E

RUSSELL Marian

SCHOFIELD G

SCHOFIELD Mary

SCRATCHER M C

SEDGWICK Emily

SEIRS Anne

SHAW M

SHEPPARD Mary

SHERIDAN Sarah

SHOOSMITH E

SILCOCK M

SMART Alice

SMITH Annie M

SMITH E

SMITH Ellen

SMITH Sybil

STANILAND S

STEWART Amelia

STREET Louisa

SYKES Edith

TAYLOR Fanny

TAYLOR Mary

TAYLOR S

TURNER Mary L

VALENTINE M

VENES Lily

WALKER Jane E

WALKER Lizzie

WALSH Elizabeth

WARD Eliza

WATSON D M

WEBB Mrs

HORRIDGE B
HOWINGTON Nora
HOWLES E H
HUGHES Rose
HUXLEY Martha
JACKSON Ethel
JENKINS Jane
JENNINGS S A
JOHNSON M A
JONES Lizzie
JONES Maggie
JUBB Bridget
JUDE Emily
KEENAN Annie
KELLY Mary A
BONSALL Elsie M

PERRY Annie
PORTMAN F
POST Alice
POWER Agnes
PREECE Ellen
PRESTON Louisa
PRITCHARD G
RAINBOW E
REID Gertrude
ROACHE Edith E
ROBERTSON B
ROBINSON Elsie
RODGERS G
ROFE Alice
ROSECOE M
RUSHTON Elizabeth

WELSH Agnes
WEST Elizabeth
WEST Mary
WHIDGETT V
WHITELEY F
WILLIAMS Alice
WILLIS Dorothy
WILSHAW Sarah
WILSON Agnes
WOOD Rose
WORSLOP Ida
WORTLEY May
WRAY Florence M
WYATT Doris M
YEATES Olive
CLARKE Mary E

Women's Screen Twelve
York Minster
Women's Forage Corps

BETTIS Edith
BISHOP May V
CLARKE Daisy K
COLES Gertrude
GATES Eva
GEORGE Bessie

GREEN Ellen
HANCOCK Clara M
HOWE Annie
JOHNCOCK M A
KANE Lilian
KNIGHT Julia W

PALMER Ada
SMITH Ethel
SMITH K M C
WHALEY Mary Ann
WILLIAMS Elsie
WILTSHIRE Elsie

Women's Legion Motor Transport

BUTCHER R E
CUMMING C M

EMBLETON F
MAY Rhoda

MCMAHON A G
WATKINSON R Mrs

Serbian Relief Fund

BURY Vivyan
CLARK Nellie

DEARMER Mrs M
FERRIS Lorna
FRAZER Violet T

HARLEY Mrs K M
HAVERFIELD Hon Mrs E
HOMBERSLEY Mary

Friends' War Victims Relief Committee

POWICKE Gertrude Mary   HENWOOD Sarah

Women's Emergency Canteens

GARTSIDE-TIPPING Mrs

Young Men's Christian Association

MCARTHUR M M   PEARTON Edith   ROWE Edith F
NISBET E M   PICKFORD E A   STEVENSON Betty

Women's Land Army

HAMMOND Mrs F A   POPPLEWELL Annie   PORTER Ellie
NICHOLLS Mary L   GIBBINS Maud W
CHAPMAN Mrs   GARMAN Blanche   PETTER Mrs
DAVEY Lily   NUTBURN Louisa

General Service
PARSONS Sylvia

ABBREVIATIONS

AEC Army Educational Corps

AFS Auxiliary Fire Service

AMS Army Medical Services

ANS Army Nursing Service

APMMC Almeric Paget Military Massage
Corps

ARCW Archives and Records Council,
Wales

AS Army Schoolmistresses

ASC Army Service Corps

AANS Australian Army Nursing Service

AGC Adjutant General's Corps

ATS Auxiliary Territorial Service

BAOR British Army Of the Rhine

BBC British Broadcasting Corporations

BEF British Expeditionary Force

BL British Library

BRCS British Red Cross Society

BSC British Service Corps

CAMCNS Canadian Army Medical Corps
Nursing Service

CBE Commander of the British Empire

CHR Civil Hospital Reserve

CNA Colonial Nursing Association

CPGB Communist Party of Great Britain

CWGC Commonwealth War Graves
Commission

DBE Dame Commander of the Most
Excellent Order of the British Empire

EMNS Emergency Military Nursing Service

FAA Fleet Air Arm

FANY First Aid Nursing Yeomanry

FIBIS Families in British India Society

GC George Cross

GCCS (or GC&CS) Government Code and
Cipher School

GI Government Issue (term used to describe
members of the US Army)

HMEF His Majesty's Explosive Factories

HMHS His Majesty's Hospital Ship

HMIS Her/His Majesty's Indian Ship

HMSO Her/His Majesty's Stationery Office

HSC Home Service Corps

INS Indian Nursing Service

IRA Irish Republican Army

IRB Irish Republican Brotherhood

IWM Imperial War Museum

JISC Joint Information Systems Committee

JWC Joint War Committee

L d'H Legion d'Honneur

LDV Local Defence Volunteers

LMA London Metropolitan Archives

MBE Member of the British Empire

MET Metropolitan Electric Tramways

MID Mentioned In Despatches (or
Dispatches)

MM Military Medal

NAAFI Navy, Army and Air Force Institutes

NACB Navy and Army Canteen Board

NAM National Army Museum

NCO Non-Commissioned Officer

NFF National Filling Factories

NFS National Fire Service

NLS National Library of Scotland

NNS Naval Nursing Service

NUWSS National Union of Women's
Suffrage Societies

NZANS New Zealand Army Nursing
Service

OBE Order of the British Empire

ONA Overseas Nursing Association

PCNAR Princess Christian's Army Nursing
Reserve

PMRAFNS Princess Mary Royal Air Force
Nursing Service

PoW Prisoner of War

PRONI Public Record Office of Northern
Ireland

QA Member of QAIMNS

QAIMNS (R) Queen Alexandra's Imperial Military Nursing Service (Reserve)

QAMNSI Queen Alexandra Military Nursing Service for India

QARNNS Queen Alexandra's Royal Naval Nursing Service

QMAAC Queen Mary's Army Auxiliary Corps

QAS Queen's Army Schoolmistresses

RAEC Royal Army Educational Corps

RAMC Royal Army Medical Corps

RASC Royal Army Service Corps

RFC Royal Flying Corps

RMS Royal Mail Ship

RN Royal Navy

RNAS Royal Naval Air Service

RNLI Royal National Lifeboat Institution

RRC Royal Red Cross award

SAMNS South African Military Nursing Service

SOE Special Operations Executive

SoG Society of Genealogists

SS Steam Ship

SWB Silver War Badge

SWH Scottish Women's Hospital

TA Territorial Army

TACA The Army Children Archive

TANS Territorial Army Nursing Service

TFA Territorial Force Associations

TFNS Territorial Force Nursing Service

TNA The National Archives

TNT Tri-Nitro-Toluene

VAD(s) Voluntary Aid Detachment(s)

VE Victory in Europe

VJ Victory of Japan

WAAC Women's Army Auxiliary Corps

WAF Women's Auxiliary Force

WAS Women's Auxiliary Service

WDRC Women's Defence Relief Corps

WEC Women's Emergency Corps

WEWNC War Emergency Workers' National Committee

WFA Western Front Association

WHC Women's Hospital Corps

WI Women's Institute

WLA Women's Land Army

WO War Office

WRAF Women's Royal Air Force

WRNS Women's Royal Naval Service

WSPU Women's Social and Political Union

WTC Women's Timber Corps

WVR Women's Volunteer Reserve

WWI World War One

WWII World War Two

W(R)VS Women's (Royal) Voluntary Service

YCL Young Communist League

YMCA Young Men's Christian Association

YWCA Young Women's Christian Association

The National Archives: Relevant Department Codes

ADM Admiralty
AIR Air Ministry
ARP Air Raid Precautions
BT Board of Trade
CO Colonial Office
CUST Board of Customs and Excise
DV Central Midwives Board
EN Imperial War Museum
FO Foreign Office
HO Home Office
IR Inland Revenue
KV Security Service

LAB Ministry of Labour
MAF Ministry of Agriculture and Fisheries
MEPO Records of the Metropolitan Police Force
MH Ministry of Health
MT Ministry of Transport
MUN Ministry of Munitions
NATS Ministry of National Service
PCOM Prison Commission
PIN Ministry of Pensions
RECO Ministry of Reconstruction
WO War Office
WORK Ministry of Works
ZJ The *London Gazette*
ZLIB British Transport Historical Records

The National Archives: Report of the War Cabinet committee on women in industry (Cmd. 135 of 1919); Report of the committee on women's employment (Cd.9239 of 1918) and Board of Trade Report on Increased Employment of Women (Cd.9164 of 1918).

INDEXES

Compiled by Nicholas Newington-Irving, FSG

BOLGER Kathleen   250
BOLTON A.   209
BOLTON Angela   205
BOLTON Grace   264
BOLTON Grace E.   260
BOLUS Dorothea K.   262
BOND Brian   202
BOND Ella Maude   250
BONSALL Elsie M.
BOOKER Ellen M.   258
BOOTH Polly   264
BORTHWICK Isobel: see LINDSAY Isobel
   (Lady)
BORTHWICK John (Lord)   6
BORTRICK William   vii
BOSTOCK Ida M.   258
BOSTRIDGE Mark   201
BOTHWELL (4th Earl of): see HEPBURN
   James
BOTTERILL A. (Ms)   264
BOTTLE Dorothy   18
BOTTOMS L. A. G. (Ms)   252
BOUSFIELD Mary C.   255
BOUSQET Ben   182
BOUSQUET Ben   205
BOUVERIE: see PLEYDELL BOUVERIE
   200
BOWERMAN Elsie   220
BOWMAN Hilda Mary   249
BOWMETT M. A.   20
BOWSER Thekla   64, 78, 181, 202, 255
BOYCE Ellen   53
BRACE Frances E.   250
BRADER Chris   202
BRADLEY E. I. (Miss)   229
BRADLEY Jane   252
BRADLY Irene   264
BRADSHAW F. M. M. (Mrs)   258
BRADSHAW M. A. (Ms)   263
BRAILLY Odette Marie Celine   135-136, 159,
   248
BRAITHWAITE M. D. (Ms)
BRAMALL Ethel   255
BRAMFITT M. E. (Ms)   256
BRANFORD Mary   256
BRANNIGAN Nellie   252
BRANNON Emily   263
BRAYBON Gail   202
BRAYE (Lord)   200

BRAYLEY Martin   181, 209
BRAZIER Reginald H.   202
BREARLEY Judith   209
BREAY Margaret   19, 179, 201
BRENNAN Adelle   261
BRENT Y. R. H. A. D (Ms)   256
BRETT Norah V.   250
BREWER Kate S. A.   252
BREWIS E. (Ms)   256
BRIDGE Jessie   258
BRIDGEFORD M. (Ms)   256
BRIDGET Couroy   263
BRIGGS Dorothy   256
BRIGGS G. G. B.   205
BRIGGS Phyllis Mary Erskin   167
BRIGHT Joan   208
BRIGNELL Alice   254
BRINTON Gertrude   250
BRIQUETTE M. J. (Ms)   258
BRISTOW Norah   180
BRISTOW Norah S.   36
BRITTAIN Vera Mary   78
BROAD Netta Ellen   254
BROCKLEBANK A. (Ms)   230
BROOKS Violet M.   263
BROSTER (Sister)   256
BROUGHTON E. D. (Mrs)   259
BROWN A. (Ms)   263
BROWN Agnes   263
BROWN Dorothy   263
BROWN E. (Ms)   263
BROWN E. Gladys   256
BROWN Elizabeth   263
BROWN Euphemia L.   250
BROWN F. E. (Miss)   229
BROWN L. (Mrs)   259
BROWN Marion   262
BROWN May F.   252
BROWN Norah Mary   167
BROWN Winifred   256
BROWNE Felicia Mary   101
BRUCE B. J. (Ms)   256
BRUCE Elsie   263
BRUCE M. (Ms)   262
BRUIN Mary   180, 202
BRYAN-DAUNT Z. K. (Ms)   256
BUCKERIDGE K. (Mrs)   259
BUCKINGHAM (Earl of)   200
BUCKINGHAM M. A. (Ms)   259

ELLIS F. Mary   254
ELLIS Lilian   142, 263
ELLISTON E. K. (Ms)   256
ELSTONE Jane   263
ELVINS Eliza M.   249
ELWES Emily Mary   256
EMBERTON Wilfrid   200
EMBLETON F. (Ms)   265
EMLY (Lord)   200
ENEVER Ted   209
ENGLAND (Mrs)   264
ENGLAND F. J. (Ms)   263
ENGLISH Winifred   256
ERLANGER: see D'ERLANGER
ERSKINE Harriet   20
ERSKINE M. M. E. (Ms)   262
ESCOTT Beryl   181-182, 207-208
ESTRANGE: see L'ESTRANGE
EURE (Lord)   6
EVANS Jane   250, 253
EVANS Katie   259
EVANS Margaret E.   256
EVANS Margaret M.   256
EVANS Mary   iv
EVANS Mary A.   253
EVANS Nellie   254
EVERITT Alan   200
EWES: see D'EWES
FAGG Emma   20
FAHIE Michael   207
FAIRFAX Thomas (3rd Baron Fairfax of
   Cameron)   9
FAIRMONT: see LIVINGSTONE-
   FAIRMONT
FAIRWEATHER Margaret (Hon)   143
FAITHFULL F May   256
FALCONER-GRANT L. W. (Ms)   259
FALKNER M. L. (Mrs)   259
FANNIN Teresa   258
FANNING B. B. (Ms)   256
FANSHAWE Anne   14
FARLEY Martha   250
FARMER Annie   264
FARMER Ethel   264
FARR Mabel   256
FARRAR Elizabeth   264
FAULKNER A.   20
FAWCETT Millicent   31

FAWCETT Millicent Garrett   203
FAWKES Olive   256
FEENEY Mildred   255
FEILDING Dorothie (Lady)   203, 246
FELLOWES (General)   23
FELLOWES Margaret Augusta: see
   KIRKLAND Margaret Augusta
FENTON May   255
FERGUSON Agnes   264
FERGUSON M. M. (Ms)   255
FERGUSON Mary   253
FERGUSON Rachel   250
FERNLEY Ethel   250
FERRIS Lorna   265
FETTIS Hilda   264
FEW Jane   264
FIELDING Dorothy (Lady)   71
FIGES Eva   199
FIOCCA Henri   160
FIOCCA Nancy: see WAKE Nancy Grace
   Augusta
FITZHENRY Daisy A.   262
FISHER Mabel   259
FITZGERALD C. (Ms)   255
FITZGERALD M. L. (Ms)   254
FITZGIBBON Theodora   205
FITZMAURICE M. (Ms)   264
FITZPATRICK Mary   263
FITZROY Yvonne   221
FLANNERY A. M. (Mrs)   249
FLEMING Ian   160
FLINT Doreen   255
FLINTOFF Alice   250
FLOWER H. M. P. (Ms)   259
FLYNN Maggie   264
FOGO: see ROW-FOGO
FOLEY (Mrs)   264
FOLLETTE Minnie A.   260
FOLLIOTT Amy Charlotte Melora   262
FOOT M. R. D.   208
FORBES (a historian)   207
FORBES B. G. F. (Ms)   250
FORBES: see also TREFUSIS-FORBES
FORBES KEITH: see KEITH
FORNERI Agnes F.   260
FORSTER Laura   258
FORTESCUE M. Jane   260
FOULKES Elsie   253

TAYLOR: see also HANDLEY-TAYLOR
TEGGIN Eugenie   251
TEMPEST-STEWART: see VANE-TEMPEST-
  STEWART
TEMPLE E. Stella   257
TEMPLEMAN Jean   260
TERROT Sarah A.   20
TERRY Roy   200
THEOBALD Pat   111
THOM Deborah   204
THOM Phyllis   206
THOMAS B. J. B. (Ms)   259
THOMAS Dorothy Louise   248
THOMAS E. (Mrs)   229
THOMAS Irene   114
THOMAS Lilian   251
THOMAS M. E. (Ms)   251
THOMAS Olive G.   253
THOMASSON Alice   253
THOMPSON Ada M.   261
THOMPSON H. D. M. (Ms)   257
THOMPSON M. (Ms)   260
THOMPSON M. B. (Ms)   259
THOMPSON M. H. (Ms)   262
THOMS Phyllis: see BRIGGS Phyllis Mary
  Erskin
THOMSON E. (Ms)   257
THOMSON E. R. (Ms)   251
THOMSON Ellen   253
THOMSON Kerr M.   251
THOREN: see DE THOREN   257
THORNTON Alice   8, 179
THORNTON D. M. (Ms)   253
THURBY Lucy   257
TICHBORNE M. E. F. (Ms)   257
TINDALL Fanny   251
TINDALL Mary   257
TINNISWOOD Adrian   201
TIPPING: see GARTSIDE-TIPPING
TIPU (Sultan)   141
TITLEY M. G. (Ms)   260
TODD Barbara R.   253
TODD Florence   259
TOMASELLI Phil   162, 206-209
TONKIN Edith M.   257
TOOBY Frances Mary   94, 253
TOPP S. (Ms)   263
TORAN M. (Ms)   260

TOUGH E. (Mrs)   259
TOUGH Helen F.   257
TOUGHILL C. M. F. R. (Mrs)   258
TOWNSEND Emma Jose   248
TOWNSEND F. (Ms)   254
TOWNSEND M. (Ms)   251
TOZER (Mrs)   257
TRAVERS Susan   210
TRAYNOR Oscar   97
TREFUSIS-FORBES Katherine Jane (Dame)
  129,137
TRENERRY B. (Ms)   263
TREVITHAN Rita   251
TROLLOPE Jessie   257
TRUSTRAM Myna   202
TUBMAN Esther   262
TUCKER M. Annie   254
TUCKER Mabel Grace   238
TUCKER Mary J.   259
TULLOCH Edith   251
TUPPER Addie A.   260
TURMAINE Rose J.   254
TURNBULL Elizabeth B.   20
TURNER Helen   141
TURNER John Frayn   207
TURNER Margot (Dame)   210
TURNER Mary L.   264
TURTON Alice M.   251
TWADELL Maud E.   253
TWELLS Alice   253
TWINCH Carol   206
TWIST Dorothy P.   260
TYLER Nicola   207
TYRER Nicola   210
TYSON Fanny I. O.   261
UFFINDELL Andrew   179
UNDERWOOD E. J. (Mrs)   258
URMSTON Lillian   101
URQUHART Diana   199
VALENTINE N. (Ms)   264
VANE-TEMPEST-STEWART Edith Helen: see
  CHAPLIN Edith Helen
VASS Lily F.   254
VAUGHAN Elsie M.   257
VAUGHAN Margaret   248
VAUGHAN: see also GWYNNE-VAUGHAN
VENES Lily (Ms)   264
VERNEY (Family)   201

VICKERS David   vi, 249
VILLIERS Sophia Jane   53
VINTER Bertha   251
VIVASH Irene Miawa   237
VON ARNI: see GRUBER VON ARNI
WADE Stephen   207
WADGE D. Collett   200
WAINWRIGHT D.   210
WAKE Gladys M. M.   260
WAKE Nancy Grace Augusta   160-161, 182, 209
WAKEFIELD J. (Ms)   251
WALCROFT Kitty   253
WALDIE Charlotte Ann   11
WALFORD Emma   259
WALKER Diana Barnato   146, 207
WALKER Jane E.   264
WALKER Jennie   257
WALKER Lizzie   264
WALKER Sara   257
WALKER W. L. (Ms)   253
WALKER: see also MILES WALKER
WALL Alicia   253
WALL Richard   204
WALLACE D. (Mrs)   257
WALLACE E. (Ms)   251
WALLACE Mary   253
WALLADGE Hilda   257
WALLS Emma   259
WALSH Betsy M.   253
WALSH Elizabeth   264
WALSH Sara   257
WALSHE Mary A.   251
WALTER Gladys   254
WALTERS A. M. (Ms)   209
WALTERS D. (Mrs)   229
WARD B. R.   179
WARD Eliza   264
WARD Matthew   vii
WARDLE Ida   262
WARNER Lavinia   167
WARNOCK E. (Ms)   257
WARR: see DE LA WARR
WARREN Florence   257
WASS Alice   53
WASS Elsie   53
WASS Mary   53
WATFORD Nellie   254

WATKINS (Mrs): see KING (Miss)
WATKINS Julia K.   262
WATKINSON R. (Mrs)   265
WATSON Beatrice M.   261
WATSON D. H. (Ms)   251
WATSON D. M. (Ms)   251, 264
WATSON Helen   257
WATSON Hilda   257
WATSON Jeannie   253
WATSON Mary   251
WATSON Tamar   257
WEBB (Mrs)   264
WEBB Margaret   110, 181
WEIGALL David   179, 201
WEIR M. (Ms)   263
WELFORD Alice   251
WELLER Ada E.   253
WELSH Agnes   265
WELSH Mary (Lady)   137, 247
WESLEY Mary   116
WEST Elizabeth   265
WEST Mary   265
WEST Winifred   vi, 145-146, 155
WEST: see also SACKVILLE-WEST
WESTMACOTT Dorothy   33
WESTWELL Mary   253
WHALEY Mary Ann   265
WHALL A. M. (Ms)   253
WHARTON (Lord)   6
WHEATLEY Annie   251
WHEELDON Alice   38
WHEELDON Hettie   38
WHEELER Elizabeth   20
WHEELWRIGHT Julie   200
WHIDGETT V. (Ms)   265
WHISHAW Mabel   262
WHITCOMBE Amy L.   253
WHITE-JERVIS D. J. (Ms)   257
WHITE Christopher   209
WHITE Dorothy M.   249, 257
WHITE V. C. B. (Ms)   257
WHITEHEAD Ida K.   255
WHITELEY F. (Ms)   265
WHITELOCKE Bulstrode   9
WHITTAKER E. (Ms)   253
WHITTAL Taniya   144
WHITTELL Giles   207
WHITTINGTON M. (Ms)   259

INDEX TO UNITS & PARAMILITARY ORGANISATIONS

Scheme of Entries: British Ministries
Royal Navy
Merchant Navy
Ship Index
British Army
Royal Air Force
British Military Hospitals

Royal Gunpowder Factory, Waltham Abbey
48, 217
Royal Ordnance Factory, Aycliffe 118
Royal Small Arms Factory, Enfield Lock 48

Women's Land Army etc

British Secret Organisations

Australian Armed Forces

Burmese Armed Forces

Canadian Armed Forces

Ceylon/Sri Lanka Armed Forces

Colonial Nurses

INDEX TO OTHER ORGANIZATIONS & ARCHIVAL SOURCES

See also pages 195-198 for useful archives' websites

About the SOCIETY OF GENEALOGISTS

Founded in 1911 the Society of Genealogists (SoG) is Britain's premier family history organisation. The Society maintains a splendid genealogical library and education centre in Clerkenwell.

The Society's collections are particularly valuable for research before the start of civil registration of births marriages and deaths in 1837 but there is plenty for the beginner too. Anyone starting their family history can use the online census indexes or look for entries in birth, death and marriage online indexes in the free open community access area.

The Library contains Britain's largest collection of parish register copies, indexes and transcripts and many nonconformist registers. Most cover the period from the sixteenth century to 1837. Along with registers, the library holds local histories, copies of churchyard gravestone inscriptions, poll books, trade directories, census indexes and a wealth of information about the parishes where our ancestors lived.

Unique indexes include Boyd's Marriage Index with more than 7 million names compiled from 4300 churches between 1538-1837 and the Bernau Index with references to 4.5 million names in Chancery and other court proceedings. Also available are indexes of wills and marriage licences, and of apprentices and masters (1710-1774). Over the years the Society has rescued and made available records discarded by government departments and institutions but of great interest to family historians. These include records from the Bank of England, Trinity House and information on teachers and civil servants.

Boyd's and other unique databases are published on line on **www.findmypast.com** and on the Society's own website **www.sog.org.uk**. There is free access to these and many other genealogical sites within the Library's Internet suite.

The Society is the ideal place to discover if a family history has already been researched with its huge collection of unique manuscript notes, extensive collections of past research and printed and unpublished family histories. If you expect to be carrying out family history research in the British Isles then membership is very worthwhile although non-members can use the library for a small search fee.

www.sog.org.uk

The Society of Genealogists is an educational charity. It holds study days, lectures, tutorials and evening classes and speakers from the Society regularly speak to groups around the country. The SoG runs workshops demonstrating computer programs of use to family historians. A diary of events and booking forms are available from the Society on 020 7553 3290 or on the website **www.sog.org.uk** .

Members enjoy free access to the Library, certain borrowing rights, free copies of the quarterly *Genealogists' Magazine* and various discounts of publications, courses, postal searches along with free access to data on the members' area of our website.

More details about the Society can be found on its extensive website at **www.sog.org.uk**

For a free Membership Pack contact the Society at:

14 Charterhouse Buildings,
Goswell Road,
London EC1M 7BA.
Telephone: 020 7553 3291
Fax: 020 7250 1800

The Society is always happy to help with enquiries and the following contacts may be of assistance.

Library & shop hours:

Monday	Closed
Tuesday	10am - 6pm
Wednesday	10am - 6pm
Thursday	10am - 8pm
Friday	Closed
Saturday	10am - 6pm
Sunday	Closed

Contacts:

Membership
Tel: 020 7553 3291
Email: membership@sog.org.uk

Lectures & courses
Tel: 020 7553 3290
Email: events@sog.org.uk

Family history advice line
Tel: 020 7490 8911
See website for availability